Middlebrow 2.0 and the Digital Affect

Postcolonialism across the Disciplines 30

Postcolonialism across the Disciplines

Series Editors
Graham Huggan, University of Leeds
Andrew Thompson, University of Exeter

Postcolonialism across the Disciplines showcases alternative directions for postcolonial studies. It is in part an attempt to counteract the dominance in colonial and postcolonial studies of one particular discipline – English literary/cultural studies – and to make the case for a combination of disciplinary knowledges as the basis for contemporary postcolonial critique. Edited by leading scholars, the series aims to be a seminal contribution to the field, spanning the traditional range of disciplines represented in postcolonial studies but also those less acknowledged. It will also embrace new critical paradigms and examine the relationship between the transnational/cultural, the global and the postcolonial.

Middlebrow 2.0 and the Digital Affect

Online Reading Communities of the New Nigerian Novel

Hannah Pardey

Liverpool University Press

First published 2023 by
Liverpool University Press
4 Cambridge Street
Liverpool L69 7ZU

This paperback edition published 2025

Copyright © 2025 Hannah Pardey

Hannah Pardey has asserted the right to be identified as the author of this book in accordance with the Copyright, Design and Patents Act 1988.

All rights reserved. No part of this book may be reproduced, stored in a retrieval system, or transmitted, in any form or by any means, electronic, mechanical, photocopying, recording, or otherwise, without the prior written permission of the publisher.

British Library Cataloguing-in-Publication data
A British Library CIP record is available

ISBN 978-1-837-64469-8 (hardback)
ISBN 978-1-83624-556-8 (paperback)

Typeset in Amerigo by Carnegie Book Production, Lancaster

Contents

Illustrations — vii

Abbreviations and Notations — ix

Preface and Acknowledgements — xiii

1 Introduction: The Digital Milieu of Literary Transmission — 1

2 The New Nigerian Novel as Middlebrow: Materialist and Narratological Approaches — 21

3 Algorithms of Affect: The Digital Literary Economy — 57

4 Communities 2.0: Reviewers, Reading Habits and Digital Labour — 77

5 The Verbal Performance of Affect: Emotion Terms and Patterns — 109

6 Coda: Revisiting the Digital Affect — 141

Appendix — 145
Bibliography — 169
Index — 209

Illustrations

Figures

4.1	Comparison of Reviewer Interaction	79
4.2	Top 16 Professional vs. Amateur YouTube Channels	84
4.3	Types of BookTube Videos	91
4.4.1	Demographic Data: Gender	99
4.4.2	Demographic Data: Age	99
4.4.3	Demographic Data: Race	100
4.4.4	Demographic Data: Location	101
5.1	Keywords in YouTube Reviews	112
5.2	POS Distribution of Most Frequent Emotion Terms in Review Corpora	121
5.3	Frequency of Emotion Terms across Review Corpora	122
5.4	Frequency of Emotion Terms across Novel Corpora	123
5.5	Frequency of Emotion Terms across Selected Novels	133
5.6	Frequency of Emotion Terms across Corpus of Author Videos	135
5.7	Selected Novels vs. Corpus of Author Videos	136

Tables

2.1	New Nigerian Novelists: Creative Writing	145
3.1	Review Corpora	148
4.1	Comparison of Reviewer Interaction	149
4.2.1	Top 16 Professional YouTube Channels	150
4.2.2	Top 16 Amateur YouTube Channels	151
4.3	Types of BookTube Videos	152
4.4	Demographic Data of YouTube vs. Goodreads Reviewers	153
5.1	Keywords in Review Corpora	154
5.2	Most Frequent Emotion Terms in Review Corpora	156
5.3	Frequency of Emotion Terms across Review Corpora	159
5.4	Frequency of Emotion Terms across Novel Corpora	160
5.5	Frequency of Emotion Terms across Selected Novels	165
5.6	Frequency of Emotion Terms across Corpus of Author Videos	166
5.7	Selected Novels vs. Corpus of Author Videos	167

Abbreviations and Notations

The central analytical unit of this book consists of three self-constructed corpora of reviews for 20 new Nigerian novels that were collected from Amazon, Goodreads and YouTube between March and July 2019. The following primary texts form the basis of my corpus construction. In Chapters 2 and 5, as well as the appendant figures and tables, references to the novels and the five selected e-books (Kindle format) are indicated by the subsequent abbreviations.

N01 (SN01)	Abani, Chris. *Song for Night*. 2007. Saqi Books, 2016.
N02 (SN02)	Adebayo, Ayobami. *Stay With Me*. Canongate Books, 2017.
N03 (SN03)	Adichie, Chimamanda N. *Americanah*. 4th Estate, 2013.
N04	—. *Half of a Yellow Sun*. 4th Estate, 2006.
N05	—. *Purple Hibiscus*. 4th Estate, 2003.
N06	Atta, Sefi. *Everything Good Will Come*. 2005. Interlink Books, 2008.
N07	Braithwaite, Oyinkan. *My Sister, the Serial Killer*. 2018. Atlantic Books, 2019.
N08	Cole, Teju. *Every Day Is for the Thief*. 2014. Faber and Faber, 2015.
N09	—. *Open City*. 2011. Random House, 2012.
N10	Emezi, Akwaeke. *Freshwater*. Grove Press, 2018.
N11	Evans, Diana. *26a*. 2005. Vintage, 2006.
N12	Habila, Helon. *Measuring Time*. W.W. Norton & Company, 2007.
N13	Iweala, Uzodinma. *Beasts of No Nation*. 2005. Harper Perennial, 2006.
N14	Nwaubani, Adaobi T. *I Do Not Come to You by Chance*. 2009. Phoenix, 2010.
N15	Obioma, Chigozie. *An Orchestra of Minorities*. Little, Brown, 2019.

N16 (SN04)	—. *The Fishermen*. ONE, 2015.
N17 (SN05)	Okparanta, Chinelo. *Under the Udala Trees*. 2015. Granta Books, 2016.
N18	Onuzo, Chibundu. *The Spider King's Daughter*. Faber and Faber, 2012.
N19	Oyeyemi, Helen. *The Icarus Girl*. 2005. Anchor Books, 2006.
N20	Selasi, Taiye. *Ghana Must Go*. 2013. Penguin, 2014.

Whenever I want to emphasise differences between the online reading formations, I refer to the Amazon community, the Goodreads community and the YouTube community. I use YouTube and the name for one of its particular niches, BookTube, as synonyms for stylistic reasons. Given the many overlaps between the platforms, I use umbrella terms covering all review/ers, such as online literary or reading communities and – reinforcing their key feature and function – affective online communities, altogether more often. Well aware that the notion of community is co-opted by Web 2.0 businesses, I employ the term to stress the social and emotional interests and coping strategies of my reviewers. Exceeding this study's main focus on digital reception, the fifth chapter considers additional digital material that has been gathered in September 2019. Defining my system of citation in the text (see below), I use the following abbreviations in the figures and tables presented in Chapters 3 to 5.

AR	Amazon reviews
GR	Goodreads reviews
NB	Newspaper blurbs
PB	Publisher blurbs
YA	Author videos on YouTube
YR	YouTube reviews

The overwhelming amount of resources required to investigate digital marketing and reading practices poses a challenge to the researcher who seeks to compile a full list of references. Opting for a compromise between comprehensiveness and readability, the bibliography lists the sources in accordance with the different platform settings and the varying degrees of examination of the data.

Amazon and Goodreads Reviews

Since listing all of the 14,391 Amazon and Goodreads reviews surveyed in this study would not only be unwieldy but also contradict my distant reading methods, I indicate the cut-off dates of collecting them. Applying the selection criteria that are defined in the third chapter, I gathered all available Amazon reviews up to 31 March 2019 and all available Goodreads reviews up to 30 April 2019. Whenever I quote from the Amazon and Goodreads reviews,

Abbreviations and Notations

I indicate the abbreviated name of the sub-corpus as specified in Table 3.1. For instance, when I quote from an Amazon review of *Song for Night*, I use AR01 as a reference. If readers wish to obtain the user name of an Amazon or Goodreads reviewer or the precise publication date of his or her review, they can enter the quote in the search template provided on both platforms.

YouTube Videos

The case looks different with regard to the data collected from YouTube until 31 July 2019 (reviewers) and 30 September 2019 (authors). Since readers would have difficulties locating specific YouTube reviews by using my search terms (name of author + name of novel + review) and since the fourth chapter includes detailed references to and quotes from the profiles of particular BookTubers, the bibliography lists all YouTube channels, including the video titles (with typos and other inconsistencies) and publication dates. Apart from indicating the abbreviated name of the respective sub-corpus as specified in Table 3.1, such as YR02, I mention the channel name and, in the many cases where one channel has uploaded more than one video, I also state the publication date. Whenever I relate to or cite from a profile page, I use the channel name together with the abbreviation RP (reviewer profile). References to the author videos are indicated by the abbreviation YA (see Chapter 5).

Newspaper and Publisher Blurbs

The newspaper and publisher blurbs gathered from Amazon and Goodreads in September 2019 can be found on the starting pages of the individual novels and are therefore not listed at the end of the book. References are indicated by the abbreviations NB and PB (see Chapter 5).

***

Please note that individual reviews may have been deleted since I collected and saved them. Moreover, YouTube reviewers occasionally change the names of their channels or videos. Should readers of this book encounter difficulties in finding particular reviews, contact the author at hannah.pardey@googlemail.com.

Preface and Acknowledgements

The study of the middlebrow entails exercises in scholarly self-reflection, not least because the term's evocation of a clearly defined cultural hierarchy, though deceptive, fosters ambiguous research positions (Driscoll, 2014, 1–3; Rubin, 1992, xix). To name a prominent example, Janice A. Radway (1997, 1–17) prefaces her survey of the Book-of-the-Month Club with an account of her development as a researcher. More precisely, this middlebrow studies scholar uses the introduction to *A Feeling for Books* to illustrate the ways in which her engagement with the middlebrow mediator reinforced her split sense of self. Pointing to her upbringing in "a small tract house in suburban New Jersey, furnished with one small bookcase and *Time, Reader's Digest,* and *Woman's Day* on the coffee table", she demonstrates how her initiation into the "conceptual grids and evaluative hierarchies" (4, 2) of the University of Pennsylvania jarred with the consumption modes practised at home. Eager to master the reading techniques and interpretive approaches employed in her literature classes, the "suburban girl" retained her middlebrow pleasure of books that, contrary to the titles discussed in the seminar room, "promoted physical sensations, a forgetting of the self and a complete absorption into another world" (1, 3). And yet, the established scholar leaves no doubt that the young Radway was moving in an academic landscape which demanded that she "keep [her] voracious taste for bestsellers, mysteries, cookbooks, and popular nature books a secret – a secret from everyone, including the more cultured and educated self [she] was trying to become" (2).

Writing roughly 25 years after the publication of Radway's study, and owing in large measure to her work and that of the other representatives of middlebrow studies covered in the following pages, I move in a different research landscape. Nonetheless, some reference points in my biography are strikingly compatible with the conflicting pattern Radway describes. If suburban tract houses and *Reader's Digest* issues on the coffee table are anything to go by, I have been a middlebrow reader for the better part of my life. The bookcase in the living room of my family home on the outskirts of Hanover may have slightly exceeded the library of Radway's childhood years, but certainly featured many of the same middlebrow titles. For years, I read Agatha Christie's murder mysteries and Patricia Highsmith's psychological thrillers with unreserved pleasure – and continue to do so. In fact, my research has engendered some additions to my favourites, such as Daphne du Maurier's novels, which are best devoured on train rides, on holiday, on the couch. Following my enrolment at the University of Hanover, I encountered realist and modernist classics by Charlotte Brontë and James Joyce, postcolonial novels by Chinua Achebe and J.M. Coetzee and various other titles that do not lend themselves to such consumption contexts because they prohibit the reader's sitting back, as Nicola Humble's (2011, 41–59) notorious definition of a middlebrow reading has it. University turned reading into a laborious task. More often than not, however, I found this task to be equally pleasurable, as it allowed me to put my reading history into critical perspective.

What the reading list conceals is that, at the time of my studies from 2009 to 2015, popular (and, to a lesser extent, middlebrow) literatures and cultures were already well established as research subjects. Nonetheless, and although some of my seminars focused on romances by Rosamunde Pilcher or adaptations of Jane Austen and Charles Dickens, my experience of the opposing relation between the low-, the middle- and the highbrow deviates only slightly from Radway's report. I attribute this experience to my training as a structuralist narratologist with a particular interest in postcolonial literatures and cultures. In one of my first approaches to the new Nigerian novel, I sought to discuss Chimamanda Ngozi Adichie's *Half of a Yellow Sun* (2006) and Helon Habila's *Measuring Time* (2007) as cases of historiographic meta-fiction, adhering to what Chris Bongie (2008, 281) calls the "fundamental law" of postcolonial studies. My attempt to read the novels under the signs of this pretentious label failed early on, and I recall my sense of confusion as my findings contradicted what I had learned (to believe) – that is, that the postcolonial promotes "aesthetic […] and political resistance" (Bongie, 2008, 289), not complacency. Reworking my research agenda, I came across Helen Cousins's (2011, 137–53) chapter on Richard and Judy's discussion of Adichie's novel. Here was at least some proof that the middlebrow was beginning to be applied in postcolonial contexts. By and large, however, the postcolonial middlebrow was an under-researched phenomenon in 2015, and the fragmentary state of research at the time may help explain why I started out employing the middlebrow in inverted commas, as if anxious of the consequences that the notion might have for (my attitude towards) postcolonial studies.

During the first two years of my endeavour to study the postcolonial middlebrow, confusion gave way to frustration. I had mastered the categories of narrative analysis but their application to the new Nigerian novel yielded more than meagre results. My shift from scrutinising the novels' narrative structures to investigating the material conditions of their online production, distribution and consumption, while reconciling me with my research subject, produced ambiguities of its own. Pondering her position vis-à-vis the Book-of-the-Month Club, Radway (1997, 12) relates: "Sometimes I can view the operations of the club and the tastes of the middlebrow critically, from the outside and at a distance. At other times I see them from the point of view of someone who once understood them as a participant." The exploration of middlebrow material – be it book clubs, as in Radway's case, or thousands of online reviews, as in mine – requires a considerable degree of immersion. On the other hand, and in order not to merely rehearse the aesthetic and ideological patterns under scrutiny, it calls for critical meta-perspectives. As for Radway, drawing a clear line between these two positions turned out to be challenging, not least because the digital literary economy renders a thoroughly detached viewpoint unavailable. I spent many years with my reviewers, genuinely seeking to comprehend and, every now and then, sympathising with their socio-economic aspirations. In other places, I despaired of the conservatism that distinguishes their reading practices, perhaps because it reminded me that I had come full circle, from the middlebrow reader to the researcher of the middlebrow reader. Owing to my second identity, my efforts at distancing surface in the book's academic modes of examination and presentation, including the corpus-linguistic methodology and the corresponding figures and tables, as well as the numerous quotes from the reviewers, who do much of the talking for me.

So much for the similarities between studying the middlebrow in 1997 and in 2023, for the almost three decades that separate my survey from Radway's book have seen substantial shifts in the academic world. Whereas Radway worked for the consolidation of the middlebrow as an object of scholarly investigation, I work alongside the proliferation of the middlebrow as a largely unacknowledged mode of reading in scholarly (or postcolonial) contexts. A number of episodes from my everyday academic life serve to exemplify this point. As a student, I was surprised by the extent to which the discussion of Adichie's *Americanah* (2013) and Taiye Selasi's *Ghana Must Go* (2013) in a seminar on "The Global Novel" resembled the conversational characteristics of a book club, with reading questions that concentrated on identity and belonging and course participants who continuously mused over the protagonists' feelings. As a lecturer, I was stunned when my overwhelmingly white students originating from various small towns in Lower Saxony expressed their affective identification with the main character of Buchi Emecheta's *Joys of Motherhood* (1979), Nnu Ego, an Igbo woman and mother of no fewer than nine children who forges a livelihood in colonial Lagos in the early 1930s. As a speaker at conferences, I was startled by the many comments that stressed the uniqueness of each new Nigerian novel discussed in subsequent chapters.

As an academic reader, moreover, I am baffled by the speed and frequency with which the middlebrow sneaks into critical discourses, from postcolonial studies' recent "how-to book[s]" (Carter, 1992, 293) by Elleke Boehmer (2017) or David Damrosch (2020), which recommend emotional approaches to world literature, to the countless articles on the new Nigerian novel that wallow in the "lonely existences" (Krishnan, 2014, 34) and "lost cultural identities" (Hartwiger, 2016, 10) of its characters, calling into question whether professional and lay reading modes really "persist as [...] the most meaningful sites of difference and distinction" (Procter and Benwell, 2015, 10). I leave it to the reader of this book to decide if those scholars who turn to the novels as an occasion to contemplate "the persistence of love against all odds" (Mackey, 2013, 112) or "the quotidian moments in life of love, pain, anger and frustration" (Knudsen and Rahbek, 2017, 122) can be clearly distinguished from my reviewers and their affective consumption patterns.

I do not wish to begin this book by repeating the highbrow cultural positions of Q.D. Leavis (1965), Virginia Woolf (1942, 113–19) and other cultural commentators who fuelled Britain's "battle of the brows" at the beginning of the twentieth century. Disregarding the term's analytical potential, such an evaluative approach would contradict my contribution to the middlebrow studies agenda of recognising and researching the middlebrow "as a distinctive cultural formation with both a history and a contemporary presence" (Driscoll, 2014, 1). Rather, I would like to suggest that the middlebrow can serve postcolonialists as a tool to reflect on and, if need be, readjust their critical practices, which should aim at challenging instead of confirming dominant discourses.

A word of thanks is due to the many people who have supported my endeavour to study the postcolonial digital middlebrow. Indeed, the interdisciplinary scope of this book turned the writing process into an entirely collaborative activity. My special thanks goes to Jana Gohrisch, who was most generous with her encouragement and expertise. I am grateful for the opportunity to probe into some of my contentions, presented in a freshly revised version here, in my chapter "Middlebrow 2.0: The Digital Affect and the New Nigerian Novel", published in her co-edited essay collection *Imperial Middlebrow* (2020, 218–39), and in my article "Middlebrow Postcolonialisms: Studying Readers in the Digital Age", which appeared in our special issue of *Anglistik* on *Postcolonial Cultural Studies* (2020, 67–88). On a more general note, I owe her the historical, materialist and dialectical patterns of thought that developed in our innumerable conversations and pervade (not only) this book.

A similar source of inspiration and support, Gesa Stedman provided most valuable feedback on the majority of my research results. My approach to the new Nigerian novel profited from her astute reviews of many a postcolonial middlebrow novel (most remarkably, a review of Zadie Smith's *Swing Time* tellingly titled "Global Pudding") that appear regularly on her *Literary Field Kaleidoscope* blog. Christian Huck's detailed suggestions introduced me to the intriguing work of Régis Debray, caused me to rethink Pierre Bourdieu's difficult relation to historical materialism and encouraged me to take a precise look at the Internet economy, whereas Jan Alber's comments on an earlier draft initiated the narratological fine-tuning of Chapter 2. At Leibniz University Hanover, I am especially grateful to my former colleague Ellen Grünkemeier,

Preface and Acknowledgements

who, after having toiled her way through my first and seemingly endless sample chapter on the novels' hybridity, was supportive in the study's conceptual reorientation. Janna-Lena Neumann read substantial parts of the manuscript and, as a trained mathematician, offered particularly useful commentary on the figures and tables. The corpus-linguistic method employed in this book emerged from the many inspiring discussions with Rainer Schulze, who, apart from researching tons of secondary reading material, generously shared his expertise in linguistics.

My collective thanks goes to all colleagues, including Jessica Malay, Cecile Sandten and Barbara Schaff, who expressed interest in and gave advice for the further development of the project during colloquia, conferences and workshops. Most notable among these encounters, Michael Westphal's sharp questions about one of my conference papers led to my engagement with keyword analysis, and I am very thankful for his assistance with AntConc. Katrin Berndt, Sule Egya, Rainer Emig, Peter Marsden, Brigitte Reinwald and Frank Schulze-Engler provided helpful remarks on my exposé, while Christoph Ehland gave encouraging feedback on my first published chapter. Susanne Gehrmann equally helped define the direction of the project in its early stages and, apart from inviting me to her colloquium, arranged for a cooperation with *Kindlers Literatur Lexikon*, allowing me to study the novels in easily digested doses. Thanks are also due to all people at LUP, especially to the anonymous reviewers, whose suggestions have greatly strengthened the presentation of my central arguments, and to my editor Chloe Johnson, who rendered the publication of my first book an enjoyable experience.

I thank my friends and family for their unconditional love and unwavering support. I am particularly grateful for Mandy Schwarze's magnificent skills in editing and formatting and her technical perspective on algorithms. I greatly appreciate the help of Nicolas and Tim Pardey, who, as trained economists, needed no convincing that literature is a business and took up the (at times) daunting task of familiarising their older sister with the intricacies of Excel. My final words of appreciation go to Monika Aust, whose share in my scholarly identity is much larger than she is probably aware of. It is, however, precisely because she never failed to remind me that there are more important things than reading and writing that this book is for her.

CHAPTER 1

Introduction: The Digital Milieu of Literary Transmission

This book investigates the material conditions of producing, distributing and consuming the new Nigerian novel online, paying special attention to how readers employ social media to fashion themselves as emotionally receptive members of a globalising middle-class formation. Consider Jean as a representative of the study's many protagonists. Located in Edinburgh, the twenty-something PhD student hosts a successful BookTube channel, Jean Bookishthoughts. Since her initiation into the BookTube community ten years ago, Jean has created and uploaded more than 1,000 reviews of children's and young adult books, as well as postcolonial novels that deal with issues such as gender and sexuality, race and ethnicity in an accessible way, including contemporary Nigerian diasporic fiction. Mostly shot in front of her extensive bookshelf in her living room, Jean's video reviews conceptualise reading and reviewing as recreational, social and emotional activities that exceed the boundaries of YouTube. Owing to her pervasive online presence on platforms such as Goodreads, Instagram and Twitter, as well as her blog and her podcast, Jean has established herself as a role model of online literary consumption. Created by the algorithmically defined recommendation systems of digital companies such as YouTube, Jean's expansive entourage of more than 85,000 subscribers turns to her uploads on a regular basis, using her quizzes, readathons, tags and virtual book tours as an occasion to participate in the online discussion of literature. Instructing her followers in the reading modes of the middlebrow, Jean makes sure that her affective care for the online literary community pays off financially. In addition to the list of affiliate links to Amazon or her online bookshop that accompanies every one of her reviews, she has repeatedly worked as a Baileys Women's Prize and Man Booker Prize vlogger in the last couple of years. Her peculiar mixture of private and public consumption contexts, emotional and commercial reading practices renders Jean an excellent example of this study's central research subject: online reading communities.

The principal endeavour of this book consists in analysing the extent to which the present digital literary economy refashions postcolonial production, distribution and reception practices and, as a result, creates an astonishingly closed middle-class emotional structure. To this end, the study ventures beyond the paradigm of representation and the method of close reading postcolonial literary texts by developing an innovative research design that draws on the historical materialist tradition of cultural studies or, more precisely, Régis Debray's notion of mediology. Rather than focusing on a certain medium and its socio-cultural effects, mediology is concerned with historically specific acts of mediation or transmission; in the words of Debray (1996, 16): "A historical milieu of transmission crystallizes concretely in, and through, the socialized operators of transmission. It is a space constructed by, and upon, networks of appropriators, official guarantors of reputations, regulators, go-between or middle-men." While Debray (1996, 16) has focused on the socio-technical structures of transmitting print-dominated literary culture, "with its editor-booksellers, retailers, educators, librarians, [or] organizers of reading rooms", I construct such a historical milieu of mediating postcolonial literary culture for the digital age. I do so by concentrating on the practices of two mediators in particular: first, the American university and its creation of the writing workshop; and, second, the US-based new media economy and its creation of compassionate online communities of ethnically diverse but socially balanced readers, including Jean, who use social media as a means of middle-class self-fashioning (Gohrisch, 2005, 18–21; Gohrisch, 2011, 44–67).

Adopting a medium-scale perspective, I approach the current digital milieu of postcolonial literary transmission with a self-constructed unit of analysis consisting of more than 15,000 online responses to 20 new Nigerian novels that were gathered from Amazon, Goodreads and YouTube in the first half of 2019. Combining the theories and methods of postcolonial and middlebrow studies, the digital humanities and the history of emotions, moreover, I use this specific dataset to develop a computational and reproducible methodology for examining new forms of postcolonial reader engagement that I refer to as the digital affect. Functioning as a viable tool to scrutinise the power structures of the digital literary economy, the digital affect serves to answer the following research questions: How precisely do new media technologies influence the production, marketing and reception of postcolonial literatures in general and the new Nigerian novel in particular? Why does the global and digitally mediated middlebrow provide a particularly fruitful analytical framework for investigating these influences? How does the potential egalitarianism ascribed to the Internet interact with global power structures? To what extent does the middlebrow intervene in postcolonial relations of power? What characterises the relation between postcolonial authors and their readers in the digital sphere? What are readers' motivations for forming affective reading communities and contributing to online literary discussions?

State of the Art(s): The Postcolonial Digital Middlebrow

Resulting from the interdisciplinary scope of this study's central concept, *Middlebrow 2.0 and the Digital Affect* positions itself in critical conversation with and significantly goes beyond several endeavours in postcolonial and middlebrow studies, digital reception and affect studies. Proceeding from current trends in postcolonial studies, my research design is inspired by a range of surveys that attest to the claim that "the status of literature and the literary has shifted with the move to a more culturally oriented analysis" (Huggan, 2008, 12).[1] Starting with the publication of Graham Huggan's seminal survey of *The Postcolonial Exotic* (2001), scholars such as Chris Bongie (2008), Sarah Brouillette (2007), Caroline Koegler (2018), Sandra Ponzanesi (2014), Anamik Saha (2018) and the members of the Warwick Research Collective (WReC, 2015)[2] have helpfully shifted the discipline's focus from the postcolonial text to the material conditions of its production, distribution and consumption. Strengthening the field's socio-economic lines of inquiry with the insights of middlebrow studies, I take their approaches into the Internet era to demonstrate that the literatures of an increasingly digitised "capitalist world-system" (WReC, 2015, 8) are largely defined by the writing workshop of the American university and the business schemes of US-based Web 2.0 businesses. As far as such an emphasis on the contemporary digital milieu of literary transmission redefines the postcolonial text as a "practical material activity" (Williams, 1977, 38), my research agenda equally covers one of the largest gaps in postcolonial research: the reader.

In view of the discipline's keen interest in unequal power structures, "it is [indeed] surprising that audiences, readers and reception have not featured more prominently on the radar of postcolonial studies" (Benwell et al., 2012, 6). Predominantly concerned with educating its academic audiences in *critical reading practices* (Ashcroft et al., 2007, 173; Benwell et al., 2012, 9–10; Carter, 1992, 293), postcolonialists have tended to neglect that lay readers turn to postcolonial literatures for entirely different reasons. This is not to suggest that reception studies in postcolonial contexts are non-existent. For instance, Purnima Mankekar's *Screening Culture, Viewing Politics* (1999) uses ethnographic methods to study women's television-viewing habits in India, while Shakuntala

---

1 Considering areas as diverse as art, cinema, dance, music and sports, Simon Featherstone's *Postcolonial Cultures* (2005) as well as Jana Gohrisch and Ellen Grünkemeier's essay collection *Postcolonial Studies across the Disciplines* (2013) constitute notable examples of this trend.
2 Associated with the Department of English and Comparative Literary Studies at Warwick University, the group includes Sharae Deckard, Nicholas Lawrence, Neil Lazarus, Graeme Macdonald, Upamanyu Pablo Mukherjee and Stephen Shapiro. A key representative of the discipline's materialist branch, Benita Parry assisted the collective's effort "to resituate the problem of 'world literature' [...] by pursuing the literary-cultural implications of the theory of combined and uneven development" (WReC, 2015, 6) until her death in 2020.

Banaji's *Reading 'Bollywood'* (2006) draws on audience interviews to compare the responses to Hindi films among young viewers in India and the UK. Moreover, the Africanist anthropologist Karin Barber (1997; 2006) has inspired a body of Africa-based work that engages with readers and reading cultures through the lens of popular cultural studies. Wendy Griswold's sociological survey of *Readers, Writers, and the Novel in Nigeria* (2000) or Stephanie Newell's empirical explorations of the readers of *Ghanaian Popular Fiction* (2000) and *West African Literatures* (2006) provide insights into locally specific reading formations. More recently, and resuming the dominant postcolonial take on the reader as a textual construct, Jenni Ramone's *Postcolonial Literatures in the Local Literary Marketplace* (2020) examines "fictional readers within literary texts" (19) from Cuba, India and Nigeria. However, these narrow perspectives on local reading contexts and communities do not lend themselves to consider the global and digital environments that define the reception practices of a growing number of postcolonial audiences.

In turn, scholars who focus on global contexts of postcolonial reception are rare; as Brouillette (2007, 24) rightly remarks, "few researchers have performed the detailed analyses of reading practices that might justify the identification of a characteristic mode of cosmopolitan consumption". Primarily presuming "a generalized cosmopolitan Westerner" (Innes, 2007, 200), moreover, they tend to shift the focus from resisting to responsible practices of reading. In effect, publications such as Elleke Boehmer's *The Future of the Postcolonial Past* (2017) or Marijke Denger's more recent *Caring for Community* (2019) and the contributions to the "Reading and Postcolonial Ethics" section in the edited collection *Postcolonial Audiences* (Benwell et al., 2012) tend to construct the reader of postcolonial texts in liberal humanist terms.[3]

Exceeding the reader constructs of these studies, James Procter and Bethan Benwell's *Reading Across Worlds: Transnational Book Groups and the Reception of Difference* (2015) presents the only book-length study of postcolonial consumption that comes closest to my notion of the digital affect. Procter and Benwell (11, 6) concentrate on three thematically and aesthetically related "metropolitan novels" – Zadie Smith's *White Teeth* (2000), Monica Ali's *Brick Lane*

---

3 Frequently assuming a white, Western and/or middle-class norm, the construct equally pervades non-materialist approaches to world literature, for instance by Vilashini Cooppan (2009, 30) and David Damrosch (2020, 22), an American comparative studies scholar promoting cross-border reading practices as an occasion to recognise some "common humanity". In his manual of *How to Read World Literature* (2008), Damrosch further implies that the "human" reader is "a reader confronting foreign literature" and facing "the unique challenges [of] reading across time and cultures [and] exploring today's global perspective" (cover blurb). A similar vocabulary informs approaches that credit the new Nigerian novel with supporting "discourse[s] of humanitarian sympathy" (Dalley, 2014, 132), constructing "quintessentially human" (Norridge, 2012, 28) protagonists and inviting its reader to become part of an unspecified "global village" (Hron, 2008, 45).

(2003) and Andrea Levy's *Small Island* (2004) – and their reception in altogether "30 different book groups scattered across four continents". Although they share the promising observation that the World Wide Web and "related media increasingly provide the possibility [...] of cross-cultural connections among readers and groups" (6), the authors mostly focus on face-to-face book groups and employ ethnographic methods to explore their response patterns. Accordingly, their approach to the "reception of difference", as their study's sub-title puts it, builds on a corpus of 3,400 pages of transcriptions gathered from the recorded book group discussions over a period of three years (2006–08). Presenting a careful and productive methodology for collecting and analysing data on book clubs, Procter and Benwell's survey shows that different locations of reading do not necessarily entail different patterns of response. In spite of their diverse provenances and places of residence, ranging from England, Scotland and Wales to India, Jamaica and Nigeria, the members of Procter and Benwell's book groups readily embrace "emotion [...] as an appropriate and valid currency of interpretation" (31). Paying closer attention to the work of middlebrow studies scholars on book clubs, my study offers a more comprehensive explanation for the "consistency with which book groups in different parts of the globe read" (178). More precisely, I demonstrate that the prevailing literary-sociological outlook of this swiftly diversifying research field discloses that "sympathetic engagement" (Boehmer, 2017, 17) with the postcolonial Other, rather than constituting an unselfish act of human charity, serves exercises in middle-class self-fashioning.

The middlebrow references an increasingly influential "literary-historical critical mode" (Ehland and Gohrisch, 2020, 7) of inquiry that was first adopted to investigate those authors and texts that fuelled Britain's "battle of the brows" in the early twentieth century. Striving to recover what contemporary commentators such as Q.D. Leavis and Virginia Woolf had turned into "a highly contentious term" (Humble, 2013, 97),[4] scholars of the first hour

---

4 The absence of the term in Raymond Williams's influential *Keywords: A Vocabulary of Culture and Society* (1976) implies that the middlebrow tended to evoke "anxiety and a curious sort of shame within academic circles" (Humble, 2013, 97) long after these two self-proclaimed literary gatekeepers voiced their derogatory comments. Leavis's *Fiction and The Reading Public* (1932) shows concern about the 1927 foundation of the Book Society, which, catering to the demands of newly emerging middle-class sections, affirms that "middlebrow taste has [...] been organised" (Leavis, 1965, 24). Commenting on Woolf's position vis-à-vis the middlebrow, expounded in her 1932 letter to *The New Statesman* that she never sent, few researchers take note of the writer's differentiation between middle- and lowbrow cultural practices (Humble, 2013, 98; Sullivan and Blanch, 2011, 16). Instead of rejecting *all* commercial forms of culture, Woolf (1942, 114, 115) expresses "honour and respect" for the "thoroughbred vitality" of the lowbrow "man or woman [...] who rides his body in pursuit of a living at a gallop across life", while the aspiring petite bourgeoisie "ambles and saunters now on this side of the hedge, now on that, in pursuit of no single object, neither art nor

express an interest in establishing the middlebrow as a respectable research area aimed at reassessing those fictions that, due to their incompatibility with low- and highbrow forms, have long suffered from critical neglect. In the majority of cases, this reappraisal takes the shape of feminist rewritings of modernity that show how bestselling women writers such as Stella Gibbons or Nancy Mitford have been systematically excluded from British literary history (Beauman, 1983; Light, 1991). Nicola Humble's *The Feminine Middlebrow Novel, 1920s to 1950s* (2001) was the first study that applied the term to over 60 novels by more than 30 female authors to determine their "shared generic features and ideological preoccupations" (3). Following the publication of her monograph, Humble established herself as a key contributor to *The Middlebrow Network* ("About Us") that seeks to "raise the profile of [the] middlebrow as a legitimate research theme" within literary and cultural studies.[5] The core members and various associates of the network have meanwhile produced an impressive range of publications, including a special edition of *Working Papers on the Web* on *Investigating the Middlebrow* (Brown, 2008) and a special issue of *Modernist Cultures* that seeks to locate "The Middlebrow – Within or Without Modernism" (Sullivan and Blanch, 2011, 1–17), as well as the edited volume *Middlebrow Literary Cultures: The Battle of the Brows, 1920–1960* (Brown and Grover, 2012), which strives to redefine British literary modernism by tracing the powerful presence of middlebrow authors, texts and readers. Along similar lines, other essay collections have broadened the focus to survey the intermediary role of the middlebrow in Britain's interwar period (Macdonald and Singer, 2012) or cast doubt on the term's gendered connotations (Ehland and Wächter, 2016; Macdonald, 2011).

Resulting from its establishment as a proper discipline, middlebrow studies has started to expand its spatio-temporal boundaries and attract the

---

life itself, but both mixed indistinguishably [...] with money, fame, power, or prestige". Notwithstanding her special contempt for the grovelling disposition of the second kind of consumer, recent scholarship on the Hogarth Press emphasises that Woolf's attitude towards the middlebrow may have been more ambiguous than this quote suggests (Sullivan, 2010, 52–73). Emerging since the late 1940s, American responses like Russell Lynes's "Highbrow, Lowbrow, Middlebrow" (1949) and Dwight Macdonald's "Masscult and Midcult" (1960) are marked by a more playful tone than their British equivalents. Lynes's article even inspired an illustration in *Life* (1949) that lists the different preferences in furniture, clothes, reading, salad and drinks, "firmly fixing the language of the 'brows' in the popular lexicon while softening its critical edge" (Rubin, 1992, xiv).

5 Founded in 2008 by Faye Hammill (University of Strathclyde), Erica Brown (Sheffield Hallam University) and the independent scholar Mary Grover, the network soon included US-based researchers such as Ann Ardis (University of Delaware), Janet Casey (Skidmore College) and Melissa Sullivan (Rosemont College), pursuing its agenda "to further comparative research into North American and British middlebrow cultural production and its participants, consumers and audiences" ("About Us", *The Middlebrow Network*). From 2008 to 2010, the network was funded by the AHRC ("Home", *The Middlebrow Network*).

attention of postcolonialists. Yet, although the "[m]iddlebrow is no longer solely Anglophone" nor restricted to "the historical time frame in which it originated" (Ehland and Gohrisch, 2020, 7), few studies have dared to set foot on the "uncharted territory" (Bongie, 2008, 280) where the two fields collide. Most notable among those who use middlebrow studies' "new and creative phase" (8) are the contributors to *Imperial Middlebrow* (2020), edited by Christoph Ehland and Jana Gohrisch, who investigate how middlebrow literary texts about the British empire legitimised imperial discourses. Primarily working within middlebrow studies' British – that is, text-orientated – strand, the collection goes beyond the slightly inconsistent application of the middlebrow by other postcolonialists such as Bongie (2008), Belinda Edmondson (2009) or Nadia Atia and Kate Houlden (2019, 1–23), who, according to the editors, tend to struggle with "the openly affirmed bourgeois nature of middlebrow culture" (Ehland and Gohrisch, 2020, 10).

Irrespective of this minor point of criticism, it should be noted that the contributions to *Imperial Middlebrow* undoubtedly profit from the clearly articulated frameworks of analysis that are put forward in the above-mentioned studies. For example, in "Withering Heights: Maryse Condé and the Postcolonial Middlebrow", Bongie (2008, 280–321) helpfully locates the middlebrow features of the Guadeloupian's bestsellers in their mixture of aesthetically and politically conservative and challenging modes of representation, even if his reinforcement of the "postcolonial law", according to which "any kind of premium is placed on literary value" (288), compromises the term's potential to redefine the subject matter of postcolonial studies. Similarly, in their excellent introduction to *Popular Postcolonialisms* (2019), Atia and Houlden emphasise the necessity to distinguish between popular and middlebrow forms of postcolonial production and consumption, even if the contributions to their edited collection occasionally sideline what Bongie (2008, 282) refers to as the middlebrow's "assimilative implications". Helen Cousins's chapter "A Good Authentic Read: Exoticism in the Postcolonial Novels of the Richard & Judy Book Club" (2011, 137–53), moreover, champions an approach that proves Huggan's (2008, 112) "Western model reader" from empirical perspectives, even if she establishes a distinction between the text and the reader and, in the end, circumvents the term.

While the subsequent chapter illustrates that the middlebrow can be employed as a tool of textual analysis, the predominant part of this study is inspired by the American – that is, the literary-sociological – branch of researching the middlebrow. To give an example, Joan Shelley Rubin's *The Making of Middlebrow Culture* (1992) interrogates the "role, purpose, and authority" (xvi) of American middlebrow mediators such as the Book-of-the-Month Club. Janice A. Radway's *A Feeling for Books: The Book-of-the-Month Club, Literary Taste, and Middle-Class Desire* (1997) continues Rubin's exploration of the cultural work accomplished by what Lisa Botshon and Meredith Goldsmith (2003, 4) have referred to as "the grand dame of the middlebrow". Disclosing the paradigmatic link between commerce, femininity and (desired) middle-class affiliation that renders the middlebrow consumption of literature a quintessentially emotional "event for identification, connection and response" (1997, 284), Radway's audience research has encouraged numerous studies on book club culture, including Elizabeth Long's *Book Clubs* (2003) or Danielle Fuller and DeNel Rehberg Sedo's *Reading Beyond the Book* (2013).[6] Both surveys contribute to middlebrow studies because their focus on commercial reading formations does not undermine the agency of middlebrow readers, who consider shared reading events either as "a cultural marker for distinction" (Long, 2003, 61) or as "possibilities for belonging" (Fuller and Rehberg Sedo, 2013, 211). Like the majority of audience research in postcolonial studies, however, their approaches remain restricted to examining locally specific reading events and formations,[7] largely neglecting those global and digital contexts where "reading, viewing and listening are […] activities involving mobile, exilic and diasporic audiences" (Benwell et al., 2012, 1) and common social science methods of gathering data "prove impossible to implement" (Murray, 2018, 151).

By contrast, Beth Driscoll's *The New Literary Middlebrow: Tastemakers and Reading in the Twenty-First Century* (2014) discusses contemporary middlebrow literary culture against the backdrop of "globalization and digitization" (5). Opening the concept to new research contexts, the study inspires my approach to the online reading communities of the new Nigerian novel most thoroughly. However, Driscoll's descriptive take on current middlebrow mediators along "eight key features" – "middle class, reverential and commercial, feminized, mediated, recreational, emotional and earnest" (3) – is marked by a number of shortcomings.[8] First, and despite the frequently evoked "global reach" (4)

---

6 Further research has centred on the middlebrow reading practices fostered by the first and most influential televised book clubs of Oprah Winfrey and the married couple Richard Madeley and Judy Finnigan (Aubry, 2011, 43–70; Driscoll, 2008, 139–50; Farr, 2005; Gruzd and Rehberg Sedo, 2012, 1–25; Ramone and Cousins, 2011; Rehberg Sedo, 2008, 188–206; Rooney, 2005; Woolf, 2003, 27–37). Attesting to the middlebrow's proliferation online, both Oprah's Book Club and the Richard & Judy Book Club went "entirely digital" (Driscoll, 2014, 75).

7 While Long (2003, 54) investigates book club members in Houston, Texas, Fuller and Rehberg Sedo (2013, 211) employ the notion of the "citizen reader" to stress that participants of reading events such as One City One Book seek to "belong to reading as an activity located in a place, along with others who share the same interest". Notably, these programmes frequently feature postcolonial texts, such as Adichie's *Purple Hibiscus* or *Americanah*, which were selected for the One Maryland One Book and the One Book, One New York mass reading events in 2017 ("Highlights", *Maryland Humanities*, 2017; Lobash, 2017). Venturing beyond the spatial limits of Long's research, Fuller and Rehberg Sedo do not consider how such events encourage sympathetic cross-border reading, including the pursuit of "achieving 'social cohesion' through the recognition of cultural diversity" (Procter and Benwell, 2015, 4).

8 Driscoll traces the new literary middlebrow in contexts as diverse as Oprah's Book Club, pedagogical debates about the Harry Potter novels or media reports

of middlebrow literary culture, Driscoll's monograph remains largely limited to those places where the middlebrow has developed – that is, the UK and the US – and thus does not sufficiently address how middlebrow practices modify postcolonial power relations.[9] Second, and like other cultural or media studies scholars (Aubry, 2011, 175–98; Beer and Burrows, 2010, 3–12; Jenkins, 2006; Monk, 2011, 431–77), Driscoll shows a tendency to downplay the material infrastructure of the Internet, including the software applications that can be employed to analyse digital networking and communication structures.[10] Testifying to her ongoing engagement with digital research methods,[11] Driscoll's articles "Sentiment Analysis and the Literary Festival Audience" (2015) and "Faraway, So Close: Seeing the Intimacy in Goodreads Reviews" (2019), the latter of which is co-authored with Rehberg Sedo, employ SentiStrength to analyse more than 20,000 festival tweets and 692 Goodreads reviews, respectively. Illustrating the merits of focusing on clearly defined sets of online data and their systematic study with computational tools, both articles pay insufficient attention to the software's commercial backdrop and, as a result, tend to rehearse the bourgeois affective norms of the audiences and reviewers under scrutiny.

Despite the weaknesses of SentiStrength, addressed at some length in Chapter 3, Driscoll (2015, 861–73) and Driscoll and Rehberg Sedo (2019, 248–59) come closer to devising a reproducible methodology than the media studies scholar Simone Murray (2018, 2), whose comprehensive perspective on *The Digital Literary Sphere* – "the entire institutional apparatus governing the producing, disseminating, and consuming of literary culture" – is no less influential for my endeavour to unearth the continuities between off- and online reading formations. Offering a precise look at the institutional and social agents and their positions in a remapped Bourdieusian literary

---

   on the Man Booker Prize. Seeking to illustrate the wide scope of researching the middlebrow in the new millennium, her study applies an enumerative method that differs from my conceptual contribution to middlebrow studies.
9 Arguably, her missing postcolonial perspective may help explain her celebratory conception of the middlebrow as "a source of value and satisfaction for an increasing number of readers", culminating in the concluding remark that "[t]his study has not just described the new literary middlebrow, but defended it" (201).
10 The potentially democratising effects of digital media are equally highlighted in postcolonial research contexts (Adenekan, 2021, 8, 10; Bosch Santana, 2018, 188; Hu, 2015, 7).
11 In her chapter on "The Middlebrow Pleasures of Literary Festivals", Driscoll (2014, 152–93) takes account of her observation that the contemporary middlebrow "operat[es] in a digital environment" (4) by considering roughly 3,200 online audience surveys of the 2013 Melbourne Writers Festival. Engaging with online material, she exceeds prior research on the middlebrow tastes and practices of literary festival participants (Giorgi, 2011, 11–23; Johanson and Freeman, 2012, 303–14; Ommundsen, 2009, 19–34) but, like her precursors, does not use digital humanities tools.

field that befits the Internet era, her monograph may not present a truly "transferable" methodology for examining specific online reading formations, but her thorough observations about "the institutional structures that shape reading online" (142, 152) inform my notion of the middlebrow 2.0 that, apart from emphasising that middlebrow literary culture has turned into an online venture, challenges the potentially egalitarian effects that are frequently ascribed to the digital age. Throughout the twentieth century, book societies, magazines or radio programmes provided middlebrow readers with a distinctive affective lexicon that, reducing the solutions to broader societal issues to the level of the individual, promoted a certain complacency about inequalities of all kinds (Driscoll, 2014, 25; Radway, 1997, 12–13). Since the new millennium, this task falls into the responsibility of digital corporations such as Amazon or YouTube. Discussing the proliferation of affective online communities along the socio-economic perspectives on the commercial Internet by Taina Bucher (2018), Philipp Staab (2019) or Shoshana Zuboff (2019), I contend that these capitalist companies function as the new "operators of [literary] transmission" (Debray, 1996, 16). Indeed, the following chapters illustrate that their algorithmic means of building community and structuring communication in the digital literary sphere refashion the socio-economic and thus the emotional relations of their users (Illouz, 2007, 3, 7), creating a bourgeois emotional structure with global reach.[12]

Owing to my historical materialist outlook, the next chapters point beyond Driscoll and Rehberg Sedo's (2019, 249) estimation that "emotion is a particularly important concept" in digital media environments.[13] Rather, and positioning itself at the outer end of the field's temporal spectrum, my book draws on the insights of socio-historical emotion research to offer transhistorical vantage points on the emotional responses of the online reviewers under scrutiny. In particular, Eva Illouz's (2007; 2008) and Arlie Russell Hochschild's (2003, 17, 56) surveys of the emotional dimensions of capitalism in its different stages serve to stress that emotion is neither just "stored 'inside' us" nor "independent of acts of management" but moreover constitutes "one of culture's most powerful tools for directing action" and structuring interaction, not least that of the members of the affective

---

12 A comprehensive (re)assessment of the "multifaceted category of [the] middle class, its origins, formations, lives and experiences across the globe" (Suter et al., 2020, xvii) lies beyond the scope of this book. I follow Geoffrey Evans and James Tilley's (2017, 1–6) definition of class in terms of a structure that manifests itself on socio-economic and discursive levels. Presenting heterogeneous social formations, which include ever new sections of the middle classes, the affective online communities surrounding contemporary Nigerian fiction forge a shared emotional vocabulary whose material basis is defined by Web 2.0 businesses.

13 Driscoll's monograph is marked by a similar vagueness. Anticipating the keyword analysis of my review corpora presented in Chapter 5, I did a quick document search for one of the key notions that she deems characteristic of middlebrow literary culture: the term "emotional" appears 86 times but is never clearly defined.

online communities investigated here. Scrutinising how some of the key representatives of digital capitalism (Staab, 2019) determine the feeling rules (Hochschild, 2003, 58) or affective norms of a growing Internet public, my computer-based analysis of the reviewers' emotional language use equally profits from two literary studies about nineteenth-century bourgeois emotion ideologies (Gohrisch, 2005; Stedman, 2002) that suggest that literary texts play a crucial role in defining "what is rightly owed and owing in the currency of feeling" (Hochschild, 2003, 18).[14]

At this point, however, I introduce a study that invigorates my materialist perspective on the digital literary economy and online literary discussion more generally: Christian Huck's *Digitalschatten: Das Netz und die Dinge* (2020). As the title of his German monograph implies, Huck seeks to uncover the material foundations and economic power relations that render global networking (or the Internet) possible in the first place. The author convincingly shows that digital media are set up to conceal their material basis, which only emerges from the "shadows" if technology fails and disrupts the connection between us and the rest of the world (95, 97, 116, 123, 181, 197). Presenting altogether five case studies that shine a light on the means of producing the World Wide Web, Huck's study supports the survey of my material in both direct and indirect ways. Examining the algorithmically defined communication structures of new media environments, his second case study constitutes an important reminder that the social and emotional reading practices of the online literary communities are inextricably intertwined with the commercial interests of Web 2.0 companies (43–84). On the other hand, his discussion of Cambodian workers digging pits for fibre optic cables (87–126) and Congolese miners extracting cobalt, one of the roughly 60 raw materials needed to produce smartphones (159–98), has no immediate bearing on the cultural practices of my reviewers. On closer inspection, however, his case studies serve to realise that the digital spread of bourgeois emotion discourses is premised on a combined but fundamentally uneven Internet economy (105, 118, 165).

---

14 The reason why Hochschild's *The Managed Heart* (1983), first published 40 years ago, inspires my endeavour consists in her materialist and sociological take on a specific protagonist of the 1980s American service sector: the flight attendant. Discussing the socio-economic significance of the flight attendant's smile, Hochschild (2003, 14) illustrates how an emotion "behaves like a commodity". As I detail in Chapter 3, the feeling rules of the affective online communities "fall under the sway" (Hochschild, 2003, 19) of a handful of capitalist corporations representing the commercial Internet.

Micro- and Macroeconomics:
The New Nigerian Novel in the World Wide Web

As my reading of Huck's study from a world-systemic perspective suggests, my investigation of the three online literary communities and their socio-economic dimensions profits from a school of thought that stresses the epistemological advantages of Marxism as a methodology. Resurfacing in recent reformulations of the theory of combined and uneven development by Vivek Chibber (2013, 292),[15] the Warwick Research Collective (WReC, 2015, 1–48) or Franco Moretti (2013b),[16] world-systemic perspectives serve the examination of the digital literary economy. Since such perspectives build on a continual back and forth between "analysis and synthesis" (Moretti, 2013b, 48), specific example and general pattern, I employ the new Nigerian novel to explore the "capitalist world-system" (WReC, 2015, 8) in the digital age.

First defined by Pius Adesanmi and Chris Dunton in two special issues of *English in Africa* (2005) and *Research in African Literatures* (2008), third-generation Nigerian literature or the new Nigerian novel has meanwhile turned into a staple of the global literary economy. Indeed, in one of his more recent articles, Dunton (2019, 5) confirms that "Nigeria is the powerhouse of the contemporary African novel". Drawing on a rich literary tradition established by such first- and second-generation writers as Chinua Achebe and Flora Nwapa or Buchi Emecheta and Ben Okri, Nigerian authors belonging to what Maximilian Feldner (2019, 14–17) refers to as the "new" African diaspora,

---

15 An extensive discussion of Chibber's *Postcolonial Theory and the Specter of Capital* (2013) is published in my article "Middlebrow Postcolonialisms: Studying Readers in the Digital Age" (2020, 67–88).

16 The Warwick Research Collective (2015, 7) repeatedly references Moretti's "firecracker of an article", "Conjectures on World Literature" (2000), which was first published in *New Left Review* and later appeared as a chapter in his book *Distant Reading* (2013b, 43–62). Characterised by a similar "insistence on the systematicity of world literature" (WReC, 2015, 6), Moretti (2013b, 47, original emphasis) uses world-systems theory to analyse individual literary texts from Brazil, India and Japan to substantiate and, in turn, adjust the "initial hypothesis from the world-systems school of economic history, for which international capitalism is a system that is simultaneously *one*, and *unequal*: with a core, and a periphery [...] bound together in a relationship of growing inequality". Accordingly, he introduces the following "*law of literary evolution*: in cultures that belong to the periphery of the literary system [...], the modern novel first arises not as an autonomous development but as a compromise between a western formal influence [...] and local materials" (50, original emphasis). Published 13 years after his article on world literature, Moretti's *The Bourgeois* (2013a) ensured that the notion of distant reading is now primarily applied in digital research contexts. I address the study in Chapter 5. It should be noted, however, that it focuses on eighteenth- and nineteenth-century European literature and therefore does not take into account how the Internet restructures the contemporary global book market.

including Adichie, Cole, Habila, Iweala, Oyeyemi and Selasi, have created an extensive corpus of novels. Moreover, and as Feldner (2019, 1) rightly remarks, "[t]here are no signs that this trend of internationally visible Nigerian literature is going to abate any time soon". On the contrary, names such as Adebayo, Braithwaite, Emezi, Okparanta and Onuzo herald a female-dominated fourth generation producing one successful novel after the other.

Describing the novelistic phenomenon at the point of its emergence, Adesanmi and Dunton (2008, ix) put special emphasis on the new generation's diasporic condition, which signals a deviation from the aesthetic and political occupation with the postcolonial nation that characterises the work of their precursors. The widely discussed "cosmopolitan awareness" (Dalley, 2013, 16) of new Nigerian novelists is vividly captured by Selasi's (2005) notion of the "beautiful, brown-skinned" Afropolitan who "belong[s] to no single geography, but feel[s] at home in many". Asserting that most novels show the ambiguous spatio-temporal affiliations that Selasi's fancy label suggests, scholars have tended to adopt an "either/or perspective" (Dalley, 2013, 33), focusing on the means by which third-generation writers continue or cease to engage with their predecessors' concerns (Andrade, 2011, 91–101; Bryce, 2008, 49–67; Hawley, 2008, 15–26; Hron, 2008, 27–48; Krishnan, 2010, 185–95; Strehle, 2011, 650–72; Tunca and Ledent, 2015, 1–9). As one of the field's rare monographs indicates, more recent investigations proceed along these binary lines. Feldner's *Narrating the New African Diaspora* (2019) sets out to arrange the in-depth analysis of a dozen new Nigerian novels according to whether they offer "representations of Nigeria" or negotiate "experiences of migration" (17). Since most of the texts are marked by "a dual preoccupation" (17), this strategy is bound for failure. The result echoes what has meanwhile become the dominant strategy. Locating the novels between national and global poles, Feldner creates the umpteenth description of the "transnational/ transcultural hybridity" (2) of the authors and/or their novels.

From a world-systemic perspective, both approaches are flawed. While the former tends to disregard the interdependencies of the new Nigerian novel's national and global dimensions, the latter proves inadequate to analyse power structures, including the material conditions that define them. To be sure, this does not prevent Feldner and other postcolonial critics from the enthusiastic embrace of the term; in fact, Feldner uses "hybridity" and its adjective realisation "hybrid" no fewer than 86 times. Given that the (once) critical notion signifies Homi K. Bhabha's announcement of postcolonial studies' post-Marxist phase (Boehmer and Tickell, 2015, 319; Chibber, 2013, 3–4; Zabus, 2015, 3), it is no coincidence that representatives of the field's materialist branch have addressed its shortcomings; Aijaz Ahmad (1996, 287) has remarked that the "hybrid" subject "is remarkably free of [...] class", while Parry (2004, 73) has cautioned that the term disregards "that other, economically enforced dispersal of the poor from Africa, Asia, [or] Latin America". Moving within the narrow boundaries of the "exclusive, elitist and self-aggrandizing" (Tveit, 2013) Afropolitan framework of the novels, most scholars realise that its authors are "comparatively privileged"

(Feldner, 2019, 17) or belong to the "African [...] urban upper middle class" (Guarracino, 2014, 8).[17] However, the class privileges of Adichie, Cole, Emezi, Selasi and others are hardly recognised, let alone examined as a structuring principle of their novels and the digital literary economy at large. Instead, and albeit stressing "the creative possibilities of hybridity" (Stouck, 2011, 93), many a postcolonialist pathologises the texts' third-space representations. Highlighting that the characters "struggl[e] with their hybrid identities" (Feldner, 2019, 151), "struggle to define themselves" (Klaniecki, 2020, 404) or "struggle to find a point of identification" and "create a sense of belonging" (Cumpsty, 2019, 308), they reproduce what Gohrisch (2021, 466), in a different context, has appropriately referred to as "classless identity-talk".

By contrast, I argue that the middle-class dispositions of Nigerian diasporic authors function as a means of structuring both their novels and the digital book market in which they circulate. In order to substantiate this claim, I draw on two sources that suggest that the novelists' middle-class privileges can be related to two major forces in the contemporary digital milieu of literary transmission: the US-based new media economy and American prestigious universities. Shola Adenekan's *African Literature in the Digital Age* (2021) gives ample inspiration because it adopts socio-economic perspectives on the digital literary sphere. Studying Nigerian and Kenyan writers' online production of poems, short stories and essays, he offers a range of examples that shows that "the digital space provides an alternative to mainstream ideologies, and an opportunity to create new forms of expression" (10) because it allows (aspiring) authors to circumvent established literary gatekeepers. Nonetheless, his survey leaves no doubt that "the notion of digital space is embedded in capitalist commercial mechanisms" (6), demanding consideration of "the way in which class is reified in terms of access" (7) and participation. As Adenekan makes abundantly clear, his choice to concentrate on the online literary creations of Nigerian authors is not random. Accounting for "the majority of most-talked about writers in Anglophone African literature", Nigeria equally represents one of "the most digital hubs on the continent" (8). Given that, according to the latest data,[18] almost half the population of Nigeria has access

---

17 Scholarship on Afropolitanism has exploded in the last years (Coetzee, 2016, 101–03; Durán-Almarza et al., 2017, 107–14; Knudsen and Rahbek, 2016; Wawrzinek and Makokha, 2011). I do not use the term and associated notions such as hybridity as they hamper critical perspectives on the novels. The education of the 16 novelists considered here helps elucidate this observation. Crucially, most of them not only hold degrees in creative writing but also have a training in literary and/or cultural studies. As I demonstrate in the second chapter, this factor contributes to the explanation of why their novels tend to subvert the differentiation between literary language and scholarly meta-language, undermining the analytical function of postcolonial studies' critical vocabulary.

18 Drawing on a 2012 report by the Open Society Foundations, Serena Guarracino (2014, 5) notes that the country "features one of the highest rates of internet

Introduction

to the digital sphere, "one can assume that [...] online Nigerian communities are not only populated by the educated class based in urban areas" (Adenekan and Cousins, 2014, 2). Indeed, this finding reinforces that what is referred to as "the Internet" or "the World Wide Web" designates a tremendously expansive space encompassing a variety of practices across the cultural spectrum. Even though my book reduces the scale of observation to a self-constructed unit of analysis that builds on selected novels and selected platforms of literary discussion, I agree with the proposition by Adenekan (2021, 3, 9) that "middle-class consciousness permeates digital culture" and that "much of what is portrayed in [the] fictional narratives" of the social media-savvy Nigerian authors "is based on the African middle classes".

The entanglement of Nigerian diasporic writers in a second and related structure constituting the digital milieu of literary transmission, the American (and, to a lesser extent, the British) creative writing workshop, strengthens this argument. In his article "The Global Program Era" (2018), Kalyan Nadiminti explains how the creative writing programmes of American universities encourage postcolonial writers to cultivate "a globalizing middle-class voice" and describes the outcome in terms of a "bourgeois sociolect" (377, 382). Close reading two novels by the Indian writers Kiran Desai and Karan Mahajan, he illustrates the extent to which the American university has engendered "a new realist style, one that is deeply inflected by both global capitalism and programmatic writing" (376). As the subsequent chapter demonstrates, his argument is applicable to the new generation of Nigerian authors that "has routed itself through the American university, primarily as students but also as visiting writers, lecturers, and professors" (375).[19] Like Adenekan, Nadiminti emphasises the systemic dimensions of contemporary literary production, evoking the material conditions that govern the creation of the new Nigerian novel. As Richard Jean So and Andrew Piper estimate in their article in *The Atlantic* (2016), the writing workshop "currently contributes more than $200 million a year in revenue to universities in the U.S." Accordingly, tuition fees

---

penetration: one in two Nigerians own an internet-connected device (most frequently a mobile phone), although their use is overwhelmingly concentrated in large urban areas". According to the technology magazine *Computer World*, "Nigeria now [2014] has both the largest number of internet and mobile phone users in Africa. There are more than 43 million internet users in Nigeria and the country accounts for almost forty percent of all internet traffic from the continent" (Adenekan and Cousins, 2014, 2). As of 2017, "the Nigerian Communications Commission estimates that [...] there are over a hundred million Nigerians who have internet-enabled devices" (Adenekan, 2021, 13).

19 Apart from Abani, Adichie and Obioma, Nadiminti (375–76) mentions Okey Ndibe. See Table 2.1, which was compiled through cover information, author websites and online encyclopaedia, for an overview of the degrees received by the 16 novelists covered here. Affiliation with the American or British workshop did not constitute a mandatory criterion for constructing the novel corpus but emerged as a prevalent pattern over the course of my research process.

are notoriously high,[20] and since "only 7 percent of MFA graduates are fully funded" (So and Piper, 2016), access to the renowned programmes invariably requires considerable financial resources.

The postcolonial scholar with an interest in disclosing and disputing unequal power relations will certainly notice that the new Nigerian novel, at least according to the previous paragraphs, depends on a handful of US-based digital companies and universities.[21] Against this backdrop, world-systemic perspectives gain particular significance because they underscore that the novelists, just like their international audiences, do not simply function as market-driven tools. Instead, such perspectives acknowledge that the self-positioning of Nigerian writers in the digital literary economy emerges from combined developments that create uneven effects. Arguably, Amazon's oppressive co-op contracts with publishers, discussed at some length in the third chapter, herald a new paragraph in Nigeria's "history of catastrophically low levels of book production" (Huggan, 2001, 51). The legacies of colonialism also crystallise from the fact that most of the authors receiving international recognition originate from the country's southern parts (including the Niger Delta and the country's oil reserves) and "the urban centres on the coast, especially the financial hub of Lagos" (Feldner, 2019, 21). On the other hand, world-systemic perspectives allow for the realisation that Nigerian novelists "play a crucial role in the creation of collective imaginaries" (Feldner 2019, 21) such as online reading communities. Constituting an occasion for community building in the digital sphere, the new Nigerian novel uses distinctly Nigerian literary motifs and thereby contributes in no small measure to reframing the notion of literary community as well as the social and emotional reading practices commonly associated with it.

Structure of the Book

Giving credit to the genesis of my overall research endeavour, Chapter 2 establishes narratological perspectives on the new Nigerian novel. This literary studies approach proves necessary for several related reasons. To start with, my structuralist look at the novels' recurring narrative means substantiates that market conditions are not positioned outside of but rather inscribe themselves into literature. Accordingly, demonstrating that the novels simultaneously

---

20 For instance, the website of the Graduate Office of Admissions of the University of Iowa states that, in 2020/21, the annual fees for admission into one of the graduate programmes in liberal arts and sciences, including the renowned Iowa Writers' Workshop, amount to more than 50,000 US dollars for international applicants. Students working as assistants pay close to 30,000 US dollars ("Graduate", *Iowa Graduate Admissions*).

21 This is not to mention the fibre optic cables or the smartphone, which, allowing for digital communication in the first place, point to global economic inequalities (Huck, 2020, 113, 125, 179, 180).

raise and fulfil the expectations of their readers saves the affective online communities from accusations of flattening highbrow postcolonial fiction. Along similar lines, my categorisation of the new Nigerian novel as middlebrow constitutes a prerequisite for my construction of digital review corpora detailed in Chapter 3. Since the selection of literary texts predefines the study of their audiences, at least from a literary studies perspective, one should be aware of the aesthetic features creating the responses in the first place. Locating the new Nigerian novel's key middlebrow technique in its continual repetition and variation of the *Bildungsroman* genre, I show that the texts imagine and anticipate their online reading communities, adjusting their members to the structures of digital literary capitalism on the level of narrative. Instead of relating my narratological findings to the business practices of the Internet companies or the reading habits of the reviewers, as I do in Chapters 3 and 4, respectively, this chapter resumes the dominant socio-economic outlook of my book by considering the novelists' education in the creative writing workshop. Reading Mark McGurl's astute observations about *The Program Era* (2009) through the lens of middlebrow studies, I demonstrate that the communal setting of the group workshop supports the authors' smooth transition from analogue to digital contexts of middlebrow literary production. Teaching its participants how to assume and perform an author function (Foucault, 1979, 141–60) in digital contexts, the workshop frames writing as a thoroughly social activity that feeds back into the online practices of distributing and consuming the novels.

Looking at selected conceptions of eighteenth- and nineteenth-century literary communities, Chapter 3 provides transhistorical vantage points on the three online reading formations and their material foundations. Uncovering significant continuities, a glance at some of the precursors and their means of commodifying community and emotion equally discloses how the digital literary economy, and the algorithmic software of Amazon, Goodreads and YouTube more specifically, redefines social interaction and emotional exchange. Drawing on Staab's notion of digital capitalism, I contend that the digital corporations and what I refer to as their algorithms of affect establish relatively closed and personalised "socio-technical ecosystems" (Staab and Nachtwey, 2016, 457) that create a self-enforcing bourgeois emotional structure and thus serve to explain my observations on the meso- and micro-level of the digital literary sphere presented in the subsequent two chapters. Since algorithms not only define the transmission and hence the production and consumption of the new Nigerian novel but also influence their study, I propose how to master the challenges emerging from the researcher's inescapable implication in "algorithmic culture" (Striphas, 2015) with the digital affect. Highlighting the advantages of proceeding from specific datasets as opposed to the digital literary sphere at large, the chapter concludes with an assessment of the possibilities and limitations of employing the tools of corpus-assisted discourse studies (CADS). Proving flexible and versatile enough to consider socio-historical emotion research, the corpus analysis software AntConc allows me to position the online reading communities in a bourgeois history of emotions that substantiates that the reviewers do not simply submit to but rather benefit from their regular participation in the "digital regime of cultural decision making" (Murray, 2018, 56).

Moving from the macro- to the meso-level, Chapter 4 adopts a combination of structuralist and socio-economic perspectives on the system- and user-generated meta-information about the members of the affective online communities to explore the power relations between the Internet companies and their customers or users. Whereas the previous chapter illustrates how precisely Amazon, Goodreads and YouTube capitalise on the middlebrow measures taken to promote reading as a social and emotional activity, this chapter contests one-dimensional notions of power by shifting attention to the reviewers. Examining the recurring patterns in reader profiles as well as in reading contexts, habits and motivations, the chapter presents an integrated narrative that outlines the ways in which readers profit from their contributions to the online discussion of the new Nigerian novel. My interrogation of readerly interests and desires goes beyond Huggan's notion of the postcolonial exotic and puts emphasis on the reviewers' socio-economic aspirations to affirm that they appropriate the community-building efforts of Web 2.0 companies to define themselves as emotionally receptive members of a globalising middle-class culture. The chapter stresses that social media platforms exceed clearly discernible national and/or racial borders, specifying membership primarily in terms of class and gender, not in terms of location or skin colour. Seeking to refine middlebrow studies' definition of "middle class", I suggest that the reviewers' class ambitions and affiliations primarily emerge from their peculiar redefinition and mixture of the amateur form and the Protestant work ethic. Considering scholarly approaches to both emotional and digital labour, moreover, the chapter concludes with the proposition that the digital literary economy promotes a division between paid and unpaid (or poorly paid) labour, assigning the reproductive role of caregiver to the predominantly female reviewers.

Building on the insights into the reviewers' reading habits and motivations, Chapter 5 traces the middle-class emotion ideologies of the reviewers on the linguistic micro-level. I employ the corpus linguistics software AntConc, and especially its concordance, word list and keyword list tools, to scrutinise the lexical, lexico-grammatical and semantic dimensions of the online communities' use of emotional language. Disputing essentialising notions of emotion, the chapter starts with a keyword analysis of the three review corpora to locate what Driscoll (2015, 868) refers to as verbal "emotion hotspots" and demonstrate how the reviewers render distinctions between evaluative and emotional expressions obsolete. While my approach to emotion terms draws on socio-historical emotion research to point out that the discourses of the reviewers show normative and innovative tendencies, my syntactic analysis of affect patterns highlights that their verbal performances of intimacy with fellow readers, characters and authors conceptualise emotions as public states to raise middle-class claims to universality. The final section avails itself of the comparative principle of keyword analysis to return to the middlebrow production and distribution mechanisms of the new Nigerian novel outlined in Chapters 2 and 3. Emphasising that the reviewers do not merely impose their emotions on the books, I contrast the review corpora with a range of other self-constructed online corpora to examine the feedback loops between various agents of the digital literary economy. My computational investigation of selected new Nigerian novels in e-book format, their authors' appearances in YouTube videos and newspaper and publisher blurbs allows me to contend that the digital companies' socio-technical ecosystems and their underlying algorithms of affect create a self-enforcing structure of feeling (Williams, 1977, 128–35) that serves to appropriate national, cultural and/or racial differences to the standards of bourgeois literary culture. Eventually, the digital literary economy proves inclusive of the postcolonial Other, but only with full reserve to middle-class norms and values.

The coda revisits the digital affect to reinforce the conceptual achievements of this book. Corroborating its capacity to interrogate digital literary capitalism from economic macro-, social meso- and linguistic micro-level perspectives, I suggest that the digital affect, apart from invigorating the postcolonial analysis of domination and subordination, inclusion and exclusion processes, initiates new dialogues between and charts future directions for postcolonial and middlebrow studies, digital reception studies and linguistic emotion research.

CHAPTER 2

The New Nigerian Novel as Middlebrow: Materialist and Narratological Approaches

The present chapter requires an introductory comment on the meta-level. Sketching this study's central contentions on the previous pages, I suggested that literary studies approaches to the new Nigerian novel, apart from acknowledging the development of my research agenda, provide effective means of seeing digital literary capitalism at work on the narrative level. Although appropriate, this suggestion also conceals, or at least rearranges, the different phases (of confusion, frustration, reorientation) that I went through during my long-standing occupation with this literary phenomenon. From the perspective of a trained narratologist with a particular interest in postcolonial literatures, the results of the novels' literary analysis are disappointing – that is, neither aesthetically nor politically challenging – and thus unsuitable to ascertain what Bongie (2008, 281) refers to as the "fundamental law" of postcolonial studies. On the other hand, they are not meagre enough to categorise the new Nigerian novel as popular genre fiction and consider other modes of critical inquiry right away. Consequently, it took close to 50 novels to realise that they do not lend themselves to meticulous close readings but demand approaches that take account of the material conditions of their online circulation. In other words, it is thanks to the novels' narratological and political conservatism that this book evolved into a thorough socio-economic investigation of the digital literary sphere of which the new Nigerian novel is but one, although one specifically insightful, manifestation.

Nevertheless, my strong materialist outlook does not preclude literary studies perspectives. Integrating the American and British traditions of researching the middlebrow, I read the novels as communicative acts *and* sign systems, considering literature and the socio-technical means of its transmission "systematically one by the other, one with the other" (Debray, 1999, 4). Defining the techniques of narrating the new Nigerian novel as middlebrow is crucial, as it shows that "[m]aterial technologies and symbolic forms do not constitute separate continents" (Debray, 1999, 2). Rather, the recurring narrative structures of the novels contribute to – indeed, occasion – the creation and expansion of affective online communities. Accordingly, the latter part of this chapter adopts narratological viewpoints to examine the representational means by which the texts envision their community of middlebrow readers. Starting with a discussion of the novels' ever varying repetition of the *Bildungsroman* pattern, I put special emphasis on two prevalent Nigerian motifs to confirm that they serve to construct and comply with the desires of a transnational formation of consumers who turn to the texts to carve and act out an emotionally receptive middle-class identity online. Deviating from the postcolonial practice of analysing individual literary texts, the final two sections build on a corpus of 20 novels and focus on selected case studies with a range of other examples in the background.[1] Aware that this procedure may be disappointing to those readers expecting or looking for a richer sample of the new Nigerian novel as a category of contemporary postcolonial writing, my rather unconventional perspective serves to render visible and verifiable the texts' formulaic means of representation.

Before turning to the novels, however, I present a number of socio-economic explanations for the sparse results of my narratological analysis. While the subsequent chapters interrogate the extent to which the marketing practices of the digital corporations and the reading practices of their customers influence the strategies of narrating the new Nigerian novel, the next pages discuss the authors' passage from the writing workshop to the World Wide Web, showing that the latter builds on the communal structures of the former. In order to set the scene, I read Adichie's third novel *Americanah* as a pioneering example of an emerging digital poetics – that is, the writers' meta-fictional play with the online proliferation of their texts – focusing on its oscillation between the allegedly contradictory institutional forces determining the production and, by extension, the distribution and consumption of the new Nigerian novel.[2]

---

1 The bibliography lists a range of additional titles. My choice of these novels from a considerably larger corpus results from a mixture of research interests that are related to the different disciplines covered and connected in this book. Starting from a generic definition of my case study, I noticed that specific combinations of genre patterns coincide with a notably high online visibility. While the amount of available online reviews constitutes a crucial criterion for a digital humanities scholar, my selection process was not exclusively guided by quantity. Since "[t]he object of transmission does not preexist the mechanism of its transmission" (Debray, 1999, 3), I found it equally important to consider second or third novels, as they can reveal how online literary communities develop over time and therefore promise insight into the long-term effects of the digital literary economy.
2 My reading differs from the various scholarly accounts that concentrate on the novel's "transnational hybridity" (Feldner, 2019, 118; Esplin, 2018, 73–86; Gehrmann, 2016, 61–72; Knudsen and Rahbek, 2017, 115–28; Taylor, 2019, 68–85; Ucham and Kangira, 2015, 42–50). Loosely inspired by Brouillette's (2007, 1, 68) assumptions about postcolonial writers' self-reflexive positioning in the

The Digital Programme Era: Community under Construction

Americanah tells the middle-class tale of Ifemelu, a Nigerian émigré who, equipped with clear parallels to the author's public personality, prepares to return to her home country after 13 years in the United States. Narrated in a series of long flashbacks, the text covers the protagonist's teenage years in Lagos. "[R]aised well fed and watered" yet "hungry for choice and certainty" (N03, 276), Ifemelu accepts a partial scholarship from Pennsylvania University and, in the following years, makes her way through a number of other ivy-league settings before receiving a fellowship at Princeton. Since *Americanah* begins in flashforward, the reader first encounters Ifemelu in the New Jerseyan university town. It is thus on the very first page that the text evokes "the shape of the institution" (Harris, 2014, 6) that informs the professional trajectory of both the protagonist and the writer.³ Noting "the organic grocery store on Nassau Street" as well as "the Gothic buildings with their vine-laced walls", Ifemelu maps Princeton as a venue of "affluent ease", turning her into "someone specifically admitted into a hallowed American club, someone adorned with certainty" (N03, 1). Read as a meta-fictional comment, the university appears as "the ultimate arbitrator of literary worth" (Harris, 2014, 6) that not only supports Ifemelu's career as a "race blogger" (N03, 304) but also establishes the value of the novel itself.

If the Princeton setting functions to award *Americanah* the "honorific status of literature" (McGurl, 2009, 47) from the start, it also initiates a broader meta-fictional discussion about literary taste. Like the feminine middlebrow novel of the early twentieth century, which forges its "distinctive generic identity" via recurring "scenes in which women discuss books, list their favourite authors, or imagine themselves into the plots of their favourite novels" (Humble, 2001, 54, 9), Adichie's text employs contrasting character conceptions and intertextual echoes to define "good" literature and envision

---

global literary market, I argue that Adichie's play with the blog format offers a fictional blueprint for the novel's discussion in affective online communities. By contrast, the digital mode of Braithwaite's *My Sister, the Serial Killer* and Nwaubani's *I Do Not Come to You by Chance* paints a less optimistic picture of the new media economy. Braithwaite's text engages Facebook and Instagram to investigate and disguise crime, suggesting that digital technology facilitates possibly deceptive constructions of self and other. Nwaubani's tale about a 419er, an Internet fraudster, implies that digital communication redefines global economic hierarchies, contesting the kind of transnational solidarity envisioned in Adichie's text.

3 Born in Enugu in 1977 into a professional middle-class family – her father a professor of mathematics, her mother a housewife and guardian of six children – Adichie left Nigeria at the age of 19 to study communication at Connecticut State University. Her career in the American academy encompasses an MA in Creative Writing from Johns Hopkins University, an MA in African Studies from Yale University and a temporary position as Creative Writing lecturer at Princeton University (Table 2.1).

its "ideal" reader. Pondering the reading tastes of her African-American boyfriend – and university professor – for instance, Ifemelu notes Blaine's "ridiculously high-minded" preference for "novels written by young and youngish men and packed with *things*, a fascinating, confounding accumulation of brands and music and comic books and icons, with emotions skimmed over, and each sentence stylishly aware of its own stylishness" (N03, 346, 11–12, original emphasis). Rejecting both his claim to literary superiority and the choice of novels that results from it, Ifemelu cultivates habits of reading that come close to the female middlebrow reader, who, following Humble (2001, 8), "ranges widely in her interests, encompassing many genres of literature, and combining high- and lowbrow interests in a daring disregard for conventional [Blaine's] judgements".[4] Correspondingly, the reader witnesses her taking equal pleasure in African-American novels by Ann Petry and Gayl Jones (N03, 313), thrillers by the British writer James Hadley Chase (N03, 60) and Mills & Boon novels that, though largely "silly", are "jolted by a small truth" (N03, 58).

Given that the middlebrow marketing of *Americanah* stimulates biographical reading modes, it is not hard to recognise why both academic and amateur readers approach the novel as "another instalment of the writer's public persona" (Guarracino, 2014, 3) or "think of Ifemelu as a thinly veiled Adichie" (GR03). In fact, a comparison between Ifemelu and Adichie's "feelings, thoughts and ideas" (GR04) about writing and reading realist fiction yields noteworthy overlaps. For instance, in her speech "To Instruct and Delight" (2012), which was first delivered at an event of the Commonwealth Foundation, Adichie emphasises that the "skimming over" of emotions by no means corresponds to her authorial self-conception; sketching her location between borders, both literally and figuratively, she stresses that her novels "transmit this sensibility [...] that we share, with everybody in every part of the world, a common and equal humanity". A similar tendency to claim universality by means of bourgeois emotion discourses distinguishes the author's agenda to spread "emotional truth" – "a quality that exists not in the kind of fiction that explains but in the kind of fiction that shows" (N04, P.S. Section, 9) – and thus sets fictional examples of cosmopolitan sympathy.

Arguably, *Americanah* realises Adichie's "liberal ideal of multicultural diversity and attentiveness to global issues" (Brouillette and Coleman, 2020, 584) via

---

4 Indeed, Ifemelu is fully aware of "that gently forbearing tone he used when they talked about novels, as though he was sure that she, with a little more time and a little more wisdom, would come to accept that the novels he liked were superior" (N03, 11). At another instance, "she felt like his apprentice: when they wandered through museums, he would linger at abstract paintings, which bored her, and she would drift to the bold sculptures or the naturalistic paintings, and sense in his tight smile his disappointment that she had not yet learned enough from him" (N03, 312–13). Remarkably, both the novel's narrative perspective and plot construction work in favour of Ifemelu's reading practices. Marked by unbridgeable differences in literary and cultural taste, Ifemelu and Blaine's romantic relationship is bound for failure.

literary experiments with the blog format. Evoking the digital networks of power and communication that structure the world-literary system, Ifemelu's blog writing may well be read as a meta-fictional comment on another (and allegedly opposing) production context of the novel (Guarracino, 2014, 3). Interspersed throughout the main narrative, the many entries from her blog *Raceteenth* complement the novel's negotiation of diasporic experiences. Shifting the narrative perspective from third- to first-person narration, the blog serves to compare and contrast distinct means of narrating migration. That blogging promises more immediate and personal modes of communication is suggested by the events that surround the creation of the blog. Following the breakup with her "Hot White Ex" Curt, Ifemelu emails her observations about the racial prejudices that complicated the relationship to her university friend Wambui. Wambui's electronic response raises two aspects about digital communication that concern me throughout this study: "This is so raw and true. More people should read this. You should start a blog" (N03, 295). Permitting instant and continual reactions from "readers […] all over the world" (N03, 304), Ifemelu's blog apparently provides a virtual meeting point that possesses a special "emotional value" (Guarracino, 2014, 14) for the writer and her audience.[5] The second feature is reinforced by the fact that Blaine's highbrow disposition clashes with the kind of communication model that Ifemelu has in mind: "She did not ask for his edits, but slowly she began to make changes, to add and remove, because of what he said. […] Her posts sounded too academic, too much like him" (N03, 312). Rather than writing academic papers that "include details about government policy" (N03, 314) and other "serious" sources, Ifemelu conceptualises blogging as a means of encouraging personal exchange about care products for black hair ("A Michelle Obama Shout-Out Plus Hair as Race Metaphor", N03, 296–98) or sharing her experience of depression ("On the Subject of Non-American Blacks Suffering from Illnesses Whose Names They Refuse to Know", N03, 158).[6]

---

5 The media studies scholar Jodi Dean (2010, 63, 112) contends that blogs create a "productive affective space" because "networks are not only networks of computers, protocological and fiber-optic networks. They are also affective networks capturing people." Building on her insights, Huck (2020, 64–65, 76–77, 80–83, 121) suggests that the algorithmic recommendation systems of Amazon and other digital companies function to foster a sense of familiarity among their users. I revisit his argument in Chapters 3 and 4.

6 Illustrating the extent to which Adichie blurs the line between her public persona and her protagonist and turns both of them into durable products, Ifemelu's second blog *The Small Redemptions of Lagos* continues on the author's official website. The first post, "Ifem & Ceiling 1", establishes the blog's exclusive focus on the romance between Ifemelu and her childhood sweetheart Obinze, which is rekindled towards the end of *Americanah*: "Ceiling and I have been spending a lot of time in Enugu. I love Enugu, the sense of restfulness; it has a certain ambition about it – the mall, the new roads – but it retains a small-town feel. Here, strangers still greet one another. […] Yesterday, after a brief rain, we […] sat

That the divide between the academic and online spaces of producing the new Nigerian novel is less definite than *Americanah*'s meta-fictional comments make the reader believe is implied by McGurl. In his article "Everything and Less: Fiction in the Age of Amazon" (2016),[7] he establishes at least an indirect link between the creative writing programmes of renowned American universities and the world's leading online retailer: "At the moment, one would have to say that they are merely adjacent literary-historical phenomena, although there is nothing standing in the way of their partial convergence in, say, the publication as KDP e-books of otherwise dead MFA theses" (451).[8] Drawing on my reading of *Americanah*, I seek to create a more immediate connection between the two institutional forces that determine the position of the new Nigerian novel in an increasingly digitised world-literary system. I argue that the writing workshop constitutes a significant training ground that functions to prepare new Nigerian novelists' presence in the digital literary sphere. Translating the workshop's collective structures into their novels and the digital spaces that define their public discussion, Nigerian diasporic authors not only occasion the formation of affective online communities but also contribute to the discursive means by which their members negotiate their socio-economic and, by extension, their affective belonging to bourgeois literary culture.

My argument expands upon two surveys that, taken together, outline the development of the creative writing programme since its proliferation in American universities in the 1950s. Presenting the first substantial investigation of the programme, McGurl (2009, ix, 63) rewrites "postwar American literary history" by adopting literary-sociological viewpoints on the fictions of Ken Kesey, Joyce Carol Oates, Philip Roth, John Updike and other postwar authors who wrote "under the auspices of creative writing instruction". Paying particular attention to the socio-economic conditions that turned the university into "the most important patron of artistically ambitious literary practice in the United States" (22), the book historian relates the programme's rise to the emergence of a post-industrial service economy and the concomitant need for and growth of white-collar professions (13–14):

---

on that bench in the evening cool, and ate boiled corn and ube. Bliss" ("Ifemelu's Blog", *Chimamanda Adichie*, 2014, original emphasis).

7 McGurl has meanwhile published a monograph, *Everything and Less: The Novel in the Age of Amazon* (2021), which offers further discussions of his central contentions.

8 The abbreviation KDP refers to Amazon's Kindle Direct Publishing, an initiative "designed to circumvent the traditional gatekeepers of American literary production, ushering in a new age of self-authorized popular creativity and low-cost literary entertainment" (McGurl, 2016, 449). Of the 20 novels investigated in this book, one is indeed a final thesis: Iweala's debut *Beasts of No Nation* was originally supervised by Jamaica Kincaid and Patricia Powell at Harvard University but published by Harper Perennial and not via Amazon's KDP (N13, xi).

In the 1940s, fewer than 10 percent of traditional college-age Americans were attending college of some kind; by the 1980s more than half of them were doing so, and the very concept of the delimited college age, with the rise of continuing education, job retraining, and other part-time extension initiatives, was beginning to weaken somewhat. During this period universal access to higher education became a widely shared, if only partially realized, national ideal embodied in educational grant and guaranteed loan programs offered to individual students on an unprecedented scale. (282)

Correspondingly, McGurl (2016, 453) describes the writing programme as part and parcel of a large-scale higher education movement serving to transform "industrial relations of production into postindustrial relations of service". In other words, the university system promoted a substantial shift in the conception of the writer and his or her task. Offering authorship as a middle-class occupation, it converted the author into a provider who worked for the reader, imagining and mediating the changing socio-economic, cultural and emotional relations of postwar America in literary form.[9]

Locating the postwar American writer within "the history of bourgeois liberal individualism" (Brouillette, 2016, 82), McGurl (2009, 60) demonstrates how mass higher education "substantially narrowed" the social divide constitutive of the interwar modernist period. His discussion of three creative writing "imperatives" – "write what you know", "find your voice" and "show don't tell" – suggests that the programme created a rather homogeneous set of authors and texts in conformity with middle-class values such as "self-discipline" and "self-creation" (23, 81, 3). However, and as Nadiminti (2018, 379) cautions, it would be an oversimplification to view the programme's creation of "a distinctly bourgeois, professionalized consciousness" as entirely "streamlined". Rather, McGurl (2009, 66, 67) stresses "the amorphous potentiality and mobility of the American middle class" and discerns three modes of writing, including the "technomodernism" of "an upper middle class, for whom economic security is a given and higher education is understood as a virtual birthright", such as Richard Powers or Thomas Pynchon, and the "lower-middle-class modernism" of Raymond Carver or Jayne Anne Phillips, who created "probably the most characteristic [...] product" of the programme. The third strand, "high cultural pluralism" or "multiculturalism", is represented by so-called "ethnic writers"

---

9 Reading Illouz's *Cold Intimacies* (2007), one may conclude that the American writer investigated in McGurl's study negotiated these relations in "a new [...] therapeutic emotional style" (6). Although Illouz does not focus on the American creative writing programme, her study illustrates that, "as American society became oriented toward a service economy [...], a scientific discourse that dealt primarily with persons, interactions, and emotions was the natural candidate to shape the language of selfhood in the workplace" (16). In a similar vein, McGurl (2009, 16) describes the programme in terms of a "therapeutic educational enterprise".

who are "called upon to speak from the point of view of one or another hyphenated population" and combine programmatic writing with their "own repository of storytelling tradition", such as Sandra Cisneros or Toni Morrison (McGurl, 2009, 57, 236).

Building on his expertise in twenty-first-century South Asian and African diasporic fiction, Nadiminti (2018) updates McGurl's investigation of the "ethnic writer" and his or her relation to the American university system.[10] No longer occupying a marginal position in "the project of American multiculturalism", which involved temporary visits to the literature departments across the country, the global South writer "has now become an integral part of a financialized creative class" (380, 376).[11] Giving equal attention to the similarities and differences between the postwar and the "global program era", as the title of his article has it, Nadiminti (377) confirms that the expansion of the programme beyond national borders did not substantially modify its functions: "Just as the postwar writing program nurtured a hegemonic middle-class voice as the stabilizing force of American letters, [...] the post-9/11 period builds on the historical legacy of the writing program to produce a globalizing middle-class voice as the bedrock of non-Western anglophone writing." Following Huggan and other representatives of the discipline's materialist branch in assuming that the conditions of production, distribution and consumption manifest themselves in the literary text, the second part of Nadiminti's article shifts the focus towards Kiran Desai's *The Inheritance of Loss* (2006) and Karan Mahajan's *The Association of Small Bombs* (2016). His analysis of the two Anglophone Indian novels illustrates that the literary production of Otherness currently expresses itself in the mode of "vernacular anglophone realism" – a "strategic reification of linguistic difference toward ultimately strengthening a global, English language-dominated market position" (378). Viewing the programme through the postcolonial studies lens, Nadiminti convincingly clarifies why the systematic production of postcolonial writing yields assimilative effects. Since the "professional position as [a] member of the creative class within the American university" offers financial assurance, one may well comprehend why Desai and Mahajan, just as their Nigerian colleagues, avoid all too obvious "gestures of protest" (393). Largely neglecting how the economic and social circumstances that created the workshop reverberate in the global and increasingly digital programme era,

---

10 In fact, Nadiminti (376) accuses McGurl of "ignor[ing] the prominence of global South writers within American educational institutions". As his use of the term "global South" highlights, his postcolonial outlook gestures beyond McGurl's (2009, 381) narrow conception of an "*American* writer of color" (original emphasis).

11 For instance, Achebe's short-term position as a lecturer at the University of Massachusetts Amherst markedly differs from the permanent or long-term assignments of Nigerian diasporic novelists such as Cole, Evans or Obioma (Table 2.1). Hinting at Achebe's Chancellor's lecture about "Racism in Conrad's *Heart of Darkness*" (1975), Nadiminti (2018, 380) notes that "Achebe was hardly a pliant professor" but rather retained his critical perspective on American institutions of (stereotypical) knowledge production (about Africa).

though, Nadiminti pays scant attention to the functions and effects that the globalising middle-class voice serves beyond individual monetary interests.

By contrast, I propose that the programmatic voice of the new Nigerian novelists takes the service concept of postwar American authors to a "New Economy" level.[12] Writing under the conditions of a digitised service economy, Adichie and her creative writing peers (or protégés) neither possess nor provide the technological means of reconfiguring the relationships among their readers but doubtlessly have their fair share in envisioning and negotiating them. As their creative writing degrees indicate, Nigerian diasporic writers anticipate their online communities of readers from middle-class positions – and to middlebrow effects. Other than their reputation as "central conservators of modernist literary value" (McGurl, 2009, x) implies, universities and their creative writing programmes are not incompatible with the practices that this study identifies as middlebrow. On the contrary, McGurl and Nadiminti's historical and materialist perspectives on widely different fictions illuminate that, in the words of Fredric Jameson (2012), the university is hardly "that great vacation which precedes the real life of earning your living, having a family, finding yourself inextricably fixed in society and its institutions"; instead of existing as an autonomous "enclave", the neoliberal university is firmly implicated in economic power structures. The American creative writing programme constitutes a specifically "big business" (So and Piper, 2016) that, ever since the foundation of the Iowa Writers' Workshop in 1936, has steadily increased. McGurl (2009, 24) estimates that, by the turn of the millennium, American universities housed "350 creative writing programs" and adds that, "[i]f one includes undergraduate degree programs, that number soars up to 720". And, although the programme is, "in sum, as American as baseball, apple pie, and homicide" (McGurl, 2009, 364), it has long made its way into British, Australian and other institutions of higher education. Adichie's Farafina Trust Creative Writing Workshop (2009–16) proves that the model has reached Nigeria.[13] Contributing a yearly revenue of 200 million US dollars to American universities alone, creative writing may well be described as "the largest system of literary patronage for living writers that the world

---

12 McGurl (2016, 448) discusses Amazon as a key representative "of the so-called New Economy, and of the centrality of information and communication technology thereto". His characterisation of the American service economy as "a form of *social relation*" (453, original emphasis) is compatible with the research of Illouz (2007, 3, 7), which, starting from the assumption that "social arrangements are also emotional arrangements", suggests that a new "emotional style takes place when a new interpersonal imagination is formulated". Like McGurl, Illouz (2007, 5) traces the continuities between the postwar and the post-millennial service economy when she discusses how online dating sites structure their users' emotional relations according to "the logic of economic relations".
13 The workshop was renamed Purple Hibiscus Trust Creative Writing Workshop in 2018 and advanced the international literary careers of newcomers like Emezi (Table 2.1).

has ever seen" (Fenza, 2006, 1). These numbers reinforce that the university, similar to Oprah's Book Club or the Man Booker Prize, interweaves "artistic and commercial goals" (Driscoll, 2014, 152).

Owing to its middle position between the autonomous and heteronomous poles that delineate Pierre Bourdieu's (1996, 121, 142) literary field model, the programme has always evoked the same debates about literary quality or value that characterise the historical middlebrow. In his "Preface" of an essay collection titled *The Unprofessionals* (2015), for instance, Lorin Stein (x) bemoans that the workshop creates "lower standards" because it pays "less regard for artistic, as opposed to commercial, success". Furthermore, noting that "clonal fabrications of writers proliferate in these programs at an astounding rate", John W. Aldridge (1990, 33) voices the same concerns about the institutionalised production of formulaic fiction that inform Leavis's critical remarks on the Book Society. The mission statement of the Iowa Writers' Workshop ("Philosophy") addresses the highbrow fear that everyone with an appropriate training can write thus: "Though we agree in part with the popular insistence that writing cannot be taught, we exist and proceed on the assumption that talent can be developed, and we see our possibilities and our limitations as a school in that light."

Deconstructing "the Romantic ideal of the lonely, humble artist" (So and Piper, 2016), creative writing programmes thrive on the neoliberal educational beliefs and desires of the middle classes. Given that their affiliates (and aspirants) have justified their socio-economic authority via distinct emotion ideologies all along, as I elaborate in subsequent chapters, it is certainly no coincidence that the workshop – with its "'sticky' group dynamic" – adopts a "notoriously amorous approach" to literature in general and to the act of writing in particular, encouraging a sense of "pleasure in study" (McGurl, 2009, 7, 6), literary creation and discussion among its ethnically heterogeneous participants. Pondering his training at Brown University, for instance, Rick Moody (2005) remarks that his instructor John Hawkes

> wanted us to believe in literature. He felt he had done his job if we could explain why [Vladimir Nabokov's] *The Real Life of Sebastian Knight* was a masterpiece, from the standpoint of language and construction. Hawkes played favorites, which was bad; and he loved women a lot more than men, which was bad too; and he allowed us to drink wine in class, which in my case was an incredibly bad idea, since I was developing a drinking problem. All these things were inadvisable, but what was not was the idea of emotional commitment to the process.

Moody's account serves to illustrate McGurl's (2009, 96) conceptualisation of the workshop as "a small-scale 'pathological public sphere'" that, turning the writing act into a collective effort, encourages feelings of familiarity and fellowship among its likeminded trainees.

Many postcolonial scholars have pointed to the online presence of Nigerian diasporic authors (Cruz-Gutiérrez, 2019, 66–79; Darroch, 2020,

135–50; Guarracino, 2014, 1–27; Pahl, 2016, 73–87; Shringarpure, 2020, 1–22; Toivanen, 2016, 135–61). Few have done so to consider the "middle-class consciousness" (Adenekan, 2021, 3) or community-building agenda and effect that distinguishes the marketing of their novels on social media. To the best of my knowledge, none has hitherto related their fictional and digital contributions to the creation of affective online communities to their vocational training in the writing workshop. I suggest that the common creative writing background of the new Nigerian novelists proves instrumental in forging digital literary communities that rest on shared middlebrow practices of reading and bourgeois discourses of feeling. Exceeding the national efforts of the postwar American writer, Adichie, Cole and other representatives of third- or fourth-generation Nigerian writing project the motif of self-realisation that emerges from the workshop's diasporic-academic connection beyond the seminar room to strengthen the socio-economic and affective supremacy of the globalising middle classes in the digital literary sphere.

In fact, a preliminary glimpse at the three reading formations investigated in this book discloses the extent to which literary community building in the World Wide Web feeds on the "sociable spirit", "communal endeavor" and "therapeutic educational enterprise" that McGurl (2009, 5, 16) deems characteristic of the group workshop. Following the middlebrow pattern of consumption, members of the online communities consider "awe towards" (Driscoll, 2014, 22) and identification with writers a vital prerequisite for selecting and enjoying a literary text, frequently expressing their "boundless admiration" (GR10) for or their wish to connect with the new Nigerian novelists. Adhering to the workshop principle of "writing what they know", Nigerian authors considerably enhance this sense of intimacy with them and their literary texts, which is confirmed by the reviewers' many references to and quotes from paratextual sources. Adichie's "The Danger of a Single Story" (2009) and "We Should All Be Feminists" (2013), which started life as highly acclaimed TED Talks[14] and are meanwhile available on YouTube, are mentioned in my review corpora no less than 41 and 45 times, respectively.[15]

---

14 Founded in 1984 as an annual conference, TED ("Technology, Entertainment, Design") has quickly turned into an online venture, providing a plethora of "short, powerful talks" ("Our Mission", *TED*) on various themes, including business, science and culture. The mission statement defines the work of the NPO in terms of building "a global community, welcoming people from every discipline and culture who seek a deeper understanding of the world" ("Our Mission", *TED*).

15 Promotional paratexts such as the "Author's Note" in Okparanta's novel, which frames the fate of her lesbian protagonist as part of the writer's "attempts to give Nigeria's marginalized LGBTQ citizens a more powerful voice" (N17, 325), continue to circulate in analogue form. Emezi's "Transition" article in *The Cut*, an online magazine "for women with sharp, stylish minds" ("About Us", *The Cut*), in turn, indicates that the marketing of authorial life narratives has moved online. Supporting their readers' diversity management, Emezi (2018) describes their sex reassignment surgeries as a choice "to move toward myself". Listed in the

Constituting the "first encounter" with the writers, as an Amazon reviewer called Student2 (AR04) states, these paratexts not only decide whether a reader picks up a novel but, significantly, serve as prevalent interpretation frames. Accordingly, Student2 (AR04) notes that *Half of a Yellow Sun* "presents her [Adichie's] principles from her TED Talk", while Amanda Elise Carina (YR03) remarks that *Americanah* "feels like an extension of that speech".

Ensuring that readers approach the new Nigerian novels as autobiographies of their authors and understand them as "the expression and manifestation of the individual psychic life" (Brouillette and Coleman, 2020, 586), these "marketing stories" (Squires, 2007, 119–46) foster middlebrow discourses of authenticity, honesty and trust. Reviewers take offence at supposedly "inauthentic" accounts that contradict "the frame of the author's personal experience and views" (Driscoll, 2014, 168). Discussing Iweala's civil war narrative *Beasts of No Nation*, an Amazon customer states that "I felt a little betrayed knowing that he had not been a child soldier" and "started enjoying the book less" (AR13). In a similar vein, one Goodreads reviewer laments the "white British accent" (GR05) of the speaker who reads the audiobook version of Adichie's *Purple Hibiscus*, as it reduces the credibility of the characters.[16] Abiding by the workshop rules, which bear a conspicuously close resemblance to the "Community Guidelines" of Amazon, Goodreads and YouTube,[17] new Nigerian novelists almost unanimously avoid accusations of "inauthenticity" by securing that their protagonists correspond to their own biographies and public personae. Of the 20 novels covered in this book, merely one complicates the equation of main character and author in gender terms. Yet although *I Do Not Come to You by Chance* features the male scammer Kingsley, Nwaubani's novel proves "an honest [enough] attempt" to be received as "a true depiction of [Nigerian] society" (GR14).

The marketing promise of "authentic" fiction increasingly assumes digital dimensions, offering "authors unprecedented opportunities to directly shape and constantly micromanage their public image" (Murray, 2018, 24).[18] While

---

bibliography of author videos, Adichie's TED Talks are approached with corpus linguistics software in Chapter 5.

16 The same sense of betrayal that the reviewers express in view of such perceived "inauthentic" accounts informs Oprah Winfrey's handling of the controversy surrounding James Frey, whose memoir, *A Million Little Pieces* (2003), proved to be invented. Stressing the ethical agenda of her reading pattern, Winfrey publicly accused Frey of abusing her audience's trust (Driscoll, 2014, 72–74).

17 The middlebrow register that characterises the "Community Guidelines" of these platforms, including the appeal to "[b]ring your authentic self" ("Community Guidelines", *Goodreads*) to online discussions, is addressed in Chapter 3.

18 As the recent social media controversy involving Adichie and Emezi indicates, the new Nigerian novelists employ their Instagram and Twitter accounts or official websites not only to market their novels but also to initiate meta-discussions about the influence of new media technologies on authorial self-fashioning (Flood, 2021).

these opportunities increase emerging authors' "financial and time burden for publicizing and marketing their own work", established writers use the possibility of "bypassing [...] publisher and media gatekeepers" and employ their new media accounts as "a direct channel of communication with their readerships" (Murray 2018, 37, 36). Indeed, the large majority of the 16 new Nigerian novelists engages in the same practices that characterise their middlebrow readers: they run their own websites, regularly post messages on their Facebook, Instagram and Twitter or enable Amazon customers to follow them and thus keep track of their new publications. The status as "Goodreads Author", moreover, entails the public sharing of writers' "reading lives", with the profiles detailing their reading schedules, current reads and blog posts, allowing the reviewers to envision them as "people like you and me" (AR05) or entertain "possibilities of friendship and connection" (GR03) across the globe.[19]

The specific socio-economic contexts of creating the new Nigerian novel and its online communities of readers entails what Humble (2001, 54), in view of the early twentieth-century middlebrow novel, has described as "a distinctive generic identity".[20] Similarly, and shifting from materialist to narratological means of categorising the new Nigerian novel as middlebrow, I read the novels' characteristic genre mixing as a middlebrow strategy of addressing a variety of readerly concerns. Blending the prevalent *Bildungsroman* pattern with generic features of the romance, Gothic and crime fiction, the historical novel and/or the novel of migration, they meet the online reviewers' preference for texts that are "complex and simple at the same time" (YR02, Ellen), "most unique" (GR10) and yet accessible and, to a certain degree, compatible and consistent with prior experiences of reading (new Nigerian fiction). Securing their reception as "[r]eally excellent *literary* fiction" (AR02, my emphasis), the novels' continual variation of the *Bildungsroman* formula caters to the bourgeois ideal of "intellectual growth" (AR16). Considering that they write in the digital programme era, it is no coincidence that third- or fourth-generation authors, in contrast to their precursors, produce *novels* in the *realist* mode.[21] A middle-class invention that, according to Moretti (1987, 4), served eighteenth- and nineteenth-century

---

19 Chapter 5 takes account of the observation that new Nigerian novelists are "all over YouTube at the moment" (YR04, Kitty G, 23/07/2016) and presents a corpus-linguistic analysis of selected author videos.

20 "[T]he middlebrow novel is one that straddles the divide between trashy romance or thriller on the one hand, and the philosophically or formally challenging novel on the other: offering narrative excitement without guilt, and intellectual stimulation without undue effort" (Humble, 2001, 11). Although Humble has little to say about the imperial discourses pervading her corpus of primary texts (Gohrisch, 2020, 116), her study provides inspiration on the methodological level as it relates the formal features of the middlebrow novel to the socio-economic interests of a growing female and middle-class reading public in interwar Britain (Humble, 2001, 3, 13–14).

21 Adesanmi and Dunton (2008, viii) discuss the "phenomenal revival of the Nigerian

readers to manage "the new and destabilizing forces of capitalism", it proves just as supportive in adjusting twenty-first-century audiences to the economic structures of the World Wide Web.

Discussing the middlebrow aesthetics of Sunjeev Sahota's *The Year of the Runaways* (2015), Zadie Smith's *Swing Time* (2016) and Mahsuda Snaith's *The Things We Thought We Knew* (2017), Gesa Stedman (2020, 209) observes that the novels "teach their middle-class, white, largely female audience something which this audience is not so familiar with". Drawing on my insights into the online communities' demographic structures in Chapter 4, I would like to modify this observation, which resonates with Huggan's (2008, 112) assumptions about a "Western model reader". Instead of catering exclusively to the "exotic" desires of white readers, the new Nigerian novelist addresses an ethnically heterogeneous audience that, apart from readers who are located in Nigeria, includes numerous members of the "new" African diaspora, encompassing second-generation migrants who have never seen or only sporadically visit the home country of their parents.[22] Correspondingly, I propose that the new Nigerian novel mixes bourgeois realist means of representation with two Nigerian motifs, the twin and Biafra, to fictionalise both the fragmentation and reconciliation of its affective online communities, simultaneously creating and fulfilling the emotional needs of readers who seek participation in the globalised and digitised literary economy of the twenty-first century.[23]

---

novel" as a defining feature of third-generation writing. Jane Bryce (2008, 52) notes that "recent novels by Nigerian women are predominantly realist".

22 Feldner (2019, 15) states that "more than thirty million Africans [are currently] living outside their homelands". The scope of the African diaspora is so extensive that the African Union refers to it as the continent's "sixth region" since 2005 (Quayson, 2013, 629). Evoking a centuries-long history of colonialism, the "new" African diaspora points to a period of "comparatively voluntary emigration from Africa in the second half of the twentieth century" (Feldner, 2019, 15). Some diaspora studies scholars further distinguish between three different migration waves to the United States and other countries in the global North. The third wave of migration, beginning with the turn of the century and continuing to this day, is commonly ascribed to the "unyielding desire" of skilled and unskilled Africans "to pursue global economic integration" (Arthur et al., 2012, 4). As the notion of the new Nigerian novel implies, the model has been instrumental in conceptualising Anglophone Nigerian writing in terms of three phases or generations of authors (Adesanmi and Dunton, 2008, vii–xii; Dalley, 2013, 15–34).

23 My argument is modelled on Timothy Aubry's (2011, 1, 10) contention that "contemporary therapeutic fiction", including such novels as Khaled Hosseini's *The Kite Runner* (2003) and David Foster Wallace's *Infinite Jest* (1996), "imagine[s], address[es] and interpellat[es] their readers", potentially "construct[ing] the desires that they purport to satisfy". Albeit covering different primary texts, Aubry inspires this chapter, as the new Nigerian novel may be categorised as middlebrow fiction with a therapeutic twist.

The Trope of the Twin: Fragmentation

Without doubt, the twin motif constitutes a staple ingredient of the new Nigerian novel, pervading the debuts of Emezi and Evans, Oyeyemi and Selasi, Adichie's *Half of a Yellow Sun* and Habila's *Measuring Time* alike. The number of examples further increases if one includes novels featuring an aesthetics of "twinning and doubling" (Cooper, 2008, 61) on the level of setting and/or character, such as Adebayo's *Stay With Me*, Adichie's *Purple Hibiscus* and Atta's *Everything Good Will Come*. The trope of the twin occupies a central position in Anglophone Nigerian literature, appearing in Achebe's landmark novel *Things Fall Apart* (1958), the poem "Abiku" (1961) by the Nobel Prize laureate Wole Soyinka and Okri's Booker Prize-winning novel *The Famished Road* (1991), to name but a few titles. Elisha P. Renne (2001, 63) implies that the literary archetype of the "ogbanje" or "abiku", which derives from Igbo or Yoruba mythology, respectively, addresses the allegedly high rate of twin births in Nigeria that, by medical accounts, shows a "four-fold difference [...] compared with European populations". Chikwenye Okonjo Ogunyemi (1996, 61–62), on the other hand, relates the trope to Nigeria's high infant mortality. Whereas its origins are hard to determine, the notion of the spirit child and the many rituals and objects designed to honour it attest to Nigerian cultural beliefs in the supernatural power of twins (Oruene, 1985, 209–10; Renne, 2001, 66). Signalling "the mystical, unsettled condition of simultaneously existing in several spheres" (Ogunyemi, 1996, 62), the trope has served Nigerian writers to "comment on the complexity of the interfaces of identity, particularly [...] in relation to evolving postcolonial African worlds" (Ouma, 2014, 188). Set around the period of Nigerian independence in 1960, Okri's novel realises the abiku via the protagonist Azaro, who comes to signify the eternally "unfulfilled destiny" (Berndt, 2007, 75) of Nigeria: "a spirit-child nation, one that keeps being reborn and after each birth come blood and betrayals, and the child of our will refuses to stay till we have made propitious sacrifice and displaced our serious intent to bear the weight of a unique destiny" (Okri, 1992, 494).

Conventionally considered as "the most sophisticated expression of magical realism in African literature" (Quayson, 2009, 173; Berndt, 2007, 75), *The Famished Road* employs a distinctly Nigerian literary motif to enunciate an unequivocal political commitment to postcolonial nation-building. Contemporary literary representations of the ogbanje or abiku undoubtedly resonate with this and other precursors. However, owing to the new Nigerian novelists' diasporic condition, the trope overwhelmingly serves to narrate the migration experiences of young Nigerian girls and women. Repeating the novels' discursive means and interpretive approaches, various scholars describe the female redefinition of the trope along the narrow lines of hybridity. Discussing Evans's *26a*, Irene Pérez-Fernández (2013, 292) argues that Bessi and Georgia "identify themselves as hybrid diasporic identities". In a similar vein, Jordan Stouck (2011, 107) reads Oyeyemi's *The Icarus Girl* "as embodying the conflicts and losses of hybridity and exposing the dissolution of identity that hybridity can [...] entail". Adopting biographical perspectives, Brenda Cooper (2008, 52) notes that the texts' use of twins provides "a coded language for the writers' own splitting, doubling and questing for their identities", while Madelaine Hron (2008, 30) confirms that it enables a "new generation of Nigerian writers to explore its own hybrid position in contemporary postcolonial society".[24]

Distancing myself from such readings, I interpret the novels' pervasive twin motif as a significant means of staging the national, cultural and racial heterogeneity of their affective online communities. Placing their young and predominantly female protagonists between American or British and Nigerian points of reference, novels such as *The Icarus Girl* or *Freshwater* offer possibilities of affective identification for heterogeneous middlebrow audiences who seek membership in the globalising middle classes. Instead of fostering national/ist discourses, the ogbanje or abiku constitutes Nigeria's contribution to a global self-help industry (Illouz, 2008). Demystifying the magical realism of earlier generations, new Nigerian novelists integrate the trope of the twin into the bourgeois realist structures of the *Bildungsroman*, providing both their academic and amateur readers with a profitable addition to the therapeutic lexicon that pervades middlebrow literary culture online. Inviting debates about "mental problems" such as "bipolarity" (Feldner, 2019, 147) or "psychological suffering in immigration" (Hron, 2008, 37), the motif of the twin serves middle-class readers to publicly affirm "their sense of themselves as deep, complicated, emotionally responsive human beings" (Aubry, 2011, 1).

That the new Nigerian novel is not primarily or exclusively concerned with narrating the post-independence nation emerges from the plot constructions, spatial representations and character constellations of two examples. Negotiating the experiences of second-generation Nigerians, *The Icarus Girl* and *26a* are mainly set in the suburbs of London, inviting the reader into the "houses of the striving middle classes" (Cuder-Domínguez, 2009, 279). Divided into three parts of varying length, Oyeyemi's novel unfolds in 1990s Cranbrook and is merely framed by the Harrison family's visit to the mother's home in Ibadan. However, it is here that the main conflict is both evoked and resolved, for the protagonist's trip to Nigeria engenders TillyTilly, a mysterious girl "around her own age" and with "an exact match of [her] voice" (N19, 47), whom Jessamy (Jess) can only cast off after one year of countless temper tantrums. Covering a period of 25 years that starts with the twins' birth and closes with Georgia's suicide, Evans's novel is prominently set in 1980s and 1990s Neasden but also locates the most pertinent of its 14 chapters in Sekon, a fictional place in Nigeria, which heralds a break in the twins' "twoness of oneness" (N11, 69).

---

24 For related readings of the two novels, see Cuder-Domínguez, 2009, 277–86; Feldner, 2019, 147–63; Gunning, 2015, 119–32; Mafe, 2012, 21–35; Ouma, 2014, 188–205.

While the journeys to the maternal home country provide key means of advancing plot and character development, both texts present "a catalogue of commonplace routines" instead of "diasporic routes" (McLeod, 2010, 47). Comparing *26a* to the Black British *Bildungsromane* by David Dabydeen or Bernardine Evaristo, John McLeod (2010, 47) observes that "the novel does not overtly explore the problems of a Black British community", just as the Hunter family does not inhabit "a visibly prejudicial or discriminatory environment". Rather, the suburban life of the twins appears "unspectacularly aligned with the public travails of national happenings" (McLeod, 2010, 47): for instance, when Bessi and Georgia deliberate on the impending divorce of their parents while watching the royal wedding of Charles and Diana (N11, 15–25) or have their first sexual encounters while Michael Jackson performs at Wembley (N11, 119–25). Ironically, the twins stress their "Britishness" by marking the front door of their attic room in 26a Waifer Avenue with their initials G+B: "This was the extra dimension. The one after sight, sound, smell, touch and taste where the world multiplied and exploded because it was the sum of two people" (N11, 5). Unifying and dividing the protagonists at the same time, the plus sign foreshadows a rupture in the twins' exceptional bond that is, however, not directly related to Bessi and Georgia's dual heritage. If anything, it is their parents' marriage that bears the burden of migration.[25] Similarly, Jess exhibits limited knowledge of Nigeria. Neither does she identify with her Yoruba name (N19, 21) nor does she make any endeavour to learn her mother's language (N19, 51). Instead, she calls a Yoruba dish the "'prawn thing'" (N19, 204) and frequently mispronounces Yoruba terms (N19, 200, 294), consistently printed in italics to emphasise Jess's outside perspective on Nigeria (Hron, 2008, 36). Just as in Evans's novel, then, the consequences of migration tend to play out between the protagonist's parents.[26] Briefly but effectively relocating the plot

---

25 The novel's negotiation of cultural difference revolves around domestic banalities such as cooking and furnishing (Cuder-Domínguez, 2009, 281). Evoking the image "of someone who [...] had never fully arrived" (N11, 18), Ida only glances at the "books on English cookery" (N11, 15–16), denies her husband Aubrey his pudding (N11, 19) and, in attempts at defying the bad weather, "warm[s] everything up" (N11, 18). The Neasden household's interior underlines that "[t]here were three thousand miles between [Ida's] rocker and [Aubrey's] chocolate armchair" (N11, 23). In the childhood home of the twins, a "carving of an old spirit woman with horns" (N11, 37–38) and "an eyeless black mask" collide with "miniature watercolours of the English countryside" and "a [...] tapestry of the Derbyshire dales" (N11, 38).

26 Fluent in English and Yoruba, Jess's mother Sarah left Nigeria to study English literature, much to the annoyance of her father, who takes her decision as an act of "cultural and racial betrayal" (Cuder-Domínguez, 2009, 284). Like the Neasden household, Jess's Cranbrook home is characterised by her parents' continual conflict over educational issues. When Jess shouts at her father because she does not want to dine at school and Daniel assures his wife that he will "handl[e] that" (N19, 206) with words, Sarah comments that "[i]f that had been *my* father 'handling that,' she would've been flat on the floor with a few teeth missing" (N19, 206, original emphasis).

to Nigeria, though, both novels deliberately disturb the "fragile peace" (N19, 4) that characterises the protagonists' childhood in suburban London.

Jess's reaction to the approaching journey is indeed remarkable. Hiding away in a cupboard, the eight-year-old girl envisages "Nye. Jeer. Reeee. Ah" (N19, 10) as a monster,

> looming out from across all the water and land that they had to cross in the aeroplane, reaching out for her with spindly arms made of dry, crackling grass like straw, wanting to pull her down against its beating heart, to the centre of the heat, so she would pop and crackle like a marshmallow (N19, 10).

Complying with Jess's characterisation as "*a half-and-half child*" (N19, 14, original emphasis), the narrator makes repeated use of the term "half" to highlight the "sense of incompleteness" (Hron, 2008, 37) that the family trip to Ibadan evokes. For instance, the home country of Jess's mother is described as "half a world away" (N19, 32), causing the faint anxiety that being Nigerian "might hurt" and feel "like being stretched" (N19, 268). Throwing one of many tantrums on the plane, Jess "struggle[s] and thrash[es], screaming, half dangling headfirst out of the seat" (N19, 10). Arriving in Ibadan, her maternal grandfather "half said, half announced" (N19, 20) her Yoruba name, which, to her, "sounded like another person" and "[n]ot her at all" (N19, 21). Titiola, whom Jess inadvertently turns into a double by calling her TillyTilly, addresses the protagonist as "JEssY" or "halfway between Jessamy and Jess" (N19, 44), underlining their shared fate of being "half a twin" (N19, 305). Undoubtedly, Jess's trip to Nigeria causes her "fragmenting and becoming double" (N19, 262), vainly "looking to belong" (N19, 261) until the novel's closing pages.

Bessi and Georgia show equally confused reactions on the prospect of visiting Nigeria:

> The whole thing was getting out of control. They were losing their home. They were losing Christmas. They were going to summer when it was winter. They were going against the grain of their lives. [...] They'd grow older, and become foreign. "Will we be Nigerians?" Bessi asked her mother, sitting next to Kemy on a suitcase that Ida was trying to zip closed. [...] She paused to answer Bessi's question: "What do you mean? You are Nigerian now," she said. "But only half," Bessi pointed out. "If we live there, will we be *all* Nigerian?" (N11, 44, original emphasis)

The plot and character constructions of *26a* suggest that Bessi and Georgia do not fit into such unambiguous categories. Georgia's sexual abuse by the Nigerian watchman Sedrick destroys the comfortable "land of twoness in oneness" (N11, 69), forcing the twins to consider for the first time "what oneness must feel like" (N11, 130) when, shortly after their return, Bessi leaves for St Lucia and Georgia tumbles into depression.

Causing Jess's sense of doubling and Bessi and Georgia's actual split, the journeys to Nigeria add a magical realist dimension to the novels' use of

Western genre conventions. As many critics have argued, *The Icarus Girl* and *26a* juxtapose "English and Nigerian cultural references" (Feldner, 2019, 149; Mafe, 2012, 33; Ouma, 2014, 195, 202) to parallel the protagonists' ambivalent cultural positions and invite different interpretations of the twin motif. I propose that the novels combine the pattern of the *Bildungsroman* with tropes of the Gothic novel and magical realist elements to address three desires of their middlebrow reading communities. Promising "a chill down the spine" (AR19), the novels' genre mixing provides the readers with an occasion "to learn a bit about Nigeria's traditional belief system" (GR19) while negotiating their own "psychological problems" (AR19) as a means of invigorating their affective authority in the digital literary sphere.

The first indication of *The Icarus Girl*'s generic ambiguity evolves from the paratext. The novel opens with a few lines from an Emily Dickinson poem – "Alone I cannot be – / For Hosts – do visit me – / Recordless Company" – and closes with the English translation of a Yoruba poem titled "Praise of the Leopard" (N19, 335). Arguably, these "metaphorical bookends" locate Jess's development "literally between cultures and traditions" (Mafe, 2012, 33). Similarly, "the extra dimension" (N11, 5) – that is, the attic of Bessi and Georgia – is haunted by British and Nigerian spectres alike, as allusions to Charlotte Brontë's *Jane Eyre* (1847) intermingle with a mythical tale about twins (N11, 63). Just like the grandfather's story in *26a*, the Yoruba poem evokes the male-dominated "magical-realist lineage following Amos Tutuola or Ben Okri" (Feldner, 2019, 149).[27] Although Oyeyemi can be said to participate in the trend of redefining the ogbanje or abiku from female and diasporic viewpoints (Bryce, 2008, 49, 46), her novel also echoes male novelists such as Iweala by employing animal imagery to characterise Jess and TillyTilly. For instance, Sarah is shocked to hear that Jess was "BITING someone – like some kind of

---

27 Reinforcing the new Nigerian novel's aesthetic coherence, the leopard resurfaces in Iweala's civil war narrative. The name of the protagonist Agu, which translates to the English leopard, signals one of the many Igbo myths about twinship (Gehrmann, 2012, 217). Using his idiosyncratic voice, Agu retells the story of the twins thus: "[T]hey are loving each other so much until one day they are changing into different animal. One is becoming ox [...] and the other is becoming leopard so that he can be hunting in the bush. Leopard was hunting hunting, but he is not finding anything to be killing so he is coming back to find his mother and his father. When he is coming to the river, he is seeing this ox just standing there drinking and he is saying, oho I will be killing this thing and bringing food back for my family to be eating. He is coming to Ox very quietly until he is so close he is biting Ox on the neck, but at the same time Ox is fighting him and chooking him in the heart with his two big horn. Since they are wounding, they are changing back into human being and seeing that they are brother and not enemy and so they are crying crying until they are dying right there and their blood is just running into the river and turning it to brown." (N13, 49–50) Foreshadowing Agu's transition into one of the titular *Beasts of No Nation*, the myth functions to highlight the dehumanising effects of war (Gehrmann, 2012, 217).

animal" (N19, 120, original emphasis). First appearing before Jess, TillyTilly's "head was tipped to one side and she stood, the legs apart, like a bird poised for flight, observing a dangerous animal that was about to lash out" (N19, 46). And when Jess, following a car accident, goes into a coma and sets foot in "the extra dimension", she hears "some wild animal calling to her in its own pulsating tongue" (N19, 331). Like the leopard in the poem, TillyTilly, whose repetitive name alone marks her as a spirit child, assumes the role of Jess's "[g]entle hunter" and [p]layful killer" (N19, 335), offering one of the novel's possible explanations for the protagonist's fractured sense of self.

Refraining from the use of animal imagery, Evans's novel constructs "the extra dimension" of Bessi and Georgia via shifting modes of narration. Mixing external and internal perspectives, the narrator characterises the twins' birth in terms of a near-death experience. Positioned at the roadside, Bessi and Georgia, "two furry creatures with petrified eyes staring into the oncoming headlights" (N11, 3), scream on crossing over into the human world, "land[ing] freezing cold in surgical electric white, hysterical, blubbering, trying to shake the shock from their hearts" (N11, 4). Underlining both their extraordinary connection and precarious condition as twins, the first chapters of the novel represent the consciousness of Bessi and Georgia in near-identical fashion. Seeing her twin sister return to St Luke's Hospital, Bessi experiences "that strange sinking back to the road" (N11, 4). During her sexual abuse, Georgia "s[ees] the headlights" and "hear[s] the engine" (N11, 68), and, before Bessi embarks on her trip to St Lucia, they hug and become "the only ones again, like before they got here, before the headlights" (N11, 135). The mythical story of their Nigerian grandfather provides one of the novel's interpretations of the twins' dwindling sensation of "twoness in oneness" (N11, 69):

> [Baba] told them of a woman who once had two girl twins who were best friends from the very beginning, even before they were inside their mother's womb, when they were spirits. Their names were Onia and Ode. Onia was first. Ode was second – they set her on fire. When Ode was burnt [...] Onia got sick and wouldn't eat at all until Ode's ghost entered her body. The ghost came in, and Onia began to eat again from her mother's breast. But Ode could only stay for one year, because that was how long it took for the soul to be ready to leave the earth. (N11, 63)

Irrespective of the fact that Georgia "was born [...] forty-five minutes first" (N11, 4), the story constitutes a precise foreshadowing of her pull into the spirit world. The novel presents this supernatural intervention by means of a shift to the first-person narration of Georgia's spirit, who enters the body of her twin sister for a period of three months. Like Jess, who, in the final chapter of *The Icarus Girl*, roams through the "wilderness of [her] mind" (N19, 200), Georgia walks

> [m]iles and miles through the forest. I was carried in the body of a child and her dress had turned to rags and her name is Ode in Onia. There were birds

crying in the trees above my head and the howls of witches in feathered skirts. There was fire in the distance.
I remember that story.
The thorns on the ground cut my feet as I ran and I could hear you all in the house, all the howling. I tried to shout but my voice would not carry. I began to wonder whether I would make it at all. But then I found you.
You found me.
I climbed up your ribs.
Moved into me.
Yes. (N11, 212)

Turning the spirit child Georgia into a first-person narrator, *26a* arguably redefines male representations of the ogbanje or abiku and "effect[s] a retrieval of the feminine repressed" (Bryce, 2008, 49). A similar argument can be made about the "Icarus girl" Jess, whose authorial characterisation points to the novel's "subversion of traditionally androcentric narratives" (Mafe, 2012, 22). These claims about the novels' female redefinition of Nigerian (and Greek) mythology comply with feminist readings that interpret Georgia and Jess as ghostly apparitions in the Gothic tradition that "indict[s] patriarchy, critique[s] the 'othering' of women, and represent[s] the suppressed Feminine" (Mafe, 2012, 23).[28]

Promising female empowerment, the novels' appropriations of the spirit child and the madwoman key in with their prevalent therapeutic horizon that

---

28 Accordingly, TillyTilly represents Jess's alter ego, "a stronger *version*" (Mafe, 2012, 24, original emphasis) who dares to do all the things that Jess is too scared to do, such as breaking into an amusement park (N19, 69–71) or wreaking vengeance on one of Jess's classmates (N19, 100–06). Moreover, TillyTilly proves her "potential to do significant damage" to the "male domain" (Mafe, 2012, 30) epitomised by the grandfather's house library that accommodates "the wine-coloured leather bindings of his specially commissioned copies of [Achebe's] *Things Fall Apart* and [Soyinka's] *A Dance of the Forests*" (N19, 52) or valuable collections by the British poet Samuel Taylor Coleridge (N19, 57). As TillyTilly threatens to set the books on fire (N19, 56), the novel offers an alternative perspective on the spirit child as the "monstrous female Other" (Mafe, 2012, 30) presenting Jess's "truest and darkest double", as Sandra M. Gilbert and Susan Gubar (2000, 360) called Brontë's Bertha Mason. The Western madwoman tradition, which constructs "madness [as] the consequence of the silencing of women" (Cooper, 2008, 54), is equally traceable in *26a*. Georgia haunts the attic room and her twin sister before and after her suicide. The fact that she "escapes into madness" (Cooper, 2008, 54) after her sexual abuse allows for a reading of Georgia as the "suppressed Feminine" who suffers from overbearing male power. Charting the changing relation between the twins after the incident, the novel highlights men's capacity to unhinge female bonds: "Georgia tried to think about how she could put [...] Sedrick's belt opening into words that were sayable. It was the first time ever, in this land of twoness in oneness that something had seemed unsayable." (N11, 69) Retaining the ambiguity of the archetype after which she is partly modelled, Georgia's suicide reinforces male oppression *and* female solidarity, especially in view of her hopes to protect her sister from "see[ing] the dark" (N11, 181).

provides middlebrow readers with an abundance of opportunities to affirm their "belief that everyone suffers the same kind of psychological hardships" (Aubry, 2011, 24). Indeed, the reviewers of my corpora are as quick as Feldner and Hron to make diagnoses. An Amazon reviewer called Audrey Georgia (AR19) notes that "[i]t wouldn't surprise [her] if Jess has been diagnosed with Asperger's Disorder or something else on the Autism spectrum". Equally delighted by Oyeyemi's "clear insight into mental illness", Anne-Marie (GR19) suspects "schizophrenia", whereas Kelsey (GR19) asserts that Jess shows the symptoms "of every psychological disorder, including schizophrenia, dissociative identity disorder, ADHD, depression etc." The character of Georgia triggers very similar responses. Whereas various reviewers wonder why no character in the novel cares to "get Georgia some medical help", Hanna Fawcett (GR11), sharing her "own account of depression and its debilitating effect on everyday tasks", frames clinical depression as a universal phenomenon when she remarks that Evans "perfectly sums up the challenges faced by anyone who feels they're slowly sinking into despair".

Testifying to the pervasiveness of what Illouz (2007, 6), in a different context, refers to as a "therapeutic emotional style", the reviewers' patterns of discussing the novels, just like the platforms' group therapeutic structures, are extensively addressed in subsequent chapters. Suffice it to say at this point that the "therapeutic educational enterprise" (McGurl, 2009, 16) of the creative writing programme inscribes itself into Evans and Oyeyemi's texts, providing an affective vocabulary that both underlines and undermines the potentially empowering effects of their magical realist and Gothic elements. The therapeutically inflected bourgeois realism possibly turns "the extra dimension" into a mere symptom of the protagonists' mental disorder. Deviating from magical realist classics such as *The Famished Road*, where "the universe of action is located simultaneously within both the real world and that of spirits" (Quayson, 2009, 173), *26a* and *The Icarus Girl* establish a hierarchical distinction between the two. Oyeyemi's narrator emphasises ab ovo that the events are filtered through the perspective of a child who cannot properly "see" (N19, 4, 9, 153, 172, 213). References to Jess's "enormous imagination" (N19, 139) or "big imagination" (N19, 287) equally serve to render TillyTilly a chimera of Jess's nightmares (N19, 138, 167, 194, 219), which tend to conclude with the narrator's assurance that "none of that happened" (N19, 302). The narrative situation in *26a* creates a less definite separation between the real and the supernatural. Except for the ending, though, it does not interweave the two spheres either. The reflector-characters mostly flout the conventions of magical realism that, following Ato Quayson (2009, 164), should not evoke a "sense of surprise or alarm [...] on the appearance of the magical". As in *The Icarus Girl*, the narrator of *26a* repeatedly highlights that "[t]he twins were traumatised" (N11, 64).

Crucially, both novels demystify their magical realist elements by employing psychologists who offer medical explanations for the characters' condition. Jess's psychologist Dr McKenzie affirms that "we have a situation where Jess has discovered a need of an outlet for emotions" (N19, 288), while Georgia's therapist Katya recommends "acceptance and good management" (N11, 184) before assuring both her client and the reader that "the monsters [...] are not real" (N11, 185). Against this backdrop, the suicide of Georgia does not read as a magical pull into a realm beyond the Neasden household but rather as a consequence of her incapacity to manage daily trivialities such as buying milk (N11, 149) or to realise the "DIY happiness" (N11, 152) that is advised in the self-help books stacking her shelves and bearing titles such as *Your Breath, Your Life*, *The Essential Guide to Aromatherapy* or *The Detox Bible*. However sarcastic the novel's remark on this kind of "holistic alternative self-care literature" (N11, 153) sounds, *26a*, just as well as *The Icarus Girl*, may well be considered Nigerian examples of the genre.[29]

The new Nigerian novel stages what Illouz (2003, 38), discussing *The Oprah Winfrey Show* (1986–2011), has referred to as "psychic events", creating a sense of split within and among their international readers while equally making them "feel a little less alone" (AR03).[30] A more recent example of how Nigerian diasporic authors adapt the motif of the twin to a globalising middle-class culture of self-help and suffering comes from the US-based newcomer of Igbo and Tamil descent, Emezi, who identifies as non-binary and whose debut has been marketed as an account of the "author's realities" (N10, cover blurb). Dedicating their novel to "those of us with one foot on the other side", Emezi dramatises their status as a "writer [who is] based in liminal spaces" (N10, cover blurb) in ethnic and sexual terms. The story of the child protagonist, Ada, makes consistent use of Igbo mythology as nine of the altogether 22

---

29 The possibly therapeutic effects of literature are implied by the authors, who relate the stories of their protagonists to their own experiences. In an interview with *The Guardian*, Oyeyemi (quoted in Sethi, 2005) describes her childhood in suburban London as a "really, really oppressive" period in which she developed a depression and took an overdose; asked about her coping strategies, Oyeyemi replies: "reading and reading and reading". Evans links her writing career to the suicide of her twin sister Paula, to whom *26a* is dedicated (Evaristo, 2005, 33). Additionally, Cole's novels suggest walking as a therapeutic measure. While Julius, the protagonist of *Open City*, spends his residency in psychiatry roaming the streets of New York, the unnamed first-person narrator of *Every Day Is for the Thief* visits Lagos to look for "a solid assurance" (N08, 161) of where he belongs.

30 Illouz (2003, 36) elucidates that, taken together, the psychic events of *The Oprah Winfrey Show* create a "therapeutic narrative" – that is, "a story about the self, and about the events that have helped the self achieve health, or, more frequently, that have caused it to fail. Like all narratives, the therapeutic narrative is structured by the tension between a goal, psychic well-being or 'health', and obstacles to that well-being – pathologies or dysfunctions that constitute [...] a complication." The distinct therapeutic narrative of Oprah is based on her biography of "failure", including "sexual abuse, overweight and failed romantic relations" (32, 33), which allows her to continually perform psychic events and their resolutions in therapeutic terms.

chapters are narrated by the collective "we" of Ada and the two spirits inhabiting her:

> The first time our mother came for us, we screamed. We were three and she was a snake, coiled up on the tile in the bathroom, waiting. But we had spent the last few years believing our body – thinking that our mother was someone different, a thin human with rouged cheekbones and large bottle-end glasses. And so we screamed. The demarcations are not that clear when you're new. (N10, 1)

Despite the novel's idiosyncratic narrative situation, its comparatively "slender plot and relatively little social interaction" (Dunton, 2019, 12), Ada shows notable similarities with Jess and Georgia. Just like the heroines of Evans and Oyeyemi's debuts, Ada "feel[s] the unsettling our mere presence caused" (N10, 15) and suffers from "terrifying dreams" (N10, 16), "los[es] her temper frequently" (N10, 22) or starts to "br[eak] skin without fully knowing why" (N10, 32) at the age of 12. Echoing the plot design of *26a* and *The Icarus Girl*, all of these symptoms exacerbate as she moves from Umuahia to Virginia to go to college. Unsurprisingly, the reader witnesses Ada "read[ing] lists of diagnostic criteria, things like disruption of identity, self-damaging impulsivity, emotional instability and mood swings, self-mutilating behaviour and recurrent suicidal behavior" (N10, 140). Although Asughara, one of Ada's spirits, interrupts the novel's therapeutic discourse by commenting that "I could have told her that it was all me, even that last one" (N10, 141), her narrative presence hardly subverts the middlebrow reader's appropriative consumption patterns but rather serves to look at Ada's "psychological condition [...] from this different cultural perspective" (YR10, Eric Karl Anderson, 02/12/2018).

Standing in the realist tradition of Achebe or Emecheta, Selasi's debut *Ghana Must Go* illustrates that the psychological redefinition of the twin motif does not hinge on magical-realist representational means. The novel's central themes of mobility and migration emerge from the title, which alludes to "the Nigerian government's summarily deporting two million Ghanaians" (N20, 237) from Nigeria in 1983. Judging by the plot and character design of the family saga, the reference to the expulsion is as misleading as its evocation of "the cheap market plastic bag" (Gehrmann, 2016, 66) that has been associated with migration across West African borders ever since (N20, 316). Neither expelled nor poor, the Sais represent a professional middle-class family of Ghanaian-Nigerian descent who have managed to establish a "*Successful Family*" (N20, 123, original emphasis) life in the suburbs of Boston:

> There was "him," straining daily to perform the Provider, and Fola's star turn as Suburban Housewife, and Olu's as fastidious-cum-favored First Son; the Artist, gifted, awkward; and the Baby. Then she. Determined to deliver a flawless performance, to fly from the stage chased by thunderous applause, Darling Daughter of champions, elementary school standout, the brightest of pupils in bright-eyed class pictures. (N20, 123)

"Too precious, too perfect" (N20, 234) to be believable,[31] the "performance" is bound to fail, and the text uses shifts in setting and narrative perspective to explore why the family members find themselves dispersed across the globe when the novel begins. Sadie, the youngest of the four prodigies of father Kweku and mother Fola, spells out what the concerted perspective of the six reflector-characters suggests: the Sais are a family with no "roots spreading out underneath them, with no living grandparent, no history, a horizontal – they've floated, have scattered, drifting outward, or inward, barely noticing when someone has slipped off the grid" (N20, 146–47). The chance to become a "family with gravity" (N20, 146) presents itself towards the distinctly happy ending when, following Kweku's death from a heart attack – or, to adopt the novel's pathetic parlance, "the heartbreak he fled from" (N20, 86) – the children reunite in Accra for his funeral.

Significantly, the narrow focus on the six family members renders the reasons for and features of "their struggles with identity" (GR20) entirely homegrown and individual. Suffering the fate of the youngest child, Sadie develops an eating disorder and, paralleling the destiny of Bessi and Georgia, the twins Taiwo and Kehinde go separate ways after their sexual abuse by a Nigerian uncle. Just like *26a* and *The Icarus Girl*, the novel advises therapeutic treatment:

> The thing that he does, that he hates himself for doing, the mute-and-immobile act, locked off in space. Why does this happen? he'd asked Dr. Shipman. Can you stop it? Can you fix me? I'm a coward, I'm a punk. I stand in the chamber behind the glass walls, I can see all the people there passing me by, but can't *get* to them, can't speak to them, can't tell them I'm *in here*; I can't break the glass, and they can't hear me shout.
> "Protection," said the doctor.
> "Protection from what?"
> "From your fear, from your hurt, from your anguish, your rage."
> "I'm not angry," said Kehinde.
> "You are, and you should be. Allow it, your anger. Permit it to be."
> "But it's not. I'm not angry."
> "You aren't? With your mother? Your father? Your uncle? Your sister? Yourself?"
> "*Not my sister*," he'd say, but too sharply, too quickly. (N20, 174–75, original emphasis)

Exceeding the diasporic contexts of Emezi and Selasi's texts, novels such as *Purple Hibiscus* or *Everything Good Will Come* use the twin motif to narrate

---

31 Noting the (class) privileges of the Sais, numerous scholars refer to the characters as "prototypical Afropolitans" (Gehrmann, 2016, 67; Feldner, 2019, 127–45; Tunca and Ledent, 2015, 4). As highlighted in the first chapter, I do not use the term because its application tends to rehearse the new Nigerian novel's structures and ideologies. Indeed, Feldner's (2019, 137) surmise that the novel was "written for the very purpose of illustrating the concept" proves to be a dead-end street because it does not allow for analytical meta-perspectives on *Ghana Must Go*.

postcolonial Nigeria. Coming of age in the 1980s and 1990s, Adichie and Atta's young heroines, just like the couple in Adebayo's *Stay With Me* or the brothers in Obioma's *The Fishermen*, develop alongside a nation that, "damaged and derailed by the legacies of colonialism" (Mullaney, 2010, 32), determines their "*individual destiny*" (Jameson, 1986, 69, original emphasis). Drawing on Jameson's definition of "third-world" national allegories, critics have noted the new Nigerian novel's tendency of "representing a politics of the family while quietly but clearly telling stories of the nation" (Andrade, 2011, 91; Bryce, 2008, 49–67; Dalley, 2014, 121–46; Hron, 2008, 27–48). As the emotional responses of my reviewers show, the "new" national allegories by Adichie or Obioma have strong middlebrow appeal as they promise *affective* knowledge about or "insight into Nigerian culture" (AR05).[32] Deviating from first- and second-generation writers, contemporary Nigerian novelists unanimously stress individual over national fates. Published as early as 2003, Adichie's debut creates the blueprint for this pattern in its very first sentence (Bryce, 2008, 58). Alluding to Achebe, the "hyper-precursor" (Boehmer, 2009, 142) of Nigerian diasporic writers, the novel locates the representation of postcolonial conflict in the domestic sphere: "Things started to fall apart at home when my brother, Jaja, did not go to communion and Papa flung his heavy missal across the room and broke the figurines on the étagère" (N05, 3). Accordingly, 15-year-old Kambili narrates military rule in 1980s Nigeria through her rite of passage in a repressive middle-class household in Enugu. *The Fishermen* applies the first-person perspective of ten-year-old Ben to represent Nigeria's failed passage into democratic rule in 1993 through "a tragic chain of events" (YR16, Pull Down The Moon), among them fratricide and suicide, afflicting the Agwu family. And Yejide and Akin, the two first-person narrators of Adebayo's weepie, negotiate the rule of General Babangida through the ups and downs of their marriage, as the following metaphor shows: "Nigeria was still in the honeymoon phase of her relationship with Babangida, and like most new brides she wasn't asking probing questions, yet" (N02, 73).

The prevalent "allegorical realism" of these texts, which present postcolonial Nigeria through "tropes belonging to the narrative conventions of melodramatic romance" (Dalley, 2014, 138), equally informs contemporary negotiations of the Biafran War, as the next section highlights. If coupled with the motif of the twin, as in Adichie's postcolonial female *Bildungsroman*, allegorical realism primarily functions to dramatise the pathologies of middle-class family life, particularly the conflict-ridden relation of the postcolonial daughter to her overbearing father.[33] Placed between the stereotypical

---

32 Radway (1997, 263) uses the term "sentimental education" to describe "a distinctive middlebrow style" or tenet of literary distribution. As this chapter demonstrates, the notion can also be applied to analyse the potential effects of particular textual structures.

33 Overpowering father figures equally dominate the plot of Braithwaite's *My Sister, the Serial Killer* and Onuzo's *The Spider King's Daughter*. Mixing elements of crime

characters of her "tyrannical father" Eugene and his "cosmopolitan sister" Ifeoma (Hron, 2008, 31), *Purple Hibiscus*'s Kambili only develops into the "hybrid" title flower because of her brother Jaja. Two years apart, the siblings entertain a twin-like relation and, for the most part, behave "like two things that went together" (N05, 205). Their bond manifests itself most clearly in their non-verbal "eye language" (N05, 109), a communication system invented to ease the claustrophobic silence at home. Tacitly, they worry about Eugene's abuse of their mother Beatrice (N05, 30) or agree on secret escapes from their tight work schedules (N05, 59). Jaja attains ogbanje-status when he violates their arrangement during a stay with their aunt. Quicker to adjust to life in Nsukka, where "they laughed so easily, so often" (N05, 85) and "could say anything at any time to anyone" (N05, 120), Jaja tells his cousins about their violent father and leaves Kambili puzzled: "Had Jaja forgotten that [...] there was so much that we never told?" (N05, 145) When he takes his mother's blame for the murder of Eugene, Jaja, just as Georgia in *26a*, TillyTilly in *The Icarus Girl* or, to provide another example, Sheri Bakare in *Everything Good Will Come*, clears the path for his sister's – and, by implication, the reader's – "psychological growth" (AR05).

The Motif of Biafra: Reconciliation

If the new Nigerian novel employs the trope of the twin to pathologise the hybridity of its child protagonists and, by extension, the heterogeneous setup of its online reading communities, the motif of Biafra serves to enact possibilities of reconciliation. Allusions to the Biafran War or the Nigerian Civil War, which was fought from 1967 to 1970 and ended with the defeat of the secessionist Republic of Biafra, are so prevailing that various scholars praise Adichie or Habila for continuing the "unfinished business of national reconciliation" (Dalley, 2013, 17; Dalley, 2014, 122–27; Hawley, 2008, 15–26; Krishnan, 2010, 185–95; Krishnan, 2013, 187–208). Recent representations of the postcolonial conflict differ in the extent to which Biafra pervades plot, character and narration. Since most of the 20 selected novels are set after the civil war, Biafra tends to feature as a vague reference point in the many national allegories that construct postcolonial Nigeria through the personal hi/stories of the protagonists and their families. Strengthening the novels' consistency, these rather brief references to Biafra suggest the conflict's lasting impact on Nigerian society, politics and culture, while equally implying that third- or fourth- generation characters are frequently too young to properly remember and relate the historical event. The first-person narrator of *Everything Good Will Come* is a case in point: "born in the year of my country's

---

and romance fiction, the texts imply that their protagonists' criminal behaviour and inability to form romantic relations result from what one BookTuber fittingly describes as "daddy issues" (YR07, My Reading Days, 08/03/2019).

independence" (N06, 330), Enitan listens carefully to her father's stories about "the Wild West" and thereby acquires "as much knowledge about the events in my country as any seven-year-old c[an]" (N06, 9). Represented through Enitan's limited perspective, however, her childhood days remain unaffected by "the political overhaul" (N06, 67). It is only in retrospect, and through the lens of the narrating I, that Enitan realises

> the holocaust that was Biafra, through memoirs and history books, and pictures of limbless people; children with their stomachs bloated from kwashiorkor and their rib cages as thin as leaf veins. Their parents were mostly dead. Executed. Macheted. Blown up. Beheaded. There were accounts of blood-drinking, flesh-eating, atrocities of the human spirit that only a civil war could generate, while in Lagos we had carried on as though it were happening in a different country. (N06, 86)

Standing in marked contrast to first- and second-generation civil war fiction, such as Emecheta's *Destination Biafra* (1982), the novel's temporal positioning towards Biafra indicates that new Nigerian novelists face "the interpretive challenges of narrating [a] civil war" (Dalley, 2014, 122) that they have no first-hand experience and knowledge of. And, while many of their peers confine themselves to symbolic side notes on the Biafran War,[34] authors such as Okparanta accept these challenges. Categorising her debut *Under the Udala Trees* or Adichie's *Half of a Yellow Sun* and Habila's *Measuring Time* as historical fiction, various researchers point to the new Nigerian novel's capacity to open up "a space for collective memorialization" (Krishnan, 2014, 34) and thereby reconcile national readers with Nigeria's colonial legacies (Dalley, 2014, 126–27). Even a cursory glance at these texts and their paratextual frames proves that they, "[m]ore than most other novels of the Nigerian diaspora", creatively engage with "national identity formation" (Feldner, 2019, 37). *Half of a Yellow Sun*, in particular, signifies the Igbo descent and "Biafran sympathies" (Adichie, 2008, 50) of its author. In the first place, the novel's title creates a direct connection with the civil war, as it refers to the Biafran flag: "swaths of red, black, and green and, at the centre, a luminous half of a yellow sun" (N04, 163). Unfolding in varying parts of Nigeria before and during the war, the novel narrates Biafra's secession and breakdown through the perspectives of three

---

34 Like Atta's novel, Obioma's debut *The Fishermen* features a child narrator, Ben, who can merely hint at the (infrastructural) legacies of the Biafran War. For instance, crossing over the Omi-Ala River, he and his brothers use a bridge that was erected by Biafran soldiers "after blowing up the main bridge during the Nigerian civil war, as an alternate bridge by which they could cross in the event of an invasion by Nigerian troops" (N16, 84). Elsewhere, Ben reports his father's words, revealing that his understanding of the war relies on the perspectives of others: "Then he brought the talk down to Nigeria, down to the corruption that had eaten the entrails of the nation and finally, as usual, he berated Gowon, a man we had grown to hate, the man he's repeatedly accused of bombing our village several times – the man who killed very many women during the Nigerian civil war" (N16, 300).

characters who belong to or seek membership in the Igbo minority group. On the paratextual level, the novel offers a verse from Achebe's "Mango Seedling" (1968), a poem dedicated to Christopher Okigbo, a well-known Nigerian poet who lost his life fighting for Biafran independence. A laudatory blurb in which the "father" of the Anglophone Nigerian novel credits his literary offspring with "the gift of ancient storytellers" (N04, cover blurb) further invigorates the intergenerational bond between Adichie and Achebe. Additionally, the novel's dedication to Adichie's grandparents, witnesses and victims of the war, and an author essay at the end of the book, "In the Shadow of Biafra" (N04, P.S. Section, 9–12), arguably construct a national readership that is strongly encouraged "to collectively acknowledge what happened" (Adichie, 2008, 53; Dalley, 2014, 126).

In the "Acknowledgments" section of her novel, Okparanta, who was born in Port Harcourt in southern Nigeria, refers to Achebe and Soyinka as "my predecessors, my guiding lights" (N17, 327) and, like Adichie, thanks a family member "for her war songs and war stories, for her folktales, without all of which this book might not exist" (N17, 328). Indeed, the story of her protagonist Ijeoma begins in

> 1967 when the war barged in and installed itself all over the place. By 1968, the whole of Ojoto had begun pulsing with the ruckus of armored cars and shelling machines, bomber planes and their loud engines sending shock waves through our ears. By 1968, our men had begun slinging guns across their shoulders and carrying axes and machetes, blades glistening in the sun; and out on the streets, every hour or two in the afternoons and evenings, their chanting could be heard, loud voices pouring out like libations from their mouths: "Biafra, win the war!" (N17, 4)

Presenting yet another national allegory, Okparanta's novel establishes immediate ties between personal and political hi/stories. Highlighting that the developments in the secessionist state soon lead to "Mama's sending me off" and "Papa's refusal to go to the bunker" (N17, 4), Okparanta, just as Adichie or Habila in their literary approaches to the war, "juxtaposes the making of a single person against the destruction of national hope" (Andrade, 2011, 93).

Expanding the geographical borders of Nigerian civil war fiction to the country's north, Habila appears less outspoken about his personal motivations for narrating Biafra. However, the "Acknowledgements" section of *Measuring Time* promises an intertextual reference to Okigbo's poem "A Shrub Among Poplars" (1971). On the textual level, Biafra is explicitly evoked by the character Haruna, the uncle of the twin brothers Mamo and LaMamo, who comes back to the fictional village of Keti several years after the end of the war and eventually commits suicide. Marking a short though decisive episode in the life of the adolescent boys, Haruna's return constitutes the novel's "foundational moment" (Krishnan, 2014, 34). Kindling Mamo's longing for the "fame and wealth" (N12, 55) of a local historian, Biafra serves as a prompt to experiment with new and communal forms of "re-creat[ing]" and preserving "cultural memory" (Krishnan, 2014, 31).

Just as the trope of the twin, the motif of Biafra discloses that the new Nigerian novel is not "discontinuous with what came before" (Dalley, 2013, 17). And, just as its redefinition of the ogbanje or abiku, the new Nigerian novel's "engagement with a primarily local, territorially demarcated political sphere" (Dalley, 2013, 17) does not contradict its authors' "international outlook and global orientation" (Feldner, 2019, 18). In what follows, I challenge the widespread critical assumption that Adichie's, Habila's and Okparanta's novels about the Biafran War exclusively serve to inspire "identity construction in contemporary Nigeria" (Feldner, 2019, 38), imagine a "national community" (Dalley, 2014, 126) of readers or experiment with possible approaches to "national reconciliation" (Dalley, 2013, 17). Exceeding the implied reader constructs of these positions and considering the thousands of online reviews investigated in later chapters, I assert that the novels' representations of Biafra invite postcolonial reconciliation in the digital literary sphere. Which narrative techniques do the novels employ to anticipate community? How do they define access? And what kind of language do they propose to address and move beyond colonial legacies?

The character constellation and narrative situation of *Half of a Yellow Sun* imply that the novel imagines community along inclusive and emotive lines. Shifting perspective between Ugwu, a houseboy who comes to Nsukka to work for the university professor Odenigbo, Olanna, a London-educated sociologist and Odenigbo's partner, and Richard, a British expat who admires Igbo-Ugwu art just as much as Olanna's twin Kainene, the novel emphasises that class, gender and race influence the representation of national turmoil (Dalley, 2014, 124). However, a closer look at the plot design and narrative perspectives reveals that the text's allegorical realism tends to smooth out differences between the three protagonists. Narrating national change with "the language of domestic melodrama" (Dalley, 2014, 134), all three reflector-characters foster bourgeois emotion discourses across national, cultural and racial borders. The text's inverted chronology of events or Olanna and Ugwu's perspectives prove this contention.

The "back-and-forth chronology" (Dalley, 2014, 124) of the plot, in particular, invites affective approaches to the Biafran War. Separated into four parts, *Half of a Yellow Sun* switches between prewar and war times. Evolving in "The Early Sixties", parts one and three zoom in on Odenigbo's middle-class household, paying special attention to the characters' budding relations. Playing out in Biafra in "The Late Sixties", parts two and four foreground the political events engendering the civil war. Paralleling the realist mode of *Purple Hibiscus*, the exchange of parts two and three shifts the focus from the national conflict to the characters' middle-class problems – that is, "sexual insecurity, personal betrayal, [and] family breakdown" (Dalley, 2014, 138) – which dominate parts one and three. Indeed, the coups, the Igbo massacres or the secession of Biafra pale in the light of the following pressing questions: Is Odenigbo the father of Baby (N04, 107)? Why is Richard no longer visiting Olanna and her partner (N04, 151, 168)? Why does Ugwu try to forget "those weeks before

Baby's birth" (N04, 200)? Why did Kainene rip Richard's manuscript to pieces? (N04, 182)? Constantly "interrupt[ing] the narrative of the escalating war", *Half of a Yellow Sun* places prime "emphasis on the conflicts within the family" (Feldner, 2019, 47). Such a plot design may well motivate readers to view the political processes through "the full scale of [their bourgeois] emotions" (YR04, andyreadsbooks), especially those who "know very little about Biafra" and seek to be "a more aware and better person" (AR04) who is literate enough to acknowledge colonial injustices.

Providing individualised vantage points on postcolonial conflict, the reflector-characters function as middle-class "vehicles for lessons in Nigerian history" (AR04). Albeit all of them "call for empathetic witnessing and affective response" (Dalley, 2014, 132), I concentrate on Olanna, who negotiates Biafra through middle-class domesticity and empathy, and Ugwu, whose *Bildungsroman* strand adapts the motif to formulate a plea for middle-class progress through education. Olanna invigorates the novel's larger "discourse of humanitarian sympathy" (Dalley, 2014, 131) by providing sexually explicit descriptions. Pondering the character's potential functions for non-Nigerian readers, Zoe Norridge (2012, 35) remarks that Olanna's language use encourages "intimate form[s] of involvement". Repeatedly relating the details of her sexual intercourse with Odenigbo, Olanna forges an affective lexicon that allows her and her readers to process and appropriate experiences of pain and loss. In an attempt to cope with the memory of her murdered Kano relatives, for instance, she reaches for Odenigbo's hand and, "press[ing] it against her breast", says:

> "Touch me." She knew he didn't want to, that he touched her breasts because he would do whatever she wanted, whatever would make her better. She caressed his neck, buried her fingers in his dense hair, and when he slid into her, she thought about [her cousin] Arize's pregnant belly, how easily it must have broken, skin stretched that taut. She started to cry. (N04, 160)

Attesting to anything but her "quintessentially human" (Norridge, 2012, 19) perspective on the Biafran War, Olanna's corporeal identification with Arize rather points to the novel's peculiar entanglement of class and sexuality. Although Olanna struggles with "being a part of the gloss that was her parents' life" (N04, 34), her class privileges doubtlessly inform her mediation of national conflict, which is primarily rendered as a sacrifice of material and sexual comforts. Following the extended family's movement to rural Abba, for instance, Olanna bemoans that "their stove and toaster and pressure cooker and imported spices were left behind in Nsukka" (N04, 185). Consequently, her relation to the female villagers is heavily affected by perceived class distinctions: "She felt bitter towards them at first, because when she tried to talk about the things she had left behind in Nsukka – her books, her piano, her clothes, her china, her wigs, her Singer sewing machine, the television – they ignored her and started to talk about something else." (N04, 185) By contrast, reviewers such as Caradee Wright (AR04), who "cannot imagine having to leave my house and my possessions instantly never to return", show no such barriers. This is not to deny Olanna's support of the Biafran cause. She does so, however, from a position of middle-class superiority, as her patronising gestures of setting up a village school (N04, 291) or sharing supplies with the mother of a sick child (N04, 327) imply. Operating in the mode of a sympathetic yet detached charity lady, Olanna's approach to the Igbo community provides an instruction for the middlebrow reader who views the fictional universe of poverty and disease with a similar mixture of empathy and disgust. Paralleling her material sacrifices, the family's relocation to ever tinier and shabbier lodgings influences the sexual relation between Olanna and Odenigbo. Arriving at a desolate shelter in Umuahia, she inspects "the bed, two yam tubers, and the mattress that leaned against the dirt-smeared wall" (N04, 327) and cannot imagine having sex there. Accordingly, the couple lie "with their backs turned to each other" (N04, 337) from now on.

That the text's "engagement with history, cultural affiliation, and collective consciousness" is less "multidimensional" (Krishnan, 2013, 193) or inclusive than the three reflector-characters insinuate, at least in class terms, is further highlighted by the *Bildungsroman* thread presenting Ugwu's middle-class development from houseboy to historiographer.[35] Initially appearing as "the ignorant, wide-eyed African" (Cousins, 2011, 1 46), Ugwu does not lend himself to middle-class identification but invites middle-class benevolence. Showing rather than telling the character's thought processes, the narrator merely surfaces in the use of phrasal conjunctions or a stylistic technique that Daria Tunca (2014, 68, 71) refers to as "underlexicalisation". Hardly fluent in English, Ugwu marvels at "the alien furniture" (N04, 5) in his master's middle-class household but misses the proper words to describe what he sees, including a "box studded with dangerous-looking knobs" (N04, 5, a radiogram), "something that look[s] like a woman's coat" (N04, 9, a dressing gown) or "the white thing, almost as tall as he was" (N04, 6, a fridge). Poking gentle fun at the houseboy, the

---

[35] Including an involuntary enlistment in the Biafran armed forces, Ugwu's rite of passage echoes the genre of the child soldier narrative that, contrary to *Half of a Yellow Sun*, transforms "the Biafra template into broader [...] probings of the travails of the subject in the context of war and trauma" (Adesanmi and Dunton, 2008, x). Drawing on Ken Saro-Wiwa's *Sozaboy: A Novel in Rotten English* (1985), Abani's *Song for Night* and Iweala's *Beasts of No Nation* (and its 2015 Netflix adaptation, directed by Cary Fukunaga) employ the "archetypical figure" (Gehrmann, 2012, 210) of the child soldier to "suggest that a very different understanding of global relationality – of the 'human community' is necessary" (Mackey, 2013, 108). Instead of taking the generic path of middle-class progress, as Ugwu does over the course of Adichie's historical novel, the main characters of Abani and Iweala's "monologic novels" (Gehrmann, 2012, 213), My Luck and Agu, foster the creation of caring online communities by addressing the middlebrow reader's sense of ethical responsibility about human (and especially children's) rights issues (Driscoll, 2014, 44; Hron, 2008, 45).

technique also functions to construct a reader who, in compliance with Ugwu, does not (yet) speak the language and has not (yet) attained the level of "global attention" (GR17) required to belong to the affective online communities. That Ugwu anticipates the reviewers' desire for "learn[ing] a lot about this period in Nigeria's history and a lot about human nature in general" (AR04) is emphasised by the "wide piece of paper" that Odenigbo uses to acquaint Ugwu with "strange places" (N04, 10, a world map).

In line with the structural and ideological pattern of the *Bildungsroman*, the rift between the novel's covert third-person narrator and the reflector-character gradually disappears as Ugwu exceeds the status of "a normal houseboy" (N04, 17). Indeed, Odenigbo and Olanna not only give him "a comb and a shirt" (N04, 47–48) and instruct him to cook with an adequate amount of oil (N04, 48) but also supply plenty of books and newspapers (N04, 17). In effect, Ugwu increasingly seeks to distinguish himself from the inhabitants of his village and cannot wait to "impress [his sister] Anulika and his cousins and relatives with his English, his new shirt, his knowledge of sandwiches and running tap water" (N04, 86). By degrees, the houseboy comes to approximate the middle-class pretensions of his master and mistress. Visiting his family in the chronologically later parts of the novel, he finds "[h]is mother's food [...] unpalatable", craving to return "to Nsukka and finally eat a real meal" (N04, 119). In contrast to Anulika, moreover, he has by now resolved that he will "not marry until he ha[s] become like Master, until he ha[s] spent many years reading books" (N04, 176). The Biafran War not only forms the backdrop of Ugwu's passage into adulthood but also offers an occasion to continually work on his "unfinished knowledge" (N04, 142). As Biafra's secession looms on the horizon, Ugwu "read[s] the newspapers more carefully" and "listen[s] more closely to Master and his guests" (N04, 142). Just as the members of the online literary communities, Ugwu realises that social distinction presupposes educational progress.

Having evolved alongside the nation's rise and fall, Ugwu has arguably earned "the right and responsibility" (Boxall, 2013, 174) to make use of and share the knowledge he has acquired in the novel's meta-text: "The Book: The World Was Silent When We Died". Discussing this meta-text as an instance of "writing back", many scholars underscore that Ugwu's account of Nigerian history heralds "the exit of the Western subject [Richard] from narrative control" (Novak, 2008, 40). Indeed, Ugwu's authorship highlights that, "in the wake of globalization" (Feldner, 2019, 8), the task of community building cannot be accomplished by a British writer such as Richard, who, despite seeking belonging to the newly emerging Biafran community, occasionally reveals "a racism that has perhaps always been at work in [his] exoticising fantasy" (Boxall, 2013, 177).[36] And, while the novel's meta-text may well

---

36 Richard's racism surfaces repeatedly, as for instance when he imagines beating up his houseboy Harrison, who has just informed Kainene about her partner's affair with Olanna: Richard "wanted to cane Harrison. It had always appalled him,

be read as an intertextual echo of the closing lines in Achebe's *Things Fall Apart*,[37] I am inclined to challenge the assumption that Ugwu writes "from the perspective of below" (Gehrmann, 2012, 228). Rather, "The Book" invigorates Ugwu's position as a fresh member of the educated middle classes and, instead of questioning the reviewers' quest for affective knowledge, functions to mitigate their "embarrassment of having known nothing" (GR04) about Britain's share in the Biafran War.

The central meta-text in Habila's *Measuring Time*, tentatively titled *Live and Times*, equally gestures towards postcolonial reconciliation on social media. After several failed attempts at writing the local history of Keti, Mamo envisions a biographical approach because biography "*deals with the human element*" and "*realizes more than history does that we are all human and fallible*" (N12, 186, original emphasis). Considering the novel's playful rearrangement of multiple (fictional) intertexts such as Reverend Drinkwater's *A Brief History of the Peoples of Keti* and the entries in the diary of his wife Hannah or the letters that Mamo's twin brother LaMamo sends from the trenches of numerous unspecified African war zones, critics have tended to read *Measuring Time* as a metahistorical novel that suggests "a new concept of historiography" (Schulze-Engler, 2013, 277; Anyokwu, 2008, 21; Gehrmann, 2012, 232; Roy, 2011, 18). Challenging these critical assumptions about the novel's postmodern play, I claim that Mamo's biographical history anticipates an international middlebrow readership that nurtures the vision of "unity-in-diversity" (Dalley, 2014, 121), predicated on the allegedly "universal emotions" (AR02) of happiness and acceptance. Even if *Lives and Times* remains "placed under the ambiguity of a conditional tense" (Krishnan, 2014, 36), the novel *Measuring Time* fixes Mamo's idea within its pages, illustrating that the inclusion of meta-fictional elements does not necessarily preclude the unquestioned rehearsal of liberal humanist commonplaces:

> He wouldn't be seeking for parallels between lives [...] because he saw that as already given: all lives are already parallel; each life is comparable to another life regardless of circumstance. People desire the same things; they only differ in how they allow their aspirations to be modified by the dominant values of their society. All aspire to be happy. (N12, 358)

While Adichie and Habila's novels imagine a middle-class reader who deems emotion a panacea against postcolonial conflict, Okparanta's coming-of-age novel broadens the conception of the online reading communities by developing a plea for sexual diversity. Paralleling "[e]xternal wars and internal

---

the thought that some colonial Englishman flogged elderly black servants. Now, though, he felt like doing just as they had done" (N04, 225).

37 On the very final page of Achebe's novel, the point of view shifts "from the familiar Igbo to the alien British, from Okonkwo to the District Commissioner" (Andrade, 2011, 92), who plans to reduce the story of Umuofia to "a reasonable paragraph" (Achebe, 2001, 150) in his forthcoming book.

wars" (GR17), *Under the Udala Trees* highlights how the onset of the Biafran War triggers Ijeoma's lesbian desire. When Ijeoma's mother, following the death of her husband, sends her ten-year-old daughter to the household of a childless couple, Ijeoma meets Amina, who, despite her Hausa background, shares the protagonist's sense of "loneliness, raggedness, disorientation, and hunger" (Pucherova, 2019, 116). Ijeoma

> felt a shadow following me, a shadow other than my own. It crossed the roads with me, hopped over the puddles with me. It appeared to tap the leaves with me, or at least it stood close behind me as I did. I stopped in order to allow the shadow to pass me. I found a large rock near where an udala tree stood and sat down there. I waited on the rock, hoping that the shadow would continue along, but it did not. Instead, it set across from me, on another rock, eyes bright, like a pair of light bulbs. She was no longer a shadow. [...] The moment our eyes locked, I knew I would not be leaving without her. (N17, 104–05)

Locating the two girls "under the udala trees", the text "provocatively interrogates prescriptive notions of femininity" (Pucherova, 2019, 116). Yet, although Ijeoma and Amina's budding love cannot come to fruition, Ijeoma engages in a sexual relation with Amina and, at a later point in the novel, leaves her husband to live with a woman. Put differently, Okparanta's novel uses the Biafran War to promote the "tolerance of otherness" (Pucherova, 2019, 116), envisioning Nigerian society and, by implication, the affective communities of online reviewers as places "where love is allowed to be love, between men and women, and men and men, and women and women just as between Yoruba and Igbo and Hausa and Fulani" (N17, 321).

The middlebrow features of the new Nigerian novel, to recapitulate the key arguments developed in this chapter, can be affirmed from both materialist and narratological viewpoints. On the level of narrative, the novels' middlebrow characteristics manifest themselves in their varying realisations of the *Bildungsroman*, unanimously representing migration and the nation through the individual fates of their child or adolescent protagonists. Whereas this chapter related the novels' prevalent narrative techniques to the authors' creative writing background, the remainder of this book seeks socio-economic explanations on the levels of transmission and reception. Starting with an overview of the historical precursors of online literary communities, the next chapter scrutinises the structures of the digital literary economy, and particularly the business practices of Amazon, Goodreads and YouTube, to disclose the socio-technical means of marketing community, emotion and the new Nigerian novel.

CHAPTER 3

Algorithms of Affect: The Digital Literary Economy

Arguably, promoting "books as a tool for readers to develop ideas about their membership of larger communities" (Driscoll, 2014, 42) is no invention of Amazon, Goodreads, YouTube and the like. A quick glance at some of the precursors of online literary communities reveals that socially orientated reading practices entertain a long-standing relation with trade and commerce, evoking a history of capitalism that has fostered the socio-economic and affective superiority of the middle classes all along. Illustrating that the large-scale proliferation of print technology since the eighteenth century encouraged the formation of national public spheres across Europe, the German sociologist Jürgen Habermas (1989, 37) contends that community access was limited to those "who – insofar as they were propertied and educated – as readers, listeners, and spectators could avail themselves via the market of objects that were subject to discussion".[1] Similarly, Benedict Anderson (2006, 77) investigates eighteenth- and nineteenth-century "imagined communities" to suggest that membership in a national collective presupposed the financial means to afford both the print publications – that is, daily newspapers and realist novels – and the leisure time to consume them.[2] Class equally features as a central analytical category in two studies

---

1 First published in 1962, Habermas's study was translated into English only in 1989. Paying special attention to the British "centers of criticism" against state and church authorities, he demonstrates how coffee houses or salons nurtured the idea of an "inclusive public of all private people" (32, 35) that was unanimously bound to the emerging capitalist market and the various assets required to participate in it.
2 As the sub-title of his monograph highlights, Anderson principally employs the notion of community to invite *Reflections on the Origin and Spread of Nationalism*. Evoking the national borders of community, he emphasises that membership required middle-class affiliation. Contrasting two fictional factory owners in Lille and Lyon to "traditional aristocracies", he asserts that, as "they did not [...] marry

that explore how the shared consumption of sentimental novels by female readers triggered the development of affective reading communities in eighteenth-century Britain (Barker-Benfield, 1992) and nineteenth-century America (Berlant, 2008). In addition, and albeit placing less focus on literary community, Gohrisch's *Bürgerliche Gefühlsdispositionen in der englischen Prosa des 19. Jahrhunderts* (2005) and Stedman's *Stemming the Torrent: Expression and Control in the Victorian Discourses on Emotions, 1830–1872* (2002) scrutinise a broad range of nineteenth-century fictional and non-fictional material to illustrate that the heterogeneous British middle classes strengthened their supremacy in the newly developing industrial capitalist market economy via specific emotion discourses.[3]

Invigorating my historical and materialist outlook on the online literary communities of the new Nigerian novel, these studies not only hint at striking continuities between industrial and digital literary capitalism.[4] If the Industrial Revolution, including capitalist literary production, caused the emergence of "a specifically middle-class emotional culture" (Gohrisch, 2011, 44), the main beneficiaries of digitisation may well be regarded as what Hochschild (2003, 75), in a different context, refers to as "keepers of feeling rules". Refashioning the socio-economic and, by implication, the emotional relations among an ever-increasing number of social media users, including the ways in which they approach literary texts, Internet corporations such as Amazon, Goodreads and YouTube exercise tremendous power over "what the world expects of the heart" (Hochschild, 2003, 58). The new socio-technical means by which they bring the emotions of their customers or users "under their sway" (Hochschild, 2003, 19) and some of the reasons why these means create a challenge for the researcher are discussed in the subsequent

---

each other's daughter or inherit each other's property", they had no other "reason to know of one another's existence" except for "print-language" (77).

3 Further studies exploring the affective dimension of eighteenth- and nineteenth-century British reading cultures include Ablow (2010), Cohen (2009), Hughes (2011) and Williams (2017). My approach to the affective lexicon of the online literary communities is principally informed by Gohrisch and Stedman's studies, which examine nineteenth-century bourgeois emotion discourses most thoroughly. To give equal credit and weight to their studies, I quote from Gohrisch's "Negotiating the Emotional Habitus of the Middle Classes in *The Mayor of Casterbridge*" (2011).

4 This claim is supported by Ernest Mandel's periodisation of capitalism that, in the words of Jameson (1984, 78), distinguishes between "three fundamental moments in capitalism, each one marking a dialectical expansion over the previous stage". Structured along the lines of "quantum leaps in the evolution of machinery under capital" (Jameson, 1984, 77), the model may be complemented by a fourth – that is, digital – stage. The expansion of the Internet since the 1990s shows remarkable parallels to the "[m]achine production of steam-driven motors since 1848" or "electronic and nuclear-powered apparatuses" (Mandel, 1975, 18) since the 1940s, shifting private ownership from "factories, mills and workshops" or "multinational corporations" (Barker, 2004, 19) to Amazon or Google.

sections.⁵ I propose that digital companies such as Amazon and YouTube ensure their monopoly status in the digital literary economy by establishing closed ecosystems that, building on socio-technical algorithms of affect, function to enhance a middle-class affective pattern that encompasses both the labour relations (Chapter 4) and emotional expressions (Chapter 5) of the online reading communities under scrutiny.

Structuring community and communication in the World Wide Web, algorithms equally determine the study of digital literary consumption. Whoever engages with online material will quickly realise that a position "outside" the Internet economy is unavailable, which is part of the explanation why "the intellectual work of understanding reading online [is] seemingly always still to be done" (Murray, 2018, 147). In fact, and as the introductory chapter of this book indicated, Murray (2018, 141–67) investigates reading practices on social media without clearly delineated datasets, while Aubry (2011, 176) or Driscoll and Rehberg Sedo (2019, 249) do not pay sufficient attention to the economic bedrock of online literary discussions, including its implications for the selection of computational software. Delineating my conception of digital literary capitalism, this chapter advances the digital affect by stressing the advantages of approaching the social and emotional reading practices of online communities through specific datasets and with computerised methods derived from corpus linguistics.

The Creation of Affective Online Communities: Amazon, Goodreads and YouTube

How can one grasp the digital literary sphere in economic terms? Highlighting that, in the current "transitional environment, long-standing concerns about the political economy of the book world do not disappear", Murray (2018, 54) suggests an update of Bourdieu's oeuvre. Expounded in such surveys as *The Field of Cultural Production* (1993) or *The Rules of Art* (1996), the numerous concepts and models employed by the French sociologist to examine cultural behaviour are so well established that several of the studies referred to in this book make use of them without further justification. Proving its productivity across the disciplines, Bourdieu's critical terminology pervades the postcolonial approaches to the global book market by Huggan (2001, 4–5, 212–14) or

---

5 Other than the national scope of the above-mentioned studies may suggest, the challenge does not result from "the Internet's structural undermining of national boundaries" (Murray, 2018, 2). Primarily invented to confirm "middle-class lifestyles and values" (Aubry, 2011, 26), the novel has always been a "global" genre in the sense that its formal and ideological conventions rested on colonial exploitation. What the thoroughly international scope of the online literary communities examined here shows is that digital literary capitalism, contrary to its precursors, grants affective authority to the postcolonial Other.

the contributions to *Bourdieu and Postcolonial Studies* (Dalleo, 2016) published in LUP's "Postcolonialism across the Disciplines" series and including chapters by Bongie (2016, 53–79) and Brouillette (2016, 80–101). Bourdieu's notions of capital and habitus also feature in the literary-sociological research of middlebrow studies scholars such as Aubry (2011, 6, 15) and Driscoll (2014, 12–17) or the socio-historical emotion research of Gohrisch (2005, 39–40; 2011, 47–48), Illouz (2007, 63–64, 67) and Stedman (2002, 3–5).[6] Evoking his theory of the literary field, the title of Murray's monograph, *The Digital Literary Sphere* (2018), equally underpins her attempt at "reframing" Bourdieusian terminology "to engage meaningfully with twenty-first-century digital cultural phenomena" (18). Indeed, and in spite of her macro-level perspective on the digital literary sphere, Murray demonstrates that Bourdieu's literary field theory can serve the investigation of the digital literary economy. Tackling the algorithmic "Challenge to the Bourdieusian Field", Murray (55–58) provides exceptional insights into Amazon's business schemes. Ranking among a "tiny body of critical analysis that offsets a vast and mostly celebratory genre of business journalism and corporate hagiography", her endeavour is much appreciated, not least because it dissolves the misleading distinction between human agents and computer software by elucidating that algorithms do not "function without social or political investments" (54, 57). Notwithstanding, I would like to put forward that Bourdieu's work does not lend itself to conduct a proper historical materialist analysis of the digital literary economy.

This contention can be supported by taking a closer look at Bourdieu's notion of capital. Primarily received as extensions of an economic concept into the spheres of society and culture, Bourdieu's distinct forms of capital – social, cultural, symbolic – are problematic for two reasons, at least from a materialist perspective. For one, and as the sociologist Mathieu Hikaru Desan (2013, 336) contends, this common reception results from the reductive assumption that "Marx's conception of capital is economistic". Instead of defining capital in monetary terms, Marx (1981, 953) uses the notion to refer to historically variable modes of exploitation that determine the entire structure of a given society: "a definite social relation of production pertaining to a particular historical social formation, which [...] takes the form of a thing and gives this thing a specific social character". Subverting the extension model further, Bourdieu (1990, 122) characterises economic capital as merely one "particular case of a general theory of the economy of practices" and thus not only disregards the socio-historical dimensions of the concept in the Marxist sense but also "tends to take the economic field [...] for granted" (Desan, 2013, 318). In sum, and in the words of Desan (332), what Bourdieu "extends is [...] only capital's appearance as a power resource. In insisting on calling these [...] power resources 'capital' without developing a concept of capital as

---

6 Amending the two notions, Gohrisch and Stedman speak of an emotional habitus, whereas Aubry and Illouz and, more recently, Adenekan (2021, 6, 47, 105) refer to psychological, emotional and digital capital, respectively.

such, Bourdieu obscures the relations of exploitation which Marx's concept of capital renders legible", providing melodious metaphors rather than thorough tools for socio-economic analysis.

A comprehensive Marxist analysis of the digital literary economy lies beyond the scope of this book. However, rather than drawing on a Bourdieusian analytical framework, my approach profits from the materialist and sociological perspectives on the Internet economy developed by Bucher (2018), Huck (2020), Staab (2019) and Zuboff (2019), among others. Staab's notion of digital capitalism is particularly well suited to examine the socio-economic and emotional relations of power that structure online literary communities. Positioning digital corporations such as Amazon, Facebook and Google at the outer end of an overarching history of capitalism, the German sociologist shows that their business practices are both contingent with and different from prior capitalist production models. Rather than dominating specific market areas, they operate as and become increasingly identical with privatised or proprietary markets that regulate an ever-expanding number of production and consumption sectors (30, 34, 50, 223). Deviating from other monopolists, many leading Internet companies do not trouble themselves with the resource-thrifty production of commodities but pursue and perpetuate control over supply and demand by continuously amending and expanding their digital goods and services (45). Taking after the potentially inexhaustible product range of financial capitalist companies, such as credits or shares, the production of digital goods such as software, while facilitating communication and transaction, involves no to negligible marginal costs (21, 29, 81–84; Staab and Nachtwey, 2016, 461), especially if compared with the tremendously high fees that the behemoths demand for functioning as proprietary markets.[7] In the year 2021, Amazon and its subsidiary Goodreads gained over 31 billion US dollars in advertising revenues, whereas YouTube earned close to 30 billion US dollars from controlling the communication circuits between producers and consumers (Staab, 2019, 45, 47–48).[8]

As the extraordinary amount of revenues in advertising implies, user data may be considered "the companies' primary capital" (Staab and Nachtwey, 2016, 460). Indeed, digital corporations have a vital interest in retaining old and attracting new customers and users as exclusive access to their data constitutes an essential prerequisite for successful negotiations

---

7 Notably, and contrary to telecommunications providers, energy and water suppliers or railway operators, which have to invest large sums into infrastructure before they can commence business, Amazon and the like mostly saved these expenses as they could build on already existing voice networks (Staab, 2019, 28–29).

8 The difference between Amazon and all other digital companies addressed in this chapter consists in the fact that *The Everything Store* (Stone, 2013) also makes money from the retail of books (and everything else). Accordingly, its sales revenue amounted to almost 470 billion US dollars in 2021. See below for Amazon's role as a publisher.

with producers. Unsurprisingly, then, Amazon and its competitors invest substantial parts of their revenues into the enhancement and extension of their services. As Staab (2019, 37–39, 106), referring to Ulrich Dolata (2015, 505–29), argues, these investments primarily serve to create and, in effect, control "socio-technical ecosystems" (Staab and Nachtwey, 2016, 460):

> They offer customers a number of synchronized and interlinked programs and services. The anchor product – whether it's an iPad, a Nexus, a Surface or a Kindle – serves as a digital hub for all forms of communication and coordination. Once a user is integrated into such a socio-technical space for communication – because [...] she or he stores data and files it in a specific provider's cloud – then other applications from the same provider dock into the existing structures. This results in closed systems that [...] systematically impede changing to another provider, since users would then generally face a loss of aggregated data, with unpleasant consequences. (Staab and Nachtwey, 2016, 462)

Since "they are highly personalized" (Staab and Nachtwey, 2016, 462), the distinct ecosystems of Amazon, Facebook and others follow a remarkably closed and self-enforcing logic. Whoever tries to move across different ecosystems – say, those of Apple and Google – will probably experience frustration owing to their incompatibility.[9] Seeking to reduce this impression and thereby preventing their customers' switching between providers, digital companies constantly adapt their ecosystems or, more specifically, the algorithms that these are based on, to the interests and tastes of their users.

Testifying to their pervasiveness in professional and private life, algorithms have sparked celebratory and critical commentary across the disciplines and beyond. Relating a range of common conceptions – "a type of technology", "a step-by-step instruction", a "code that tries to accommodate personal interests", "an application that determines what you see" or that is "use[d] to guarantee the best user experience possible" and "an appetizer to make you crave for more of the same" – Bucher (2018, 19) takes issue with the neoliberal service rhetoric that characterises such and similar attempts at advertising algorithms as neutral supporters of decision making. Without doubt, algorithms serve to structure "the vast amount of data produced and available on the Web" (Bucher, 2018, 3). Furthermore, as Illouz (2007, 85) reveals in her discussion of online dating sites such as eHarmony.org or match.com, in a capitalist "economy of abundance", this data is by no means confined to goods but frequently encompasses humans and the "cost-benefit and efficiency" of their romantic encounters as well. The work of Bucher and

---

9 The incompatibility of the Amazon, Goodreads and YouTube pages is less pronounced, although Amazon ensures that communication across the platforms does not threaten its "near-monopoly position" (Murray, 2018, 75) in the digital literary sphere, for instance by equipping influential BookTubers with affiliate links to its online bookstore.

Illouz is representative of a swiftly burgeoning field of research that scholars such as Tarleton Gillespie (2016, 18–30) or Nick Seaver (2013, 1–12) have referred to as critical algorithm studies. Rather than concerning themselves with the technical characteristics and improvements of algorithms, representatives of this research area study the socio-cultural "meaning[s] and implications that algorithmic systems may have" (Bucher, 2018, 29), paying particular attention to the ways in which they are generative of power hierarchies. In his early intervention into the field, Ted Striphas (2015, 396, 406) cautions about the consequences of "algorithmic culture"; heralding "the enfolding of human thought, conduct, organization and expression into the logic of big data", algorithms privatise not only decision making but culture – "the values, practices and artifacts [...] of specific social groups" – at large. Similarly, Bucher (2018, 158, 4) explores what she terms "programmed sociality" – the manner in which "algorithms 'program' ways of being together" online – to conclude that it "prescribe[s] certain norms, values, and practices". Safiya Umoja Noble's *Algorithms of Oppression* (2018), moreover, discloses the racial prejudices and sexist attitudes inscribed in man-made software. Exceeding the "black box" approach adopted by many a literary and cultural studies scholar (Driscoll and Rehberg Sedo, 2019, 258; Rauscher, 2018, 312), critical algorithm studies provides ample inspiration for my take on the new Nigerian novel's online reading communities that constitute mere examples of the many "socio-bio-technical assemblages" (Huck, 2021, 95) that pervade the Internet in general and the digital literary sphere in particular. Consequently, the insights of Bucher, Noble and Striphas encourage a precise look at the norms, values and practices that are encoded in those algorithms that "assemble the social" (Latour, 2005) and emotional relations among my online reviewers.

Drawing on the experience of constructing and examining my medium-scale case study, I contend that the ecosystems of Amazon, Goodreads and YouTube build on affective algorithms that, complying with the lucrative middlebrow model of literacy, function to create and preserve a distinctly bourgeois emotional culture. Since "all roads of online book talk lead to Amazon", I take an exemplary look at the company that fashions itself as the "Earth's Biggest Bookstore" (Murray, 2018, 75, 61) to substantiate my claim. At the outset of his article in *The New Yorker*, tellingly titled "Cheap Words" (2014), the journalist George Packer describes Amazon as

> a global superstore, like Walmart. It's also a hardware manufacturer, like Apple, and a utility, like Con Edison, and a video distributor, like Netflix, and a book publisher, like Random House, and a production studio, like Paramount, and a literary magazine, like *The Paris Review*, and a grocery deliverer, like FreshDirect, and someday it might be a package service, like U.P.S. Its founder and chief executive, Jeff Bezos, also owns a major newspaper, the *Washington Post*. All these streams and tributaries make Amazon something radically new in the history of American business. Sam Walton wanted merely to be the world's biggest retailer. After Apple

launched the iPod, Steve Jobs didn't sign up pop stars for recording contracts. A.T.&T. doesn't build transmission towers and rent them to smaller phone companies, the way Amazon Web Services provides server infrastructure for startups [...]. Amazon's identity and goals are never clear and always fluid, which makes the company destablilizing and intimidating.

In light of Packer's characterisation,[10] one can easily overlook that Amazon was launched as an online bookstore in 1995, only gradually turning into *The Everything Store* (Stone, 2013). Indeed, books have become merely one of the company's many income sources. According to McGurl (2016, 448), "by 2014 its receipts from books had shrunk dramatically as a percentage of its estimated seventy-billion dollars in yearly revenue, to something like 7 percent".[11] While these figures may verify Packer's (2014) contention that the sale of books mostly served to ensure Amazon's "world domination at the beginning of the Internet age", McGurl (2016, 448) rightly remarks that the company keeps a "uniquely intense and ongoing self-association with literature". Its firm "commitment to the idea of literature, to getting inside literature" not only manifests itself in its acquisition of Goodreads or its establishment as "a traditional publisher with fourteen separate imprints" (449, 450). It also transpires from the bookish anecdotes about Bezos or his former wife McKenzie, a creative writing graduate and the author of novels such as *The Testing of Luther Albright* (2005) and *Traps* (2013), who, notably enough, "studied under Toni Morrison at Princeton" (Packer, 2014).

A key representative and beneficiary of what McGurl (2016, 452) calls the new economy – "a postindustrial economy of services facilitated by technology" – Amazon arguably exceeds the service concept of the postwar writing workshop discussed in the second chapter. Conceptualising the company in terms of "a possible successor-formation of the Program Era", McGurl (452, 448) highlights "the aggression with which [Amazon] pursues its own interests under the banner [...] of *customer*" (original emphasis) – who is frequently a reader. A first indication of its "intensely reader-oriented" (Driscoll, 2014, 28) middlebrow practices, Amazon's care for customers (capital) emerges from the following anecdote about Bezos's decision to leave the Manhattan hedge fund he was working for in 1994, relocate to Seattle and found Amazon (Packer, 2014). As the journalist Brad Stone (2013, 27) relates,

> [a]t the time Bezos was thinking about what to do next, he had recently finished the novel *Remains of the Day*, by Kazuo Ishiguro, about a butler who wistfully recalls his personal and professional choices during a career in service in wartime Great Britain. So looking back on life's important

---

10 Packer reinforces his assertion of Bezos's megalomania by relating that Amazon's founder initially "thought of calling his company Relentless.com [...] before adopting the name of the world's largest river by volume".
11 It should be noted, though, that this "fraction is no small part of the book business, accounting for roughly half of all US book purchases" (McGurl, 2016, 448).

junctures was on Bezos's mind when he came up with what he calls "the regret-minimization framework" to decide the next step to take at this juncture in his career.

In accordance with Bezos's self-conception as a servant to his customer, Amazon efficiently "transforms literary experience into customer experience" (McGurl 2016, 455), serving the quick delivery of ridiculously cheap books just as well as "a sense of clubbish belonging with likeminded literate people" (Murray, 2018, 58).

Amazon's community-building services, a second indication of its middlebrow marketing schemes, result from an extensive shift in the early 2000s from "editorial suggestions" to algorithms based on "customers' history to make recommendations for future purchases" (Packer, 2014). Concealing the company's thoroughly commodified conception of community, Bezos adopts a "consciously folksy tone" (Murray, 2018, 60) to explain the workings of Amazon's collaborative filtering algorithms:

> It is a statistical technique that looks at your past purchase streams and finds other people whose past purchase streams are similar. Think of the people it finds as your electronic soul mates. Then we look at that aggregation and see what things your electronic soul mates have bought that you haven't. Those are the books we recommend. And it works. (quoted in Murray, 2018, 70)

In effect, Amazon sells not only books but tailor-made reading experiences, which, building on customers' personal reading histories, cover aesthetically and politically similar titles. Whoever purchases, say, Adichie's *Americanah* via Amazon will certainly receive recommendations for *Purple Hibiscus*, *Half of a Yellow Sun* and a range of other new Nigerian novels. Generated and improved on the basis of accumulated user data, algorithmic software does not simply govern consumer choices but rather "gives the people what they want", as James Marcus (2005, 200), one of Amazon's former editors, specifies (Bucher, 2018, 23–28, 158–59; Staab and Nachtwey, 2016, 460). In addition, and as Bezos's definition of customers in terms of "electronic soul mates" substantiates, Amazon's algorithms turn the act of reading into a genuinely social experience that promises "communal fellow-feeling" (Murray, 2018, 62) because it connects customers with similar reading tastes and patterns, encouraging them to comment on each others' reviews or search each others' reader profiles for custom-made titles. As Huck (2020, 77–76, 80, 82–83) persuasively demonstrates, algorithmic recommendation enhances the impression of familiarity with fellow social media users who, because they feel personally addressed, share more and more personal details and thus contribute to the creation of affective ties within online communities – and, last but by no means least, the creation of further capital for the digital companies.

A third and related indication of Amazon's middlebrow literacy model emerges from its "netiquette" (Rauscher, 2018, 310) or its "Community

Guidelines", which, like Bezos's explanation of collaborative filtering, cocoon the company's business interests in middlebrow discourses of authenticity, honesty and trust. Advertising the platform's interactive features as excellent opportunities of "engaging other users and sharing authentic feedback about products and services", for instance, Amazon's guidelines not only emphasise the site's capability to support friendly connections among its customers but equally caution that "[w]e take the integrity of the Community seriously" ("Community Guidelines", *Amazon*). In a similar vein, YouTube presents its policies as a means of "ensur[ing] [that] our community stays protected" ("Community Guidelines", *YouTube*). Notably, and although most digital reading platforms encourage their users to "report an abuse" (Amazon) or "flag" allegedly inappropriate reviews (Goodreads), their providers leave no doubt that "[i]t is at our sole discretion to decide when content violates our guidelines" ("Community Guidelines", *Goodreads*). Despite the recurring hint that "advertising, promotion, or solicitation" ("Community Guidelines", *Amazon*) are prohibited, moreover, the guidelines remain conspicuously imprecise about the particularities of their netiquette or feeling rules, which shine through only if one studies the reviews that, insofar as they have not been deleted, conform with the companies' conception of community.[12]

The middlebrow affective lexicon of the guidelines, just as the promotional parlance informing Bezos's definition of algorithms, effectively obscures that community building on Amazon, Goodreads and YouTube constitutes a quintessentially commercial practice that, first and foremost, serves "the harvesting of voluntarily supplied user data" (Murray, 2018, 61; McGurl, 2016, 450; Nakamura, 2013, 241–42; Staab and Nachtwey, 2016, 460) and, as a consequence, the retention of users. While the operating principle – the learning capacity of algorithms – suggests that digital companies do not simply nudge their consumers and users towards any consumption path or pattern, algorithms doubtlessly constitute powerful tools of control or surveillance that can modify purchase and consumer habits (Zuboff, 2019, 295). Whereas Zuboff's notion of surveillance capitalism invites critical perspectives on the ways in which digital companies affect the market's demand side, Staab (2019, 21–22, 32, 177–78) convincingly contends that the exclusive access to consumers is not an end in itself but rather functions to exert power

---

12 Strengthening users' "community allegiance", the "Community Guidelines" may also be read as a reaction to fake or "sock-puppet reviews" of publishers or "authors puffing their own books" (Murray, 2018, 59, 131, 134). Next to its guidelines, "Amazon has instituted various technical checks, such as linking reviewer identity with purchaser credit card records, marking reviews from those with a buyer record for the item as 'verified purchase', and appearing to elevate these up the hierarchy of review listings" (Murray, 2018, 135). All these efforts do not alter the fact that one can never "be sure who wrote a specific review" (Rauscher, 2018, 321). What can be studied, however, is how Amazon, Goodreads and YouTube choose to present their communities, as I do below.

over the supply side and producers, including publishing houses. Given the steadily increasing digitisation of the world-literary system, publishers have a vital interest in the reading tastes of countless potential customers and the favourable integration into the algorithmic infrastructure of online reading platforms. Utilising their growing dependence on "virtual shelf space and automated marketing services" (McGurl, 2016, 455), Amazon has continually increased its co-op or promotional rates, thereby causing the downfall of small and independent publishers. While strengthening their dominant position, the Big Five[13] are equally pressured: "the larger houses [...] relinquish five to seven per cent of gross sales, pushing Amazon's percentage discount on books into the mid-fifties" (Packer, 2014). Additionally, they increasingly have to compete with Amazon in its (more recent) guise as a producer of literature that systematically "circumvent[s] the traditional gatekeepers of American literary production" (McGurl, 2016, 449), as indicated by such programmes as Kindle Direct Publishing or Kindle Worlds.

It is not hard to recognise that the business schemes of Amazon and other representatives of digital literary capitalism foster a "self-reinforcing and confirmatory" (Murray, 2018, 60) system of literary transmission that, supporting repetition rather than reform,[14] renders reading outside and beyond middle-class emotional structures more and more difficult, as my study's subsequent focus on the online reviewers of the new Nigerian novel confirms. Considering the pitfalls and potentials that accompany the construction of digital review corpora, the remainder of this chapter introduces the digital affect: a computational method that not only serves to examine the reading communities of recent Nigerian fiction but, by virtue of its reproducibility, lends itself to explore the social meso- and linguistic micro-levels of other (postcolonial) reading formations online.

The Construction of Digital Review Corpora: Data Collection and Error Analysis

Indeed, the gathering, saving and editing of constantly changing and increasing online data constitutes a hugely laborious yet worthwhile task. In contrast to many a corpus linguist, I could not draw on existing corpora but had to construct my datasets of online reviews before their socio-economic and linguistic analyses could even begin. Crucially, and contrary to the broader approaches to digital communication or online readers by Huck (2020, 43–84) or Murray (2018, 141–67), my study emanated from an interest in the reception

---

13 The Big Five – the five biggest publishing houses worldwide – are Hachette, HarperCollins, Macmillan, Penguin Random House and Simon & Schuster (Packer, 2014).
14 In view of the new Nigerian novel's repetitive structures, it may not surprise that the majority of the 20 novels were published by (imprints of) the Big Five.

of particular literary texts rather than the automated recommendation systems of digital companies as such. This focus by no means disregards the influences and effects of algorithmic software on the transmission and hence the production and consumption of literature. My research conception is nonetheless significant because it renders the construction of review corpora relatively independent of algorithms.

Looking back at the development of my research agenda, the construction of my datasets comes close to a strategy that Bucher (2018, 46) describes as "unknowing" algorithms: "seeing differently, looking elsewhere, or not even looking at all" as a prerequisite to understand their cultural work. Starting from a generic definition of my case study, I did not select the novels because they were recommended in Goodreads newsletters or YouTube playlists. However, it is crucial to recognise that this strategy does not prevent the researcher's impact on the structures of communities that define power primarily in terms of clicks and views.

Following the selection of the novels, I had to make a decision concerning the platforms from which to gather the reviews. Besides Amazon, Goodreads and YouTube, the Internet offers a variety of candidates, including Facebook, Instagram, Snapchat, Tumblr and Twitter.[15] My choice was primarily informed by this study's corpus-linguistic methodology and my materialist pattern of thought, which call for text-based reviews circulating on those platforms that sell online literary discussion as "a means of social networking" (Nakamura, 2013, 239) most profitably. As the above-mentioned figures verify, Amazon, Goodreads and YouTube rank among the most powerful representatives of digital literary capitalism. This is not to suggest that Facebook, Instagram or Twitter constitute less appropriate representatives. According to Google, these companies gained approximately 115, 25 and 5 billion US dollars in advertising revenues in 2021. Seeking to ensure the efficiency of my research, I took an exemplary look at the contributions of my BookTubers to these platforms. Showing either identical or shortened versions of those video reviews uploaded on YouTube, the sample yields that it would have been superfluous to consider more representatives since different platforms do not necessarily provide different content. Highlighting that their socio-technical ecosystems are not entirely closed, this finding also indicates that the platforms employ algorithms to similar effect. For instance, the "shelfies" (shelf-selfies) and "perfectly composed photographs" (Kalpaxis, 2020) of books on Instagram (or Bookstagram) and Twitter, overwhelmingly arranged alongside a cup of coffee or a bunch of flowers, emphasise the middlebrow reader's domestic consumption context and reverential attitude towards the object of the book addressed in the subsequent chapter. Having said this, the

---

15 The next chapter points out that, in contrast to other social media sites promoting a bookish agenda, such as BookCrossing, BookJetty or LibraryThing, the reviewers included in my corpora frequently use these platforms as well.

image-heavy reviews on these platforms do not lend themselves to corpus-linguistic analyses that build on the written or spoken word.

Deviating from the research design of Aubry (2011) or Driscoll and Rehberg Sedo (2019), my study does not limit itself to reviews from one platform. Considerably increasing my investment of time and effort, the choice of three different yet interrelated social media sites and the resulting construction of three distinct review corpora bear a couple of advantages. Obviously, collecting reviews from more than one platform enables a direct comparison between the strategies of marketing literary consumption as a social and emotional practice. Promoting varying degrees of interaction, investment and impact within and across the sites, Amazon, Goodreads and YouTube serve to consider the many ways in which they redefine emotional labour (Chapter 4). Besides, contrasting the written reviews on Amazon and Goodreads with the spoken reviews on YouTube helps examine how distinct media influence the expression of emotion and the definition of affective norms (Chapter 5).

Table 3.1 details the composition of the three review corpora for 20 new Nigerian novels that I constructed between March and July 2019. In order to minimise the bias potential that results from looking at a selected sample of online reviews (Gibbons and Whiteley, 2018, 311), it is indispensable to construct review corpora in the most comprehensive way possible. As Trevor Owens in *Designing Online Communities* (2015) cautions, researchers of online reviews should consider "[w]ho constituted [a] collection of records, and for what purpose" (169). Gathering an arbitrary number of reviews, to put it differently, would conceal how the sites construct and represent their reading communities. Correspondingly, the diverging numbers across the platforms do not arise from a random selection process but rather relate to two factors that affect the construction of review corpora. One factor concerns the novels' varied degrees of prominence among the reviewers. While Adichie's *Americanah* ranks as an Amazon, Goodreads and "BookTube darling" (YR10, Barter Hordes, 19/04/2019), male novelists such as Abani or Habila triggered relatively fewer responses. Braithwaite's *My Sister, the Serial Killer*, Emezi's *Freshwater* and Obioma's *An Orchestra of Minorities* were published only a few months before I constructed my corpora, meaning that they were granted less time to generate reviews. However, the fact that they had already established a notable presence on the platforms and, more specifically, in the reviews of those who had turned to other new Nigerian novels before proves the confirmatory mechanisms of digital literary capitalism in general and the platforms' affective algorithms in particular. These mechanisms are also affirmed by the online presence of more recent Nigerian novels by the same authors, such as Braithwaite's *The Baby Is Mine* (2021), Emezi's *The Death of Vivek Oji* (2020) or *Dear Senthuran* (2021), Onuzo's *Sankofa* (2021) and Oyeyemi's *Peaces* (2021), or other Nigerian diasporic writers appearing on the digital literary scene, such as Tola Rotimi Abraham (*Black Sunday*, 2020). Unsurprisingly, these titles have already caught the attention of my reviewers at the time of revising the manuscript.

A second factor concerns the platform-specific guidelines. Limiting the act of reviewing to its customers (Rauscher, 2018, 310), Amazon does not restrict access to selected reviews, allowing me to gather all reviews available until 31 March 2019. Nonetheless, it should be noted that Amazon, like "every [other] platform, commercial or not, reserves the right to delete any specific review or user account" on the basis of their "Community Guidelines", demonstrating its power to "regulate whose voice is heard" (Rauscher, 2018, 311) and who can participate in the online discussion of literary texts. Anything but "passive conduit[s]" (Nakamura, 2013, 243), digital reading platforms, including the rules implemented to structure and organise them, undoubtedly follow "a logic of ownership, control and limited permission" (Owens, 2015, 161).

This logic becomes particularly apparent when collecting reviews from the Goodreads page. Hosting an estimated amount of 50 million reviews (Driscoll and Rehberg Sedo, 2019, 248),[16] Goodreads rates among the "largest social networking site[s]" (Nakamura, 2013, 239) but displays no more than 300 reviews per book. Accordingly, the actual number of reviews on Goodreads notably exceeds the 4,292 reviews denoted in Table 3.1. Indeed, I counted close to 50,000 reviews for the 20 novels up to 30 April 2019. Defined by an unspecified default setting, the reviews that were available for each novel probably garnered the most "likes" and comments in descending order. As I demonstrate in the subsequent chapter, such practices highlight the extent to which digital companies define "participation and expression" (Fister, 2014), rewarding selected reviewers with online visibility and tastemaker authority.

Irrespective of the constraints ensuing from the netiquette of Amazon and Goodreads, the written reviews are comparatively easy to collect and save, even if the researcher has to consider excluding reviews that comment only on the novels' shipping and packaging or use languages other than English. Saving – that is, "copying and pasting the text into a word-processing document" (Gibbons and Whiteley, 2018, 312) – is advisable because platform content is prone to change. In addition, if the researcher wishes to compare and contrast not only the different sites but also the responses to the individual novels, as I do in Chapter 5, I suggest dividing the reviews into separate sub-corpora and saving them as such. If meta-data, including the reviewer's name and location, star ratings or "likes" and "helpful" markers, are relevant to the research agenda, they are best saved alongside the respective reviews.

Since it is more time-consuming to produce video reviews, the numbers for YouTube are relatively low. Adding to the strenuous task of preparing the videos for the application of corpus-linguistic tools, their peculiar structure

---

16 In her chapter, published one year before the article by Driscoll and Rehberg Sedo, Rauscher (2018, 308) states the total number of 34 million reviews. This deviation may illustrate the pace at which reading communities in the World Wide Web proliferate.

constitutes a substantial challenge as to which sequences to include or exclude. Although YouTube offers automated sub-titles, the reviews commonly burst with incorrect grammar, spelling and punctuation. Needless to say, such and similar phenomena equally characterise the written reviews on Amazon and Goodreads but video reviews almost always require extensive editing and sometimes full transcriptions.[17] A certain amount of editing becomes mandatory if one seeks to apply computer software that commonly "operates with simple searching and matching techniques" (Rauscher, 2018, 313). However, finding a reasonable balance between close and distant reading approaches to the online responses is recommendable, not least because "some information that lies within the individual style and even wrong spelling might be lost" (Rauscher, 2018, 313) – such as the recurring observation of Amazon reviewers that Iweala's novel "flows in *pigeon* English prose" (AR13, my emphasis).

Both written and spoken reviews invariably evoke the wider digital literary sphere and its various agents, begging the question of *whose* language is actually investigated. Considering their many indirect references to and direct quotes from the novels, author interviews or newspaper and publisher blurbs, I propose to approach online reviews as intertexts or "mosaic[s] of quotations" (Cuddon, 2013, 367) that, in conventional middlebrow fashion, blur the levels of production, distribution and consumption.[18] The structural features of most videos complicate matters further. Compared with Amazon and Goodreads users, BookTubers exhibit a particular preference for the middlebrow pattern of quickly transitioning from the discussion of literary texts to the relation of personal experiences (Driscoll, 2014, 65; Long, 2003, 203). Locating "the place of reading in self-improvement through self-increased knowledge", to use Driscoll's (2014, 65) description of the pattern, BookTuber Philly Aime (YR05) performs how Adichie's *Purple Hibiscus* has her "going in one direction" before

---

17 This task can be quite nerve-racking, considering the features of spoken (as opposed to written) language generally and BookTubers' alleged struggle "to find the words that describe how I feel" (YR03, The Book Castle, 13/06/2019) specifically. To provide an example, this is how BookTuber Siwe Magadla (YR10, 15/06/2018) relates her experience of reading *Freshwater*: "I'm really ... I don't know ... I don't have the words to express this and I'm just so excited and I feel ... I don't know ... I feel a lot of things. I feel emotional as well mostly. And so, yeah, I'm so ... I'm so happy." All the same, and as the next chapter shows, YouTube videos make a particularly worthwhile addition to any corpus of online reviews. For one, they provide the most comprehensive insight into the demographic setup of online reading communities. Second, they illustrate more than the written reviews on Amazon and Goodreads that middlebrow patterns of reading constitute *activities* that considerably exceed the discussion of a given literary text.

18 Albeit acknowledging that a corpus-linguistic analysis of online reviews cannot properly distinguish between these levels, Chapter 5 suggests how the thoroughly comparative mode of keyword analysis serves to gain an understanding about the interdependence of the different agents that constitute the digital literary sphere.

"thinking of another part of [the novel] that relates to me". And Shellee (YR10, Shellee Stories, 11/11/2018) draws on Emezi's representation of "someone that may have mental illness" as a prompt to share a story about "a friend who really struggled with alcoholism", whereas Noria (YR03, Noria Reads, 17/02/2019) records her "Books That Saved My Life" series to detail how *Americanah* helped her cope with "my sexual assault".

Complying with these commitments to work through their psychological difficulties, BookTubers frequently organise their videos around book hauls, TBRs (books "to be read") and wrap-ups, all of which means that the majority of them entails the discussion of more than one novel, both encompassing and exceeding my corpus of primary texts.[19] As a consequence, the editing of YouTube reviews clearly surpasses the correction of erroneous transcriptions, demanding the researcher to decide which sequences to cut or maintain. Major text reductions may prevent significant insights into the BookTuber's reading habits, including his or her consumption contexts and motivations. Moreover, the deletion of large parts of a video review potentially obscures the thoroughly commercial orientation of YouTube videos that transpires from the simultaneous marketing of books and beauty or hair products on "lifestyle" channels. On the other hand, incorporating longer sequences that do not relate to the new Nigerian novel distort the results of a corpus-linguistic analysis aimed at responses to particular literary texts. Editing my corpus of videos, I opted for a middle path, excluding the lengthy presentations of other books and retaining the reviews' overall "script" (with greetings and farewells). I also refrained from establishing a distinction between novels that the BookTubers (claim to) have already read and have yet to read as I found both forms of discussion equally suggestive of the feeling rules constructed and negotiated in the Web 2.0 universe.[20]

CADS and Keyword Analysis: Possibilities and Limitations

The size of the three corpora, which include 15,026 online reviews, call for computerised analytical procedures. The notion of "Big Data" proliferated very much alongside the digital humanities and its quantitative methods of

---

19 See Chapter 4 for a discussion of the different video types as one of the BookTubers' strategies to cope with the demands of digital literary capitalism. In the few cases where the same review covers more than one novel from my corpus, I split the video into separate mini-reviews and allocated them to the respective sub-corpora. This procedure explains the discrepancy between the number of reviews shown in Table 3.1 and in the bibliography.

20 In addition, expressions such as "I know I will love Chimamanda" (YR04, Jasmine's Reads, 11/04/2019) hint at the participatory pressures created by BookTube and the digital literary sphere at large, suggesting that those who seek belonging have a clear idea of the feeling rules that govern online literary discussion (Ehret et al., 2018, 151; Hochschild, 2003, 18, 69).

Algorithms of Affect

text analysis. In the "burgeoning discipline" of digital literary studies, scholars have used digital tools to trace larger "patterns in literary developments" (Murray, 2018, 6, 7; Bode and Dixon, 2009; Goldstone and Underwood, 2014; Jockers, 2013; Moretti, 2013a)[21] or examine born-digital texts such as hyperfiction (Bell, 2010; Hayles, 2008; Kirschenbaum, 2008). In contrast, and in spite of the comparatively easy accessibility of millions of digital reader responses,[22] distant reading approaches to the genre of online reviews are still in their infancy. Demarcating a developing and, as a consequence, somewhat disparate field of research, digital reception studies currently covers a range of scattered articles and chapters on a variety of topics, including the analyses of online responses to heritage films (Monk, 2011, 431–77) or contemporary crime fiction (Rauscher, 2018, 307–24).[23] Studies that are computer-based and thus more immediately relevant to my research agenda, while certainly inspirational for my approach to the review corpora, testify that the analysis of digital reception is fraught with a number of challenges. Whereas Murray (2018, 142) refrains from investigating a specific set of reviews and therefore fails to suggest a truly "transferable" procedure, Aubry (2011, 175–98) considers too few Amazon reviews of Hosseini's *The Kite Runner* to devise a reproducible method for the study of my datasets. In turn, and informed by a similar neglect of the Internet economy and its impact on online reading behaviour, Driscoll's (2015, 861–73) approach to 20,189 audience tweets produced during the 2013 Australian Writers Festival and Driscoll and Rehberg Sedo's (2019, 248–59) computerised analysis of 692 Goodreads reviews with SentiStrength, while conceding its narrow perspective on emotional language, do not take sufficient account of the programme's commercial backdrop. Originating from "programs that track consumer satisfaction with goods and services" and operating on the basis of "algorithms for advertising placement and recommendations" (Driscoll, 2015, 863), the business orientation of the SentiStrength software is reinforced by its in-built rating system, which shows an uncomfortably close similarity with the star-rating systems of social media sites. Classifying emotional experiences as "positive" or "negative", the software is characterised by a

---

21 Although these studies primarily adopt "retrospective" vantages and thus do not "throw light on contemporary literary developments" (Murray, 2018, 7), they serve as an inspiration for my computer-assisted take on selected new Nigerian novels in Chapter 5. Notably, my approach avails itself of the simultaneity of literary text and reader response characteristic of the Internet era, whereas historical surveys have to make do with implied readers.
22 That is, in comparison with the "laboratory-like, experimental settings" (Rauscher, 2018, 308) that constitute the basis of many ethnographic or sociological research agendas.
23 Further examples include Peter Boot (2013) and Sebastian Domsch (2009, 221–38), who approach online literary discussions from genre theoretical perspectives, or Daniel Allington (2016, 254–78) and Ed Finn (2013), who focus on the analysis of online reviews.

strong tendency to reproduce bourgeois affective norms, as the sparse results of Driscoll's (2015, 867) efforts demonstrate: "the twitter conversation at the Melbourne Writers Festival had a positive emotional quality".

In order to curb the risk of merely reproducing the "opinion mining" (Driscoll, 2015, 863) practices of software developers, I apply the digital toolbox of CADS. Like SentiStrength, this branch of corpus linguistics "capitalises on [...] the power of computers to identify patterns in large stretches of language" (Gibbons and Whiteley, 2018, 285). Unlike SentiStrength, however, it leaves substantial leeway for "additional interpretive work from the researcher" (Gibbons and Whiteley, 2018, 285) and therefore places the power of defining and interpreting emotional expressions in academic hands. Allowing for the effective combination with other disciplines,[24] CADS enables me to bring the insights of socio-historical emotion research to bear on the study of the new Nigerian novel's online reading communities and envision their "emotion talk"[25] as the latest manifestation of an overarching bourgeois history of emotions. More precisely, my approach profits from the field's strong emphasis on the social, economic and cultural functions of discourse (Halliday, 1985, 10; Partington and Marchi, 2015, 217), ensuring a conceptualisation of the online reviewers as subjects with socio-economic interests rather than mere objects of the digital companies' "new regime of controlled consumerism" (Nakamura, 2013, 214). In this book, then, corpus-linguistic approaches do not constitute an end in themselves but serve to adopt a transhistorical and sociologically informed vantage point on the affective lexicon of online literary communities.

The quantitative procedures of CADS can be realised by many corpus software programmes, some of which "require a fee for a single-user licence or annual subscription, such as Wordsmith and WMatrix" (Gibbons and Whiteley, 2018, 285–86) or MaxQDA (Rauscher, 2018, 315). I work with a freeware corpus linguistics software called AntConc. Created by the linguist Laurence Anthony, the toolkit offers all "commonly employed statistical overview techniques" (Partington and Marchi, 2015, 217) and can thus be applied to disclose the linguistic properties of my three review corpora. In Chapter 5, I make extensive use of AntConc's wordlist and concordancing tools to uncover the lexical features and lexico-grammatical patterns of the reviewers' emotion talk. Setting

---

24 Previous research has mostly been conducted in the field of socio-political CADS, which explores "how social, cultural, and political representations, such as gender or race, are constructed and reinforced by the accumulation of linguistic patterns" (Partington and Marchi, 2015, 220). Stubbs (1996), Baker (2006), Pearce (2008, 1–29) or Taylor (2013, 81–113) analyse gender stereotypes, while Krishnamurthy (1996, 129–49) and researchers of the RASIM Project (Baker and McEnery, 2005, 197–226) consider representations of ethnic minorities.

25 The term is borrowed from Monika Bednarek (2008, 24, original emphasis) and clarifies my understanding of the reviewers' emotional expressions in terms of "a *discursive practice*" that does not "represent the speaker's [...] 'real' internal affective state" but rather signifies his or her strategic employment of emotion discourses.

the scene for my corpus-linguistic study of the reviews, AntConc's keyword list tool necessitates more detailed consideration as it evinces that CADS bears limitations of its own. Keyword analysis constitutes a significant first step in the study of online reviews because it reveals the "register-specific features" (Bednarek, 2008, 28) of my corpora. Put differently, keyword analysis highlights those terms that the reviewers employ "*with unusual frequency*" (Scott, 1997, 236, original emphasis). The term "unusual" points to the comparative principle of keyword analysis, according to which "it is only possible to both uncover and evaluate the particular features of a discourse type by comparing it with others" (Partington and Marchi, 2015, 223). Accordingly, AntConc's keyword list tool serves to compare a small and specialised corpus with a large and general reference corpus to determine those words that occur relatively frequently in the corpus under scrutiny. In this conventional instruction of how to conduct a keyword analysis (Baker, 2004, 90; Bednarek, 2008, 28), keyness emerges as some "quality which is [...] intuitively obvious", concealing that its "apparent simplicity masks some complexity" (Scott and Tribble, 2006, 55).

Presuming an undefined linguistic standard, as the term "general" used to characterise reference corpora or the definition of keywords in terms of their "unusual" frequency imply, quantitative linguistic analyses possibly overlook the multifarious power relations that inform their methods and findings. As Chapter 5 stresses, this observation applies particularly to the identification and classification of emotion terms. Anything but common (Bednarek 2008, 48) or universal (Turner and Stets, 2005, 13–15), emotion terms and their discussion along these essentialising lines rather attest to the largely unquestioned dominance of middle-class values in the academy. Instead of confirming my acceptance of linguistic norms, then, I use AntConc's keyword list tool to reflect on the socio-economic formations from which they emerge. Activating the socio-political thrust of CADS, my keyword analyses ultimately evade the norms of emotion research(ers) and employ other self-constructed online corpora to propose that the feeling rules of the online reading communities investigated on the subsequent pages constitute part and parcel of a digital literary economy that thrives on the continual exchange of bourgeois emotion ideologies.

Despite the possibilities of combining corpus linguistics with the analytical and interpretive protocols of other humanities disciplines, AntConc remains a statistical tool, premised on the mere frequency of specific words and word clusters. And while some of its applications serve to gain insight into the demographic features or the reading contexts and habits of the reviewers, the software does not lend itself to explore the versatile meta-information that accompany the reviews and invite a differentiated look at the power (or, rather, labour) relations between the digital companies and their customers and users. Building on my long-term observations of the online literary communities, then, the next chapter employs more conventional cultural studies approaches to determine the extent to which digital literary capitalism and, more specifically, the Internet companies' algorithmically defined ecosystems, transform relations of labour and levels of income.

CHAPTER 4

Communities 2.0: Reviewers, Reading Habits and Digital Labour

Taking account of the observation that computerised linguistic procedures alone fail to disclose the online reviewers' habits of reading and motivations for contributing to the discussion of the new Nigerian novel, the present chapter surveys the system- and user-generated meta-data of the communities to put the emotion talk of their members into socio-economic perspective. Shifting the focus from the capitalist interests of the Web 2.0 businesses to the socio-economic aspirations of their customers and users, I illustrate how the digital companies' ecosystems and their underlying algorithms of affect transform the material basis – that is, the labour relations and income levels informing the verbal expression of emotions presented in Chapter 5. Starting with a comparison of the platforms' page designs and their varying degrees of encouraging reviewer interaction, investment and impact, I put particular emphasis on the ways in which Amazon, Goodreads and YouTube invite middlebrow redefinitions of the amateur form. My structuralist perspective on BookTubers' favoured review types and reading occasions in the second section serves to highlight that these redefinitions combine with a digital appropriation of the Protestant work ethic that, as the demographic sample analysis in the third section proves, emerges as an attempt at confirming the "cross-cultural continuity" (Aubry, 2011, 183) of bourgeois emotional culture. The final section draws on scholarly conceptions of emotional and digital labour to assess these observations. Applying Hochschild's differentiation between private emotion work and public emotional labour to the working conditions of the reviewers,[1] I propose that the mostly female members of

---

1 Hochschild (2003, 7, original emphasis) defines emotional labour as public acts of emotion management that are "sold for a wage and therefore ha[ve] *exchange value*", whereas emotion work "refer[s] to these same acts done in a private context where they have *use value*". Crucially, she does not employ the two notions to establish a distinction between public and private, communal and individual or

the communities do not merely constitute the "means of production" (Bucher, 2018, 2), the key capital (Staab and Nachtwey, 2016, 460) or the "object[s] of capitalist accumulation" (Striphas, 2011, 183) of Web 2.0 companies. Rather, and hinting at notable continuities in terms of the "gender [...] and class patterns to the civil and commercial use of human feeling" (Hochschild, 2003, 21), the digital literary economy capitalises on the ambiguous self-positioning of female reviewers as both amateurs *and* workers by assigning the thoroughly reproductive and notoriously underpaid work of affective care to them.

Reviewer Interaction, Investment and Impact: The Middlebrow Amateur

Hosting the largest amount of available responses, the Amazon page generates comparably little interaction, with 13,451 "helpful" markers and 688 comments for 10,099 reviews (Figure 4.1, Table 4.1).[2] This finding keys in with the frequently anonymous self-presentation of the users, who, often appearing as "Amazon Customers" (611 times) or as "Kindle Customers" (127), exhibit moderate interest in increasing their recognition value or establishing personal links with other reviewers.[3] Notably, Amazon's "Top Reviewers", "Vine Voices" or "Hall of Fame" customers, who are provided with "opinion-influencer status" (Murray, 2018, 138) by the world's leading online retailer, do not necessarily constitute an exception in this respect. Contrary to Amazon's endeavour to "shift the gatekeeping power" (Driscoll, 2014, 103) to preselected readers, reviewers in possession of these badges do not compose the longest and most considerate responses or inspire the majority of community interactions. Accounting for approximately one-tenth of the total "helpful" markers and a mere handful of the 688 comments, the 186 labelled reviews in my Amazon corpus suggest that the reading community's desire for mediators who offer instruction and "confirm their mastery" (Driscoll, 2014, 27) is not solely satisfied by Amazon's chosen tastemakers. By comparison, the 25 reviews written by the most influential Amazon reviewers in my data record – Friederike Knabe, missp85, Read-A-Lot, Roger Brunyate and S.A.I. – garnered nearly 300 "helpful" markers and 66 comments alone, indicating that authority status within the community does not merely hinge on the reviewers' overt business affiliation with the company.

---

inauthentic and authentic spheres but uses them to point out how these alleged opposites continually pervade and produce each other. As I show below, a similar observation applies to the somewhat paradoxical combination of the Protestant work ethic with the amateur form by the reviewers.

2 In Chapters 4 and 5, the figures are included in the running text to increase legibility. For the same reason, the rather bulky tables on which the figures are based can be found in the appendix.

3 At the time of revising this book, Amazon has deleted the comments feature.

Communities 2.0

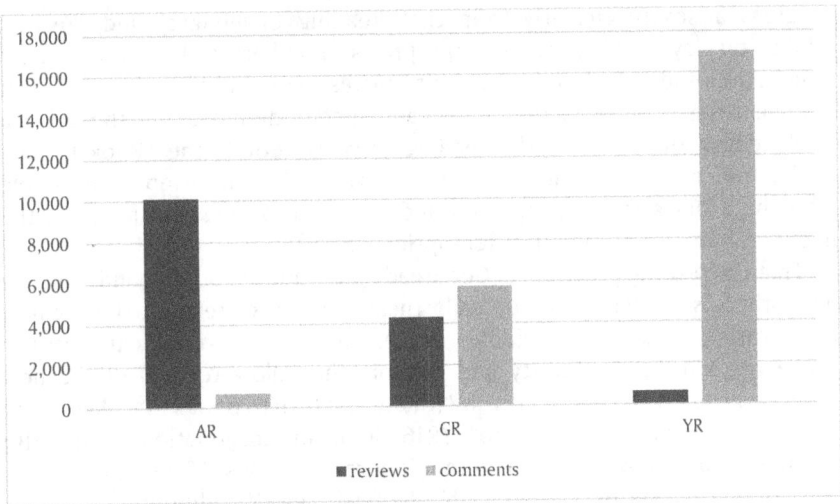

Figure 4.1 Comparison of Reviewer Interaction

By and large, Amazon hardly reaches the level of reader engagement created by Goodreads, which "has evolved to become a complex site" (Driscoll and Rehberg Sedo, 2019, 250). Goodreads reviews are, on average, longer than Amazon responses[4] and, demonstrating the reviewers' heightened investment in both their literary sophistication and the novels, often feature direct quotes from the texts, links to author interviews, newspaper reviews and online encyclopaedia such as Wikipedia. Their closer entanglement in digital reading practices further crystallises from the fact that various Goodreads users run a blog (78 times) or Twitter (24), Instagram (17) and Facebook (16) pages dedicated to the discussion of literature, keep track of the authors' activities on these sites (113) and have not seldom written and published hundreds of reviews of books, which, needless to say, exceed my corpus of novels.[5] Moreover, the thoroughly domestic architecture of the Goodreads page stimulates the exchange of personal information and thus the connection with other (registered) reviewers. Users are asked to upload pictures, provide links to personal websites, share facts "About Me" and their "Interests" or "Favorite Books", "add books to virtual shelves, allocate them star ratings, write and reply to reviews, [and] follow one another and participate in discussion forums" (Driscoll and Rehberg Sedo, 2019, 250). The middlebrow "project of self-improvement" (Driscoll, 2014, 79) and (reading)

---

4 Based on the numbers in Table 3.1, the average length of an Amazon review amounts to 97 words. The average Goodreads review, at 211 words, is more than twice as long.

5 The numbers in brackets refer to the mentions of these platforms in the written reviews.

progress arises particularly from the "Reading Challenges" and "Year in Books" displays, which measure the precise numbers of books and pages read, match individual and community tastes by listing the most and least popular titles of one's virtual library and specify details about the average book length or rating of the reading year. Moreover, the "Bookshelves" application enables the identification of and communication with people who share one's reading interests and therefore promises support in the neoliberal pursuit of (bookish) self-optimisation.[6]

That the reading practices of Goodreads users aim at sociality and intimacy with others is further substantiated by their frequent references to book clubs. Constituting paradigmatic middlebrow reading contexts, book club settings evoke the kind of familiarity and comfort that allow readers of the new Nigerian novel to "go out of my way" (GR06) and turn to books that "I wouldn't normally read" or "be exposed to" (YR16, Book Your Imagination, 15/08/2016) in the first place. With regard to my Goodreads corpus, 70 users allocate a new Nigerian novel to a "book club" shelf, whereas 71 additional reviewers either mention a virtual or face-to-face book club as their immediate reading context or recommend the reviewed novel for book club discussion.[7] In light of the cosy "at-home aesthetics" (Driscoll, 2014, 38) of Goodreads, it is hardly surprising that the friendly interaction among its users is high, as the number of "likes" (38,941) and comments (5,780) for the 4,292 Goodreads reviews shows (Figure 4.1, Table 4.1).

---

6 As Murray (2018, 157) suggests, Kobo's Reading Life app functions in much the same way: resembling a "wearable fitness-tracking device", the app measures their users' advancement – that is, the number of books read or the number of pages turned per hour – which is immediately shared with others on Facebook or Twitter.

7 By comparison, 262 Amazon reviewers refer to their participation in on- and offline reading groups or propose that a novel qualifies as a book club pick. Amazon and Goodreads references to book clubs, in particular, highlight the gendered dimension of the middlebrow, as in this statement by an Amazon customer: "I imagine that MANY all-female book clubs read and love this book [*Americanah*] while many men roll their eyes and quit reading" (AR03, original emphasis). The gender bias is less pronounced among BookTubers, who illustrate how various social media platforms may be used to organise group readings (YR17, Britta Böhler, 06/11/2016). As indicated by the names of their channels (ASMR Curls Book Club, Black Girls Book Club, Mariana's Study Corner, Unveiled Stories Book Club, Weird Book Book Club), nine BookTubers fashion themselves as book club hosts who regularly upload videos for their viewers, whereas other channels create book clubs around specific novels or literary events (for instance, Ink and Paper Blog's "Around the World in 1000 Pages" videos that concentrate on Adichie's *Purple Hibiscus*, among other novels). Apart from these more obvious references, BookTubers exhibit the greatest creativity in updating and appropriating book club activities for digital contexts that frequently require the bridging of considerable geographical distances. I discuss BookTubers' social reading practices, such as buddy reads or tagging readers, in the next section.

The homely layout of the Goodreads page and the social and intimate reading practices it promotes are firmly inscribed into the company's mission statement, which uses the same "vocabulary of communal fellow-feeling" (Murray, 2018, 62) that informs Bezos's explanation of Amazon's algorithmic software. According to founder Otis Chandler ("About Goodreads", *Goodreads*), Goodreads is constructed as "a place where I could see my friends' bookshelves and learn about what they thought of all their books". His hint at "Elizabeth, my co-founder (and now wife)", who "wrote the site copy" in their "living room", further elicits the snugness and warmth of a parlour that fosters bookish communication among family and friends (Driscoll and Rehberg Sedo, 2019, 250). Commenting on the site's in-built domestic tropes, Lisa Nakamura (2013, 240) unwittingly identifies the middlebrow's distinctive enmeshment of private and public, non-commercial and profit-oriented contexts when she remarks that the virtual Goodreads "shelves remediate earlier reading cultures where books were displayed in the home as signs of taste and status". Refurbishing the relaxed living room settings of the televised Richard & Judy Book Club or Oprah's Book Club for the digital literary sphere, Goodreads simultaneously creates and caters to the opposing desire of the middlebrow reader to establish distinction from and connection with fellow readers (Driscoll, 2014, 109–19).

Taking the domestic imagery of the middlebrow a step further, BookTubers showcase the virtual living rooms of Goodreads reviewers in literal fashion. Indeed, the vast majority of the altogether 635 videos released by 330 different channels is recorded in the domestic sphere, such as The Palm Print's "Living Room" series, and features the BookTubers next to their "enviable stacks of bestsellers, classics and YA fiction" (Kalpaxis, 2020) or in front of their expansive shelves.[8] Notably contradicting the middlebrow's online proliferation, BookTubers' "reverence for the object of the book" highlights their contradictory alignment with prestige and commerce and the resulting urge to evince "respect for elite culture" (Driscoll, 2014, 22) and purchasing power. The 20 new Nigerian novels discussed in the video reviews appear only 11 times as e-books but are shown in hardcover and paperback versions 177 and 220 times.[9] These hard copies and paperbacks are commonly purchased

---

8 The discrepancy results from the fact that 95 BookTube channels have released more than one video review, either for one or several novels included in my corpus. Channels such as SavidgeReads (RP), run by "a bookish bear" located in Britain, or The Book Castle, whose host Alice records her reviews in a bedroom in Oslo, count among the frontrunners, with 22 and 15 videos for seven different novels, respectively. Their choice of novels substantiates the interplay between the personalised recommendation system of YouTube and the programmatic production of the new Nigerian novel.

9 Apart from audiobooks (seven times), which are cherished for their time-saving qualities (see below), BookTubers also integrate pictures of the novels' covers (137), especially if they produce various reviews for the same book, as in the many TBR videos (see below), and have verified their possession of the object on previous occasions.

from Amazon, as Belle Michelle ("I did a massive, massive, massive order on Amazon", YR03) and HollaAtFola ("I have literally filled my Amazon wish list with a gazillion books", YR18) confirm.[10] Next to the assumption that BookTubers' preference for the book-as-object results from their reviewing in a visual medium, the choice of hardcovers and paperbacks conforms to the middlebrow reader's desire for corporeal readings that stimulate a variety of senses. Expressing great delight at the paperback of Iweala's *Beasts of No Nation*, for instance, Karen (YR13, The Book Rookie) remarks that "[i]t's got that nice like textured feel". That such sensuous experiences are associated with "home" is affirmed by BookTuber Amerie (RP; YR03, 19/05/2015), a "Grammy-nominated singer-songwriter and NYT bestselling author", who relates the object of the book to the domestic setting of its middlebrow consumption context when musing that "there's something about paperbacks [...] they are really cozy, I think".

BookTubers almost invariably construct reading as a profoundly private activity that is, however, readily rendered public. Undoubtedly, this paradox constitutes part of the explanation for why they enjoy an exceptional visibility in the digital literary sphere. Compared to the reviewers on Amazon and Goodreads, they establish a specifically great amount of cross references. Almost half of the 330 channel hosts write their own blogs (140 times) and show a high degree of bookish activity on Twitter (208), Instagram (182) or Facebook (65).[11] Additionally, 152 channels link to Goodreads accounts that include 24 Goodreads reviews in my corpus alone. Sharing their private sphere, both literally and figuratively, on a regular basis, their reviews are as firmly integrated in their subscribers' lives as the novels are integrated in their own lives. Accordingly, the YouTube reviews of 20 new Nigerian novels reached more than ten million subscribers and generated 1,821,168 views and 17,008 comments until July 2019 (Figure 4.1, Table 4.1). Remarkably, the contrast to the interaction figures of the Amazon and Goodreads reviews even remains significant if one excludes the comparatively few professional channels in the corpus. The 314 BookTubers that can be classified as non-professional still answered the social and emotional needs of approximately 4.5 million subscribers and garnered the incredible amount of 1,760,201 views and 16,833 comments (Figure 4.2, Tables 4.2.1 and 4.2.2).

---

10 Amazon reviewers' preference for the Kindle format (6,012 times vs. 939 hardcovers and 2,763 paperbacks) may result from the device itself, which prompts readers to leave a star rating. I thank the anonymous reviewer of the manuscript for pointing out this potential skewing factor. Against this backdrop, it should be noted that the distribution programmes of Amazon (Vine) and Goodreads (NetGalley) encourage middlebrow materiality. The altogether 107 "Vine Customer Reviews of Free Product" included in my Amazon corpus are all based on the more expensive hardcopy versions of the novels (see below).

11 The numbers in brackets refer to the mentions of these platforms in the profiles of the reviewers.

The digital middlebrow delineates an amateur cultural formation that, as I illustrate below, is precisely what leading Internet corporations take advantage of. Tracing the continuities of the historical and the contemporary middlebrow, Driscoll (2014, 36, original emphasis) argues that "middlebrow practices are *amateur*, a word derived from the Latin amator, meaning lover". Since the term was and still is employed to position the middlebrow "outside, and often against, the academy" (Driscoll, 2014, 36), one can hardly overlook its pejorative connotations that signify "a naïve surrender of critical distance based on an embarrassing inability to recognize the distinction between literature and life" (Aubry, 2011, 1).[12] Paralleling the divide between modernist and middlebrow writing that served to downplay the market success of female writers in early twentieth-century Britain, amateur BookTubers easily outnumber and exceed the influence of professional channels that provide responses to the new Nigerian novel. In contrast to the video reviews by amateurs, professional channels are marked by their overt attachment to and/or cooperation with literary and cultural institutions that, in most cases, transpires from their names. That the association of professional channels with highbrow cultural positions is, however, considerably hampered shows in the idiosyncratic mixture of institutional agents that the new Nigerian novel calls into action. The 16 channels that classify as professional here range from *The Wendy Williams Show*, an American talk show bearing a close resemblance to *The Oprah Winfrey Show*, to major television broadcasters located in the UK (Channel 4 News), the US (PBS NewsHour) or Nigeria (Channels Television), cultural organisations such as the British Council and Columbia Global Reports, a publishing imprint of Columbia University, and two Massachusetts local libraries. Figure 4.2 (Tables 4.2.1 and 4.2.2) displays the scope of the top 16 professional and amateur channels included in my corpus of YouTube reviews. Accordingly, the amateurs were not only the more active reviewers (96 vs. 40 video reviews for one or several of the 20 new Nigerian novels) but also garnered substantially more views and comments. The exception that is constituted by the respective numbers of subscribers results from the fact

---

12 Although the middlebrow has meanwhile recovered from its discursive history of disparagement, which was, often enough, told by representatives of said academy, the World Wide Web and its promise of egalitarianism revive the old "battle of the brows". To give an example, the British-American Internet critic Andrew Keen's *The Cult of the Amateur* (2007) reactivates the war imagery that defined cultural debates in the uncertain times following the First and Second World Wars (Driscoll, 2014, 8). The sub-title of his study adopts the same bemoaning tone that pervades intellectual comments on the commercial success of British women writers at the turn of the twentieth century (Driscoll, 2014, 29–32). Lamenting that *Blogs, MySpace, YouTube, and the Rest of Today's User-Generated Media Are Destroying Our Economy, Our Culture, and Our Values*, he accuses social media users of the trivialising impact that self-proclaimed cultural gatekeepers used to direct at prolific middlebrow authors such as Ivy Compton-Burnett or E.M. Delafield (Chapter 1).

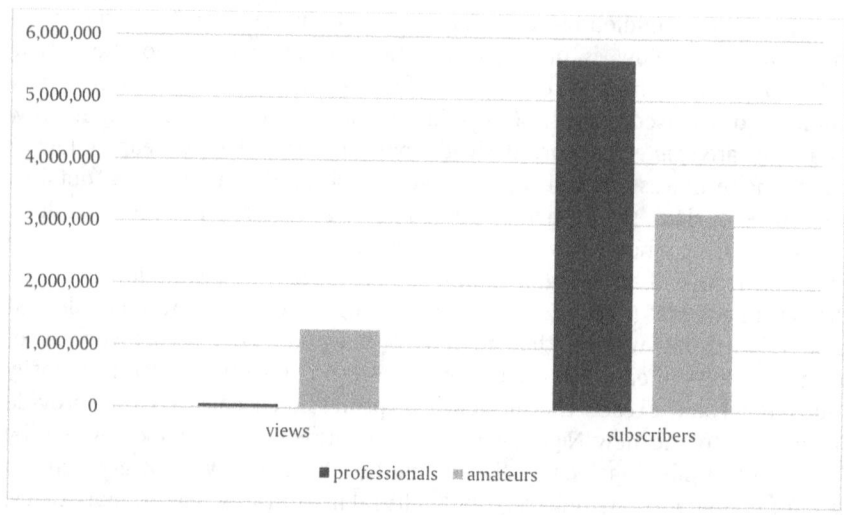

Figure 4.2 Top 16 Professional vs. Amateur YouTube Channels

that the channels of, for instance, major broadcasting companies release a variety of videos that cover a broad range of topics usually cutting across Nigerian fiction or literary issues more generally.

Compromising the association of professional YouTube channels with highbrow literary and cultural practices even more, it should be noted that the digital content of renowned institutions is not necessarily marked by radically different approaches to books and reading. To be sure, the "unboxing" of new releases is not recorded in the living rooms of the Hatfield Public Library staff; however, the ways in which the librarians Eliza and Kimber represent and recommend Emezi's debut – with its "really beautiful cover" (YR10, Hatfield Public Library) – does not differ from the unboxing videos shot in the suburban homes of Jean from Jean Bookishthoughts or Jen Campbell. Similarly, Princess Irede Abumere and the changing female guests of her BBC Africa Book Club stress their education background to justify their status as literary mediators. Yet their "hunger for African literature", including their sympathetic identification with Ifemelu's "self-discovery" (YR03, 03/11/2018) or Yejide's "obsession with having a child" (YR02, 18/08/2018), comes close to the social and emotional consumption patterns of the amateur BookTubers Anna James and Eric Karl Anderson, whose Anna & Eric Book Club focuses on novels that "we weren't just intellectually" but "emotionally impressed [by]" (YR17, A Case for Books). Notwithstanding the tricky question of who imitates whom – or the observation that the digital middlebrow, just like its historical counterpart, has a tendency to blur cultural boundaries – the figures in Tables 4.2.1 and 4.2.2 indicate that the amateurs' digital appropriation of middlebrow literacy patterns is presented as more influential.

Emphasising the anti-institutional and anti-intellectual connotations of the term, Driscoll neglects the economic dimension of the amateur form. As research in sport history suggests, being an amateur necessitates a certain level of affluence. In nineteenth-century Britain, to give an example, only members of the upper and upper middle classes could afford a position as amateur (and thus unsalaried) soccer players (Llewellyn and Gleaves, 2014, 95–116). Members of the lower and lower middle classes, in turn, had neither time nor money enough to provide their labour free of charge. Redefining the amateur form in middlebrow terms, the members of the three reading communities investigated here, and representatives of the BookTube community in particular, constantly assure that they primarily turn to books for recreational purposes to highlight their economic independence. Most of them insist that they "do not consider myself a professional" (AlleySinai, RP) or are "[j]ust a boy, his dog and his opinion about books" (Chris Bookish Cauldron, RP). If they "work in books", they present their channels as entirely private affairs – or as "an outlet just for me" (Kendra Winchester, RP). As the next section demonstrates, such and similar self-assessments stand in marked contrast to the amount of time and work that my amateur BookTubers put into their channels.

Review Types and Reading Occasions: The Middlebrow Work Ethic

Disclosing their economic interests, the most influential BookTubers turn their homes into miniature marketplaces for literary and other commodities and promote the new Nigerian novel as a means of strengthening their – and their viewers' – social and emotional ties to the globalising middle classes. Instead of constructing the domestic space as a retreat from consumer culture, as the hope that "we will all make a home here" (vuvu vena reads, RP) or the objective of developing "a deeper relationship with books" (READING in the DARK, RP) indicate at first glance, they regularly showcase that they have successfully realised the capitalist principles of perpetual productivity and growth and therefore qualify as specifically suitable model consumers in the digital age. This finding is, first and foremost, reinforced by the sheer quantity of their uploads. When I first encountered the 16 amateur reviewers listed in Table 4.4.2 in July 2019, their channels encompassed 7,182 videos with close to 350 million views. Revisiting their channels at the time of revising this book (three years later), the amount of uploaded videos and clicks had increased by more than 1,300 and approximately 110 million, respectively. The multitude of content that BookTubers produce proves impossible to watch, let alone analyse, even if the researcher adopts the work schedules of the research subjects. Distant reading methods therefore lend themselves to uncover the recurring features of BookTube channels and interrogate how precisely their hosts adapt the Protestant work ethic to the Internet era. Looking at the amateur reader profiles, one cannot fail to notice that books play merely one role, albeit a central one, in BookTubers' larger "journey" towards neoliberal selves.

In middlebrow consumption contexts, the discussion of books almost always "functions [...] as a launching pad to somewhere else" (Long, 2003, 203). Middlebrow studies scholars have suggested that this "somewhere else" overwhelmingly refers to notions of middle-class progress and the desire to "improve" or "optimise" oneself and society (Driscoll, 2014, 40, 62). The illustration of my corpus construction in the previous chapter highlighted that such approaches to reading challenge the selection of online reviews for computerised linguistic analyses. Utilising books "less as a source of aesthetic satisfaction than as a practical dispenser of advice" (Aubry, 2011, 1), middlebrow readers easily blur the scholarly focus on responses to particular literary texts. On the other hand, online reviewers' continual excursions into other aspects of their lives allow for significant insights into the precise reading contexts and, by implication, the specific functions that they ascribe to the new Nigerian novel. Taking a structuralist look at the reader profiles of BookTubers, one observes the recurring use of conceptual metaphors that construct life as a journey not just "towards bookishness" (READING in the DARK, RP) but also – and more frequently – towards "a holistic and healthy" (Chadel Mathurin, RP) "lifestyle" that rests on a broad range of consumer products. Online reviewers, and especially BookTubers, weave the new Nigerian novel into their "weight loss journey" (Comfycozyup, RP) and their "Natural Hair Journey" (Chadel Mathurin, RP) or, less specifically, their "journey to live a life that is better than average" (Abnormal Growth, RP). Of the altogether 330 BookTubers, 35 explicitly refer to their channels as "lifestyle channels" or to themselves as "lifestyle bloggers" and discuss Nigerian diasporic fiction alongside fashion, makeup and hair, physical fitness (including nutrition, diet therapies or cooking recipes) and various issues revolving around mental health, as the following examples substantiate:

> Natural hair tutorials, beauty, self-care, chit chats and so much more. (AlleySinai, RP)

> Let's talk – mostly about natural hair, a little bit about fashion, beauty and life in general! (HollaAtFola, RP)

> This is a hair, makeup, fashion, health, and lifestyle channel for the modern multi-dimensional woman. (modernmrshuxtable, RP)

> This channel is all about personal growth, mindfulness, lifestyle and holistic living. I share knowledge about [...] positivity and creativity, to help you become your best self. I deeply enjoy the process of creating a life that is abundant and fulfilling in every aspect; by embracing myself and aligning with my vision through my yoga practice, my belief in God and lessons I've learnt through past experiences. I hope to share calmness and love through my videos and I hope that I can inspire you to create the best life for yourself that you desire and deserve. (Philly Aime, RP)

> I'm talking about issues such as loneliness, anxiety, depression, worry, fear, neurodiversity, social injustice, unfairness, body positivity, sex, relationships, feminism, mindfulness, friendship and vulnerability. (Unveiled Stories, RP)

> I do have an underlying goal of lessening the stigma surrounding mental illness. I myself have DID (dissociative identity disorder), formally called Multiple Personality Disorder. [...] I'm really a sweet girl and so are all the others of me. (Acacia Ives, RP)

Attesting to the digital proliferation of a "therapeutic emotional style" (Illouz, 2007, 6), the last three quotes particularly demonstrate that YouTube reviewers deem "individual happiness [...] the fundamental goal of life" (Aubry, 2011, 17) and of reading more specifically. Accordingly, their purchase and discussion of the new Nigerian novel may well be understood as a means of publicly "perform[ing] the interior" (Aubry, 2011, 35).[13] Considering that market affiliation involves the recognition of and control by potential competitors, I propose to conceptualise the digital output of BookTubers and other amateur reviewers on Amazon and Goodreads in terms of reading diaries or reading logs that serve to publicly commit to "my new year's resolutions" (YR20, rincey reads, 28/02/2014) or "my Goodreads goal" (YR16, SCSReads, 02/02/2016). The socio-economic gains of keeping a "bookish diary of sorts" (Kendra Winchester, RP) or engaging in "book housekeeping" (GR05) point to the immense investment that "the production of a sense of belonging online requires" (Ehret et al., 2018, 160). The "really hard work" (YR10, MercysBookishMusings, 08/01/2019) performed by online reviewers not only relates to the time-consuming process of writing or recording hundreds of reviews; as one BookTuber asserts, "I spend eight to ten hours on those videos" (YR03, ForTheLoveOfRyan). Moreover, and as some channel names suggest, participation in digital reading communities necessitates the efficient organisation of "My Reading Life" or "My Reading Days", which have to accommodate more and more books that confront many reviewers with unfamiliar cultural settings. Unsurprisingly, then, they often emphasise that they "work at understanding" (AR20) the characters in Selasi's *Ghana Must Go* or "worked hard to like" (GR13) *Beasts of No Nation*.

Undoubtedly, the desire to contribute and belong to online literary communities fosters a specific "work ethic" (AR15) that Aubry (2011, 25) traces to the Protestant denominations developing in eighteenth- and nineteenth-century America. Building on his observation that "psychological discourses [have] replace[d] religious ones as the basis for meaning" (18), he elucidates that the Protestant ethic

> continues to insist, for members of the middle class, on the need for constant vigilance and work as requisites for the establishment of character and the achievement of secular well-being. And while it also continues to motivate the accumulation of wealth as one means to these ends, amid abundant material comforts, the Protestant ethic has come to redirect its

---

13 Discussing the production contexts and representational means of the new Nigerian novel, Chapter 2 provides a range of reasons why the texts are well suited to fulfil this purpose.

energy into therapeutic endeavors, finding a new realm of struggle and perpetually delayed fulfillment in the psychological. (25)

Although Aubry does not explicitly read his selection of Amazon responses to *The Kite Runner* through the lens of the German sociologist and political economist Max Weber's *The Protestant Ethic and the Spirit of Capitalism* (1904/05), his hint at the potential origin of the online reviewers' therapeutic efforts is yet remarkable because it highlights that, in Weber's (2002, 6, 19) words, "participation in capitalist commerce" presupposes an "attitude which, *in the pursuit of a calling* [...], strives systematically for profit" (original emphasis). Scrutinising the economic evolution of various European countries since the Reformation, Weber (20) relates the vocational commitment as well as the self-control and self-discipline of "the rising strata of the middle class" to Protestant Puritanism, and particularly to Calvinist religious doctrines, as his use of the term "calling" indicates. However, and irrespective of substantial shifts in the economic structure and creed informing the "intensive work rate that is [...] demanded" of digital consumers, his arguments serve to ponder the extent to which the "*spiritual motivation*" (22, 20, original emphasis) of the powerful commercial classes pressing for social and political change in seventeenth- and eighteenth-century Europe anticipates the reviewers' therapeutic work ethic.[14] Like Puritan diaries and manuals, which chronicle the ethics of hard work to prove advancement in spiritual and economic terms, the reviewers' digital diaries function to confirm the exertions required to participate in the contemporary book market. Focusing on their prevalent review types and reading occasions, I contend that my reviewers redefine the work ethic along middlebrow lines, adjusting it to the demands of digital literary capitalism.

In her contribution to *The Routledge Companion to World Literature* (2011), Ann Steiner (318) remarks that the "massive shift in international publishing structures since the 1960s", and the empowerment of "transnational media conglomerates" specifically, has engendered a "rapid rise in book publishing". Although noting that "available statistics are contradictory" (318–19), she provides figures for the year 2009, which saw "around 120,000 titles published in the UK, 90,000 in Germany, 70,000 in India, 120,000 in Russia, 275,000 in the USA [...] and probably around 150,000 in China" (318). While Steiner's (318) chapter looks at the ramifications of "over-publishing" from the perspective of publishers and thereby illustrates how the necessity

---

14 Aubry's redefinition of Weber's notion suggests that the historical traces of online reading communities go back farther than the eighteenth- and nineteenth-century literary public spheres investigated by Habermas, Anderson, Barker-Benfield or Berlant (Chapter 3). Anderson (2006, 40) substantiates this assumption by drawing attention to "the coalition between Protestantism and print-capitalism", which "quickly created large new reading publics – not least among merchants and women, who typically knew little or no Latin – and simultaneously mobilized them for politico-religious purposes".

of export creates a constantly expanding global market for books, I am interested in the effects that such numbers have on the digital middlebrow reader who measures the mastery of books, brought to him or her by algorithmically defined recommendation systems with each passing minute, in terms of personal progress.

That online literary culture is "more fraught with pressures" than most accounts by cultural or media studies scholars are willing to permit is demonstrated by Christian Ehret, Jacy Boegel and Roya Manuel-Nekouei (2018, 151). Exploring the impact of BookTube on the development of online literacy among adolescent readers, their article considers a (slightly) different group of consumers. However, linking the pressures of the digital literary sphere to corporate interests and to "publishers eager to have their books reviewed and endorsed by popular BookTubers" (159), the authors outline the same competitive structures that entangle the protagonists of my corpus of YouTube reviews. The most influential BookTubers exemplify how to handle the extensive output of a global publishing industry. Lindsey from Lindsey's Book Life (YR02) uses her video to discuss "Books 65–70" and thereby underline the amount of reading work she has already accomplished by the first half of 2018. The "2016 books #161–165" video by a BookTuber called the audiobook afficionado (YR17) proves that Lindsey shares her work ethic with fellow reviewers who actually exceed her numbers. Accepting the challenges set by the applications of the other two reading sites, Amazon and Goodreads users equally document the scope and progress of their reading lives. However, and as Mercedes, the channel host of MercysBookishMusings (YR02, 31/03/2017), notes, on BookTube, "it's certainly excessive". Offering a summary of her "statistics for the December reading month", BookTuber Kerryn (YR17, RatherBeReading) outlines the scale of her bookish work ethic thus:

> I read a total of nineteen books. I also dnfed [did not finish] one further book. The nineteen books were made up of fourteen novels, two graphic novels, one novella, one children's novel and one web comic. I read eleven books in physical copy, I read three e-books, I listened to four audiobooks and I read one book online [...]. So excluding the web comic and the audiobooks, I read eight books that I own and six from the library. I read a total of 6,158 pages in the month of December which averaged out to 199 pages per day so that's just a touch below the 200-page average that I tried to keep it at so I'm still really happy with that. The shortest book that I read in December was the fifteen-page … was only fifteen pages. That was the novella that I read. It was a very, very short little novella. And the longest book that I read was 649 pages. So we've got very different ends of the spectrum kind of going here. The highest star rating that I gave was a 4.25 stars this month and the lowest star rating that I gave was a 2.5 stars which totaled out to an average star rating for the month of 3.38 stars which isn't too bad for me.

While other BookTubers do not necessarily structure their digital reading diaries along such meticulous lines, the number of books that Kerryn finished within a mere month is certainly no exception. The performance of BookTubers' work ethic occasionally adopts playful overtones, as implied by the banter between a couple challenging each other "who's read more total pages in August" (YR13, KnightHunter Books, 07/09/2017). However, in most cases, the experience of individual failure is strikingly real. BookTuber Rincey from rincey reads (YR20, 28/02/2014), for instance, is "really worried in March that I'm going to fall behind" on the self-prescribed number of books, whereas Lauren Wade (YR09, 06/10/2016) relates that "I feel really guilty [...] if I've not read the books that I told myself to read". Chris from Chris Bookish Cauldron (YR05, 02/04/2018) resignedly pronounces that he is "just going to write March off as a failure of a month and look forward to the future". Highlighting that participation in and belonging to the digital literary economy can be "super stressful" (YR20, rincey reads, 29/04/2014), most of my reviewers abide by their self-imposed obligations and, from time to time reactivating the religious origins of their ethic, remind themselves that they "just need to be more disciplined" (YR20, rincey reads, 28/02/2014).

How precisely do BookTubers and other reviewers manage to fulfil their ambitious goals of reading and producing reviews for this plethora of books, given that their work ethic merely – if at all – feeds into an additional occupation? To begin with, the middlebrow pattern of (producing and transmitting) the new Nigerian novel may help rationalise the reading and reviewing process. Arguably, the repetitive narrative structures of the new Nigerian novel facilitate the demands on the middlebrow reader. Moreover, and despite online reviewers' attempt to present every novel as "different" or "especially special" (YR02, Gathoni Kimaru), the algorithmic recommendation systems of Amazon, Goodreads and YouTube ensure that readers are mostly confronted with titles that correspond to their individual reading histories, reducing the interpretive efforts that the mastery of actual novelties would entail. Apart from the support provided by the novels' recurring patterns and the platforms' personalised offers, BookTubers have created a number of video types that, as I propose, allow amateur reviewers to manage the ceaseless confrontation with new titles. Giving credit to the BookTubers' creativity concerning both layout and language, Figure 4.3 (Table 4.3), which is modelled after Ehret et al. (2018, 153), gives an overview of the various types of video employed to discuss the new Nigerian novel. The illustration indicates that only 207 of the altogether 635 videos can be categorised as the conventional "review of a specific book" (Ehret et al., 2018, 153).

Representing a particular version of the single-book review, the vlog shows the reviewer during the process of reading and usually covers a couple of days. The ten vlogs included in my corpus underline that middlebrow readers fashion *every* domestic activity as part of their carefully timed development towards self-realisation. A BookTuber called Natalie Meree (YR10, My Reading Days, 12/04/2019), who seeks to integrate her BookTube obligations into her

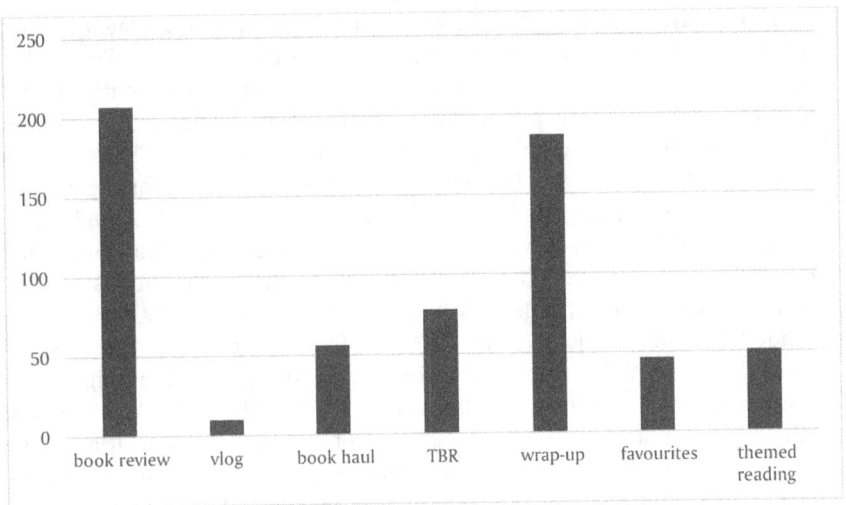

Figure 4.3 Types of BookTube Videos

suburban life as a homemaker and mother, films herself while "sneak[ing] in some more *Freshwater* [...] over some toast and tea". Along similar lines, the channel host of Comfycozyup (YR15, 08/03/2019) presents Obioma's second novel *An Orchestra of Minorities* as an essential ingredient of her "Keto diet", juxtaposing images of cooking and eating with sequences of reading and reviewing. Equally adhering to the principles of economic rationalism (Weber, 2002, 26), other vloggers prefer listening to audiobooks because they can be consumed "at double speed" (YR10, Matthew Sciarappa, 15/12/2018), "while walking or [...] working" (YR02, Lizzie Reads) and shopping for groceries (YR02, insert book pun here, 24/05/2019).[15]

Substantiating BookTubers' desire to boost the efficiency of their reading and reviewing, 418 of the 635 videos feature more than one book. As Table

---

15 As the following examples from the *Americanah* sub-corpora affirm, Amazon and Goodreads reviews also abound with references to food and drink. Emphasising the domestic context of reading, one Amazon reviewer remarks that *"Americanah* is best served with a hot drink and a couch to lay on because I feel that readers will need a comfy space in order to handle [...] the awesomeness of Adichie's novel" (AR03). Other readers stress the bodily aspects of reading when comparing *Americanah* to "a long meal" (AR03) or "the last lingering bit of chocolate on your tongue" (GR03). Yet another reviewer reinforces the therapeutic dimension of nutrition when she states that "[t]his book is good for you, but in the avocado or raspberry way" (GR03). Against this backdrop, one may well interpret the bookish resolutions of Eve's Alexandria (YR17, 10/11/2016) in terms of a reading diet: "I'm like a prepper, you know. Rather than stockpiling food and water and medical supplies, I am stockpiling pages. I'm thinking about all the pages that I need to read between now and spring."

4.3 suggests, these types can be further divided into videos displaying books that have yet to be read and books that have already been read. Falling within the first category, book haul videos display at least two but frequently around five to ten books "recently purchased, borrowed from the library, or acquired through publisher sponsorship" (Ehret et al., 2018, 153), while TBRs cover a similar amount of books and usually present the reviewer's literary selections for specific readathons, reading challenges or tags. A total of 187 video reviews can be classified as wrap-ups – "summar[ies] of books read during the previous [week or] month" (Ehret et al., 2018, 153) – such as the "BooksWeekly" series by Britta Böhler (YR02, 04/06/2017) or the "AUGUST BOOKS" video uploaded by sunbeamsjess (YR17, 28/09/2016). Occasioned by the close of the reading year (YR05, Kendra Winchester, 12/01/2019) or the anniversary of the reviewer's activities on BookTube (YR03, MercysBookishMusings, 22/01/2019), favourites videos cover a BookTuber's most popular titles, while themed reading videos such as "5 Things I've Learned About Nigerians" (YR08, African and Afro-Diasporan Art Talks, 18/09/2014) or "BAME | 5 Book Recommendations" (YR02, Jasmine's Reads, 21/02/2018) revolve around specific topics or literary phenomena.

Structured along the opposing lines of repetition and variation or generous support by and playful competition with other community members, the video types that feature more than one novel adapt the middlebrow logic of literary prizes and book clubs to the digital environment, which emerges as "a space [...] to feel validated and not so alone" (YR03, Deanna Buley). More precisely, the reviewers on YouTube not only emulate established middlebrow mediators such as Richard and Judy but also construct distinct online versions of clubbish reading practices. In fact, numerous book haul or wrap-up videos are organised around so-called buddy reads and thus geared towards shared "middle-class route[s]" (Driscoll, 2014, 55) to market affiliation. Stressing the supportive functions of literary community, Diana (YR10, diana in colour, 25/08/2018) thanks her buddy readers for the discussion of *Freshwater*, stating that "[y]ou guys made reading the book even more fun". Todd the Librarian (YR02), who did a buddy read of *Stay With Me* – "something I don't normally read" – emphasises the middlebrow prospect of joint "intellectual growth" (AR16), while Amanda Jenner (YR04) notes the therapeutic effects of a collective reading: "I really enjoyed reading this as a buddy read because it's a heavy-going novel about a fairly brutal period in recent history and it was quite nice to [...] share the pain." Transferring the middlebrow formula of creating "intimate, personal connections with books and with other readers" (Driscoll, 2014, 44) to the World Wide Web, buddy reads provide significant means of fostering emotional attachment to the digital literary sphere.

Reinforcing BookTubers' creative linguistic capacities, TBR or wrap-up videos, which are based on particular readathons, challenges or tags, serve similar purposes of socio-economic market affiliation. Set up and monitored by BookTubers with a substantial amount of followers, tags invite reviewers on BookTube and elsewhere to accomplish bookish tasks and, in turn, invite others to publicly define themselves as emotionally receptive members of the globalising middle classes. By way of example, I quote BookTuber Shawn from Shawn the Book Maniac (YR10, 07/03/2019), who specifies the reading tasks of the African Writers Tag below his response video thus:

> 1) Try to greet us in at least one African language. Look up some greetings and give it a shot. (English, German, and French don't count. We're trying to move a little beyond colonialism, even though those languages are widely spoken here.) 2) Look up a list of African countries. Which African country had you never heard of before? 3) Which African country do you want to read more about? 4) Which African country have you read most about?

Underscoring the trendsetting and community-building capabilities of influential BookTubers, such tags inspire other members to activate their work ethic, expand their reading diaries and compete in the pursuit of contributing to the digital literary economy.

That the scope of this economy creates unprecedented possibilities – indeed, requirements – to "read something from all corners of the world" (AR04) and "become more sensitive to the experiences of others" (AR03) not only emerges from the tasks set by the African Writers Tag. The names of other tags, such as the Read Diversely Tag or the Shithole Countries Tag,[16] and readathons, such as Blackathon or Pocathon, equally substantiate that the marathon-like work ethic of the online community entails the strive for *cross*-cultural competence. Janill Briones-Lopez (YR03) summarises the various challenges covered in the Blackathon below her response video as follows:

> 1. FEEL THE LOVE. Read a book (any genre) featuring a romance between two black people (or one black person + a person of color) [...] 4. MORE THAN A COLOR. We house complexity within us. Read a book starring an intersectional black character (black & LGBT, black & neurodivergent, black & disabled, etc).

And Alex from bigalbooks (YR03, 11/08/2018) outlines the reading tasks of the Pocathon thus:

> 1) Read books with main characters from three different races, ethnicities [...] 2) Read a classic book by an author of colour or a translated book 3) Read a SFF [science fiction and fantasy] book by or featuring people of colour 4)

---

16 Shawn from Shawn the Book Maniac (YR05, 21/01/2018) elucidates that the Shithole Countries Tag was created by his fellow BookTuber Diana in response to "the infamous, deeply offensive comments by the current [...] occupant of the White House", Donald Trump; rather than signalling agreement with the "linguistic abomination" of the former US president, the reading tag serves to "fight back". That BookTubers' occasional attempts at establishing an ironic distance to their reading practices yield the potential to backfire is highlighted by Shawn's and other channel names, such as Abnormal Growth, Alya Eats Books, BookNympho or RatherBeReading, which poke fun at and thereby underline their hosts' excessive consumption of books.

Read poetry by an author of colour 5) Read a book that deals with racism, prejudice or immigration.

The pervasive commitment of the digital middlebrow reader to be "there in the world" (YR10, AlleySinai), "to read more diversely" (YR20, booksandquills, 19/11/2014) and "create a more open-minded perspective" (YR03, IdaraJoy) raises pressing questions about the relation of the reviewers' therapeutic work ethic to postcolonialism and its transhistorical ramifications. Against this backdrop, it is especially noteworthy that my BookTubers, apart from revising book club activities, adopt the mechanisms of another middlebrow institution to work through the content of their TBR and wrap-up videos: the literary prize.

Acting as "standard-bearer[s] for the new literary middlebrow" (Driscoll, 2014, 151), prizes such as the Women's Prize for Fiction, the Man Booker Prize and the Wellcome Book Prize boosted the sales of Adebayo's *Stay With Me*, Braithwaite's *My Sister, the Serial Killer*, Obioma's *The Fishermen* and Emezi's *Freshwater*, especially among those online reviewers who refer to the potential accolade of a new Nigerian novel as an immediate purchasing and/or reading motivation. Exceeding the mere reference to literary prizes as reading contexts, BookTubers frequently seize the prize culture logic to enhance the online visibility of their bookish workload. Reviewers such as Jennifer from Insert Literary Pun Here (YR02, 20/05/2017) model their "Baileys 2017 series" after the multi-step process of awarding literary prestige to expand their scope of social connections in the digital literary sphere. BookTubers do not simply fall into the marketing trap laid by prize organisers but rather avail themselves of the opportunities that emerge from the separate announcements of longlists, shortlists and winners by producing numerous TBR and wrap-up videos for a manageable amount of novels. Demonstrating the efficiency of this reviewing system, Simon from SavidgeReads uses the longlisted titles of the 2019 Women's Prize to record an entire video series and nurture relations with his 16,878 channel subscribers and 21,071 viewers (counted in July 2019).[17]

Considering that BookTubers' middlebrow practices forge social and emotional connections with potential customers, it is not surprising that the most influential among them have raised the interest of and collaborate with publishers, retailers and organisers of literary events. While the last section of this chapter focuses on the Internet's fuzzy boundaries between emotion work and emotional labour and suggests how both Web 2.0 businesses and their customers or users benefit from them, I use the remaining paragraphs of this

---

17 The series includes the following video reviews: "Guessing the Women's Prize Longlist | 2019", "The Women's Prize for Fiction Longlist | 2019", "Women's Prize Longlist 2019 | Halfway Chat", "Women's Prize Longlist Thoughts & Shortlist Possibilities with My Mum | 2019" and "A Women's Prize Project | ft. All the Previous Winners | 2019".

section to turn to the dominant themes and issues around which community building on Amazon, Goodreads and YouTube revolves and ponder their relation to the reviewers' therapeutically informed work ethic. Judging by the titles of the most popular readathons, reading challenges and tags, the new Nigerian novel addresses digital communities of readers who, just as publishers and prize judges as well as school authorities, deem the recognition of and solidarity with alleged minorities – that is, black, female and queer people – "a super important thing to do" (YR17, ProblemsofaBookNerd, 02/06/2017).[18] Obviously, full participation in digital literary capitalism demands a fair amount of cross-cultural competence.

My use of the term competence serves to emphasise that "the ethical and emotional tenor of the middlebrow" (Driscoll, 2014, 86) not only dominates the digital literary sphere but also and increasingly governs school and university curricula. In fact, new Nigerian novels are often promoted as children's or YA books that conventionally encourage "the psychological development of the [adolescent] reader" (Driscoll, 2014, 99). It is thus not accidental that many of my reviewers in the younger age group state that they "got this book [...] for the purpose of completing homework" (AR01), "did a paper on it for my English class" (AR13) or "read this for a World Literature class this semester" (GR04). Other – and presumably older – reviewers reject the novels' undisguised promotion of liberal educational ideals, noting that "[t]his novel is 'Intro to Race 101' within a larger love story" (AR03) or "just seems like something I'd be assigned to read in a 'Race, Gender, Class' type class at the local community college" (AR03). Constructing my YouTube corpus, I decided to exclude the numerous videos of school projects because the detailed investigation of "the [m]iddlebrow [p]edagogies" (Driscoll, 2014, 83) practised in classrooms and lecture halls would have far exceeded the boundaries of this study. Nonetheless, my observations on the new Nigerian novelists' simultaneous entanglement in academic and middlebrow contexts of production, the middlebrow reading modes of some postcolonialists or the unacknowledged bourgeois feeling rules of many an emotion researcher lead me to contend that the cultural dominance of the middlebrow transcends the digital space. This is not to suggest that the contemporary middlebrow no longer positions itself against institutions of (higher) education. Stressing

---

18 Readers of Walter Benn Michaels's excellent *The Trouble with Diversity: How We Learned to Love Identity and Ignore Inequality* (2006) will not be surprised that *class* differences do not feature in this list. As Michaels (3, 6) convincingly illustrates, race, gender or sexuality are "extraordinarily attractive" categories because they conceal economic inequalities: "A world where some of us don't have enough money is a world where the differences between us present a problem: the need to get rid of inequality or to justify it. A world where some of us are black and some of us are white – or biracial or Native American or transgendered – is a world where the differences between us present a solution: appreciating our diversity. So we like to talk about the differences we can appreciate, and we don't like to talk about the ones we can't."

the recreational function of a middlebrow reading, HollaAtFola (YR20) affirms that her BookTube activities support her endeavour to "get [...] back into reading" because "university kind of took the love of reading out of me". Similarly, Lily Eleanor (YR17, Lily Eleanor Reads) juxtaposes recreational and educational contexts of reading, noting that the former entails different selections and practices: "I'm hoping I'll be reading a bit faster because it's now summer and [...] I'm not reading as much for school." Despite such attempts to distinguish between different modes of literary consumption, the online reading communities of the new Nigerian novel illustrate that middlebrow institutions have always catered to the educational objectives of their readers (Driscoll, 2014, 85–86).

That school and university curricula in the US and the UK tie in with the reviewers' agenda to "diversify your reading life" (YR03, bigalbooks, 11/08/2018) and become "a more aware and better person" (AR04) is not merely implied by the above-quoted statements from pupils and students. An Amazon reviewer called English Teacher (AR03) confirms that Adichie's *Americanah* "is a favorite with my seniors every year", whereas the YouTube videos of the college teacher jortizi27 blur the boundaries between the seminar room and the digital space even further. Using YouTube as a teaching tool, her video "Americanah Lecture Chapters 1–4" (YR03, 13/11/2015) serves to motivate her students to validate the "different perspectives" developed in Adichie's novel and thereby approximates the words of Goodreads reviewer ImLisaAnn (GR10), who assures her readers that Emezi's *Freshwater* "is worth the investment, particularly if reading diversely is something you value".[19] Presenting a central constituent of the reviewers' self-obligation to accomplish therapeutic work, "reading more diversely" (YR20, SavidgeReads, 27/01/2017) equally informs the school and university authorities' "ethical commitments" (Driscoll, 2014, 84) to promoting learners' cross-cultural awareness.[20]

Close reading Amazon reviews of Hosseini's *The Kite Runner*, Aubry (2011, 176) deems "the possibility of identifying with strangers [...] the defining

---

19 Notably, jortizi27 recorded her video almost five years before the COVID-19 pandemic compelled the majority of lecturers and students to enter the digital space. It remains to be seen how and to what extent digital media redefine the parameters of teaching literature.

20 The complimentary distribution of Adichie's *We Should All Be Feminists* (2014) in Swedish classrooms is another example of "the extent to which the success of the middlebrow has influenced the educational system itself" (Driscoll, 2014, 86). Ernest N. Emenyonu (2017, 2) maintains that the governmental decision was informed by "the belief that inculcating the social values advocated by Adichie [...] will help to achieve harmonious mutual relationships across genders which would carry into adult life and produce the type of gender equality that would make the world a better place to live in". Remarkably, he does not explain why Swedish education authorities chose an educated middle-class writer from the Nigerian diaspora to accomplish this mission.

project of therapeutic discourse". Elsewhere in his study, he employs the term "stranger" to stress the anonymity that characterises public spheres (36). Defining the text as "foreign", though, he places special emphasis on the "capacity of middlebrow forms of identification to mediate encounters across racial and cultural boundaries" (14). Arguably, his combined use of the terms "foreign" and "strangers" not only implies his Western perspective on the literary text but also constructs the Amazon reviewers along the same national and/or racial lines that postcolonial scholars have drawn to define a "Western model reader" (Huggan, 2008, 112). Disregarding that some, even many, but not all of the reviewers of the novel are American citizens, Aubry (2011, 189, 194) reads their therapeutic work of identifying and sympathising with the novel's Afghan characters as a means of negotiating and soothing their "guilty conscience" about the US War on Terror: "Hosseini offers a recuperative narrative that identifies humanity, through [the protagonist] Amir, precisely with sin and guilt, thus allowing readers who feel human as a consequence of their struggle to cope with the worry that they, as American citizens, are among the victimizers."

Aubry presents convincing quotes to substantiate that the therapeutic work ethic of contemporary American middle-class readers maintains the religious connotations of its forerunner. By contrast, my reviewers, instead of dealing with some form of remorse, embrace national, cultural and racial differences as an occasion to reinforce the feeling rules and standards of bourgeois literary culture. Venturing beyond middlebrow studies' primarily discursive definition of class, the subsequent section conducts a demographic sample analysis of the three online communities of the new Nigerian novel to propose that the shared middlebrow practices of reading and feeling emerge from a common material backdrop.

Reviewer Profiles: Demographic Data and Middle-Class Self-Fashioning

Apart from exhibiting the greatest creativity in refashioning middlebrow consumption practices for the digital literary sphere, BookTube provides the researcher with significant parameters concerning the reviewers' gender, age and race. In contrast, the written profiles and reviews on Amazon and Goodreads "do not necessarily reveal anything at all about the actual persons behind the screen" (Rauscher, 2018, 312). Owing to their relatively short-lived attachment to the retailer's webpages, Amazon reviewers rarely share personal information or upload pictures and thus permit only limited demographic insights. Next to numerous "Amazon Customers" or "Kindle Customers", the Amazon community created by the new Nigerian novel consists of countless Ashleys, Barbaras, Elizabeths, Lindsays, Marys and Susans and an extensive range of avid readers, booklovers or bookworms, rendering the determination of the precise number of reviewers included in the corpus, as well as their identity markers and differentials, unfeasible.

In the majority of cases, the gender and/or location of a particular reviewer can to a degree be inferred from user names such as ghanaianbeauty, kenyagal, madeira mom and trishnyc.[21] Additionally, the novels' dominant themes of migration, diaspora and hybridity encourage the readers' reflections on their countries of origin or their national and/or racial identities: while a reviewer called Ms O (AR03) discloses her descent by asserting that *Americanah* "was a book I could total[ly] relate to as a Nigerian", J. Chaille Percy (AR13) reveals her speaking position when claiming that the child soldier narrative *Beasts of No Nation* enables her "to get in touch with a point of view that is harder for Americans to relate to, hopefully never having to experience such a dreadful way of life". Confirming that the Amazon community encompasses insiders of and outsiders to Nigeria, such examples are not only hard to spot from distant reading perspectives but also appear in less definite shape. For instance, Stephanie87 (AR19) "worr[ies] whether people not from a Nigerian/African culture will really understand the symbolism" of *The Icarus Girl*, leaving it open whether her concern results from a Nigerian background or a condescending assumption about fellow "Western" readers. Owing to its reviewers' comparatively higher investment in the reading community, the Goodreads page proves more informative, with cases where profile pictures or other personal data are unavailable occurring less often.

Since BookTube turns out to be most consistent in detailing background information about its users, I look at the 330 channels to ponder the extent to which Aubry's assumption about the guilt-ridden underpinnings of the therapeutic work ethic applies to my reviewers. Attesting to the gendered dimension of middlebrow culture, 293 of the 350 different people visible in the 635 reviews of my YouTube corpus are female (Figure 4.4.1, Table 4.4).[22] Unlike other middlebrow consumption contexts, such as the Melbourne Writers Festival studied by Driscoll (2014, 164), the BookTubers are not "predominantly middle aged" but younger, with 313 falling within the bracket of 20 to 40 and at least two-thirds of these being in their early twenties (Figure 4.4.2, Table 4.4). Moreover, and subverting the construct of the "Western model reader" (Huggan, 2008, 112), the BookTube community cuts across neatly delineated colour lines, highlighting that "Western" guilt does not constitute the prime motivation for reviewers' therapeutically oriented emotion work in the digital literary sphere (Figure 4.4.3, Table 4.4).

---

21 Remarkably, numerous Amazon reviewers stress their gender and marital status by mentioning their surname in combination with Mrs, emphasising that they found "individual happiness" (Aubry, 2011, 17) in marriage.
22 Most BookTubers address their self-directed cameras alone, although the clubbish setting of a considerable number of videos results in the visibility of two or more people. BookTubers with more than one video review were counted once. The figures and tables on reviewers' gender, age and race (Figures 4.4.1 to 4.4.3, Table 4.4) specify the data by per cent to render them comparable with a sample of Goodreads data that, in contrast to BookTube, is smaller in size and does not provide information for all reviewers.

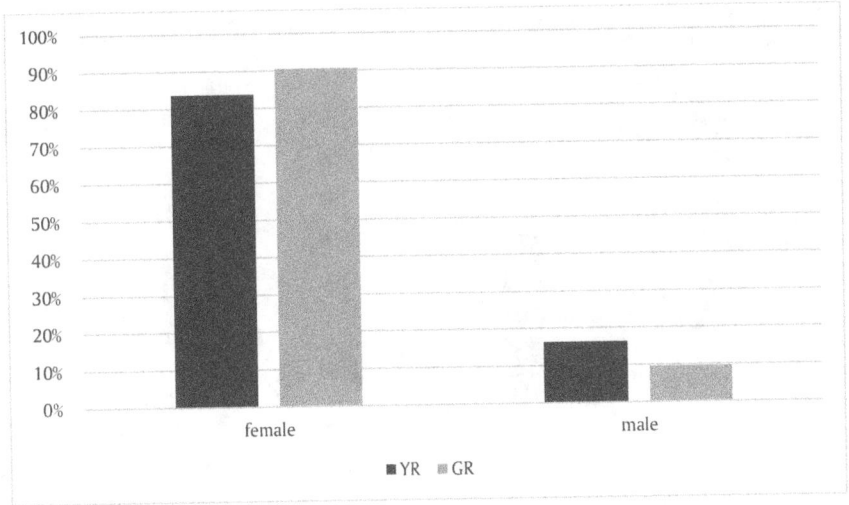

Figure 4.4.1 Demographic Data: Gender

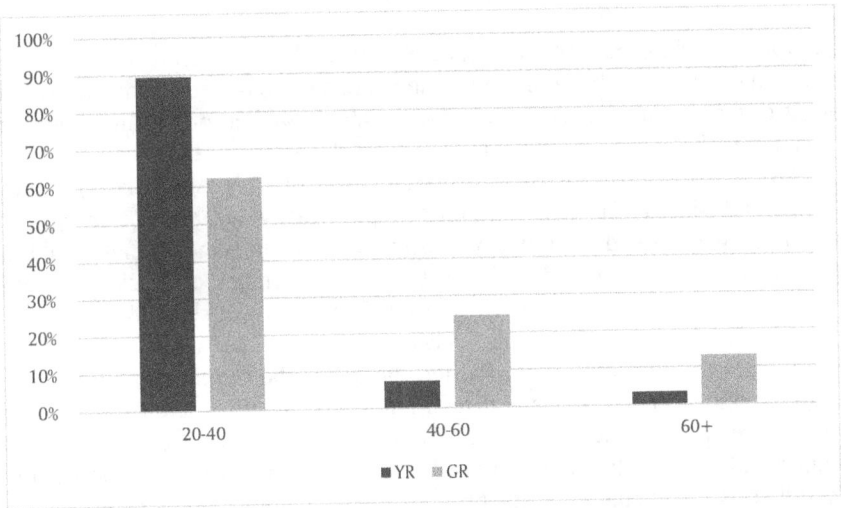

Figure 4.4.2 Demographic Data: Age

Studying BookTubers in terms of their present location and/or origin proves more difficult, as the subsequent examples show. Whereas Shawn (Shawn the Book Maniac, RP) describes himself as "[a] queer Canadian bibliophile in Tokyo", the video review of a young black woman called sugarbanana (YR17) substantiates that she currently lives in the US but originates from Nigeria. Reinforcing the diasporic structure of the BookTube community further, one equally encounters "a Nigerian living in Cape Town" (Abisola S, RP) and "a Ghanaian born, Italian raised" (Benjamina E. Dadzie, RP) reviewer among the

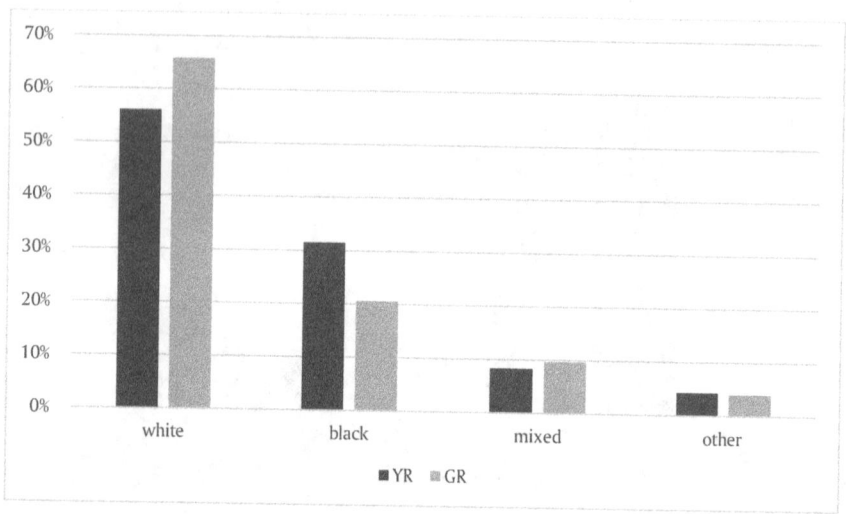

Figure 4.4.3 Demographic Data: Race

platform's "hybrid bookworm creature[s]" (Shamina Yuki Crawford, RP). The (spatial) diversity of the community members also transpires from the stated locations of the channels (Figure 4.4.4, Table 4.4). Although Euro-America dominates the picture, with 87 and 62 channels located in the US and the UK, respectively, the BookTubers also reside in Canada (12), Australia (9), South Africa and Nigeria (8), India (5), France (4), Germany and New Zealand (3).[23] Given the widespread existence of diaspora communities in (the metropolitan centres of) the UK and the US, as well as the number of black (110) and mixed-race (29) BookTubers in my corpus, it would be misleading to assume that the new Nigerian novel exclusively caters to "Western" audiences eager to work through their racial guilt. Rather, the BookTube community emerges as a geographically and ethnically diversified formation of readers who embrace the digital literary sphere as an opportunity to "feel part of a global humanity" (Aubry, 2011, 31) – that is, to strengthen their membership in the globalising middle classes via shared middlebrow contexts and practices of reception.

By comparison, the Goodreads community is structured along similarly diverse lines. A look at the 256 reviewers in the Adebayo sub-corpus, which features nine of my BookTubers and thus indicates demographic overlaps between the platforms, yields comparable findings (Figures 4.4.1 to 4.4.4, Table 4.4). The Goodreads reviewers of *Stay With Me* are mostly female (210) and equally located across the globe, from the US (92) and the UK (22) over

---

23 Here are the countries that appear once (Afghanistan, Algeria, Argentina, Ghana, Hungary, Indonesia, Italy, Maldives, Norway, Pakistan, Portugal, Qatar, Singapore, St Lucia, Switzerland, Trinidad and Tobago, Uganda) and twice (Ireland, Japan, Kenya, Netherlands, Sweden).

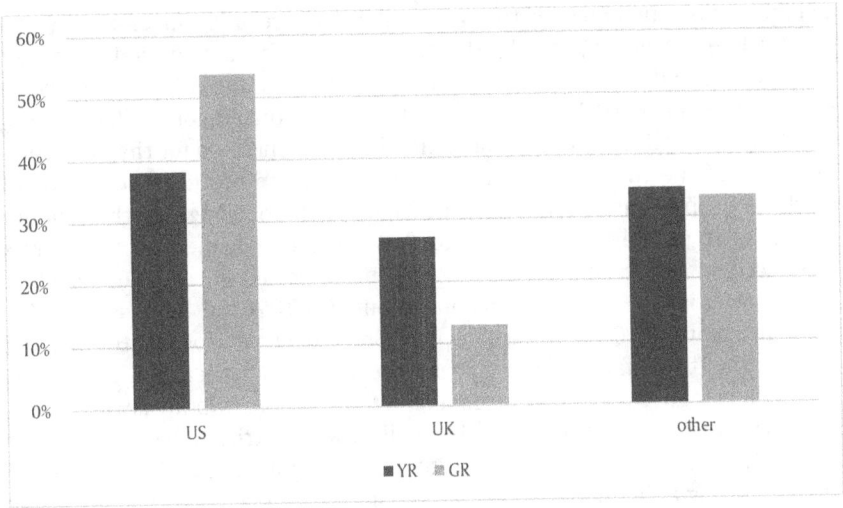

Figure 4.4.4 Demographic Data: Location

Canada (13) and Australia (6) to South Africa (5), Ireland and Nigeria (3).[24] In terms of age, the largest group of Goodreads reviewers equally falls into the category of 20 to 40 (124). However, an additional 25 and 13 per cent aged between 40 to 60 and over 60 suggests that the video format of reviewing enjoys more popularity among younger readers. Coupled with the observation that the Goodreads community is predominantly white (115) and includes fewer black (36) or mixed-race (17) reviewers as compared with the BookTube community, one may assume that visual media are particularly well suited to display the self-confidence that young black women draw from the widespread online circulation and discussion of the new Nigerian novel.

Without doubt, and as the keyword analysis of the reviews in the next chapter substantiates, the "global mode of mass consumption" that Huggan (2001, 13) calls the postcolonial exotic extends into the Internet era and its digital consumption contexts. Representing the majority – or, in the case of BookTube, more than half – of the community members, white reviewers continue to turn to a novel such as *Stay With Me* to gain "insight into the Nigerian culture" (AR02). Keen on increasing their cross-cultural competence, some of the outsiders to Nigerian society and culture may indeed read and publicly discuss the new Nigerian novel to negotiate a form of guilt resulting from the realisation that they "know next to nothing about Nigeria" (GR17) and its history of British colonisation. Yet, while the middlebrow pursuit of

---

24 Countries that appear once or twice include Belgium, Bolivia, Greece, Hungary, Indonesia, Italy, Japan, Malta, Morocco, Norway, Portugal, Sweden, Switzerland, Trinidad and Tobago, United Arab Emirates and Denmark, Germany, India, Kenya, Netherlands, Spain, respectively.

self-realisation encompasses the responsibility to "read [as] diversely" (YR04, The Maddie Hatter) as possible, the number of participants providing insider perspectives indicates that community building in the Web 2.0 universe exceeds the conceptual boundaries of the postcolonial exotic. What do the novels and their discussions in the digital literary sphere do for the non-white members of the three communities? Looking at the profiles and videos of black and mixed-race reviewers, one cannot fail to recognise the amount of emphasis placed on the need to feel represented and see themselves "reflected in media and fiction" (YR03, mynameismarines, 20/09/2016) as "ordinary citizens" (YR03, diana in colour, 05/01/2018). As Diana (YR03, diana in colour, 05/01/2018), a diasporic BookTuber who originates "from a middle-class black family" and currently resides in New Zealand, elucidates, presumably for her white fellow readers: "I think that everybody always thinks that immigrants are coming from this really poverty-stricken background and they're fleeing from Africa. But this kind of tells the more real story and my story." Hinting at her middle-class upbringing in Zambia to verify *Americanah*'s representation of Ifemelu's childhood in Nigeria, Diana corroborates that "there are just black girls in Africa who aren't [...] starving". Insiders such as Diana accomplish a crucial task within the community. Coming close to the functions fulfilled by Adichie's middle-class characters, she encourages white members such as BookNympho (YR03) to imagine Nigerians as "people [who] just live everyday lives [...] and have the normal drama", fostering the idea that "these people are just like people everywhere". What serves "as a basis for identity and solidarity" (Aubry, 2011, 36) among the geographically and/or racially divided members of the affective online communities, then, is the strategic presumption of a shared middle-class (be)longing, continually reinforced by the claim that, "[i]n the end, all hearts in the world beat the same" (GR20).

Just as in nineteenth-century Britain, the middle-class affiliations and aspirations of the reviewers manifest themselves in "economic, cultural and discursive" terms, "encompass[ing] income, educational level, occupation, domestic standards and styles, politics and leisure" (Steinbach, 2017, 116). Though the communities' practices of reading and discourses of feeling point to a common materialist basis, the social class background of their members cannot be measured in the same way as their gender, age or race. Unlike the respondents to formal inquiries, such as the Melbourne Writers Festival audience (Driscoll, 2014, 161–65), the reviewers included in my corpora do not necessarily disclose their educational background, occupation or annual income. Rather, their self-characterisation in the reader profiles suggests that the online communities consist of suburban mothers and leisured housewives, (PhD) students of literature, culture and creative writing, college teachers and university lectures, freelancers and translators alike. As stated above, few reviewers officially "work in publishing" (Matthew Sciarappa, RP) and, if they do, they almost exclusively conceptualise and promote reading as an extra-professional and recreational activity. They describe themselves as "book addict[s]" (Eve's Alexandria, RP) or "self-confessed bibliophile[s]" (Books and Headscarves, RP) and express the "hope to connect with other readers and people committed to practicing kindness, curiosity & empathy" (The Book Wanderer, RP) or "make friends" (Fred Weasley Died Laughing, RP). Downplaying their work in the digital literary economy, they stress that they are "[j]ust a stay-at-home mom with a slight book obsession" (Chapter32, RP) or "don't have a degree in English Literature" but "do have opinions" (MercysBookishMusings, RP). BookTuber Linda from LindaReads (RP) summarises the ostensible demarcation between amateur and professional reviewing thus: "I believe you don't need a specific set of skills or an arsenal of jargon [...] to talk about books. The only prerequisite, if any, is a deep passion for books." To what extent do such and similar self-conceptions, which locate the reviewers' emotion work in the private sphere, contradict the public display of their affective responses? How do they serve the commercial interests of digital companies such as Amazon and YouTube?

Class and Gender 2.0: Affective Care and the Division of Digital Labour

Most bibliophiles cannot or, more significantly, do not have to live off their reviewing activities. However, their ties with publishers, retailers and prize organisers signify the potentially profitable entanglement of private emotion work and public emotional labour. The opaque financial mechanisms of the digital literary economy make it difficult to give a precise figure for the amount of money that an amateur reviewer can earn. As Emma from emmmabooks confirms in her video "HOW BOOKTUBERS MAKE MONEY" (2016), the BookTube "community [hardly] ever talks about how money works here". Based on her tutorial as well as the channel profiles of my BookTubers, I differentiate between three major revenue streams. The first possibility for BookTubers to monetise their channels is offered by Google AdSense, an online advertising programme that supports the placement of algorithmically defined ads before or within a video review. Hinting at the programme's low barriers of access, the founder of WikiHow, Jack Herrick ("Google AdSense", *Google*), affirms that "[a]ll you have to do is drop the little AdSense code into your website and it immediately starts working". Unevenly split among the BookTuber, the advertiser and Google, the "earnings are dependent on many factors, such as how many traffic you get, what type of content you provide, where your users are located, how you set up your ads, and so on" ("AdSense Help", *Google*). For a channel to gain revenues from its videos, the BookTuber has to earn at least 100 US dollars per month. The YouTube Money Calculator of the media resource page *Influencer Marketing Hub* indicates the number of video views required to pass this threshold. With the reward for roughly 1,000 daily views ranging between three to five US dollars, BookTubers must have a substantial amount of subscribers at their disposal to profit from this advertising scheme. Unsurprisingly, only 14 of my 314 amateur BookTubers work with Google AdSense. Instead of concluding that they have no intention whatsoever of turning their private emotion work into a little extra income, I suggest a look at the other and more lucrative sources of revenue: affiliate marketing and sponsorship ("All You Need", *Influencer Marketing Hub*, 2021; "HOW BOOKTUBERS MAKE MONEY", emmmabooks, 2016).

The 86 self-generated affiliate links to Amazon (and its subsidiary Book Depository), Foyles, Mac Cosmetics, Sephora or Zara, among others, illustrate that the digital literary sphere delineates a workplace that tempts amateur reviewers to perform emotional labour on a commission basis. Even though these commissions are neither contractually agreed upon nor particularly high, as Rincey from rincey reads ("like, really small", YR16, 01/06/2018) or Dave from Wilde Reads ("I really mean tiny", YR02) remark, they insinuate that affective responses to the new Nigerian novel entail financial rewards just extensive enough to enable the reproduction of bourgeois affective norms. As the following statements by BookTubers imply, these "very small commission[s]" usually flow into "the operating expenses for this channel" (YR03, abookolive), "support my book addiction" (YR15, Comfycozyup, 08/03/2019) and "help me make more videos" (YR10, MercysBookishMusings, 08/01/2019).[25]

Moreover, the reviewer's financial and emotional investment in the BookTube community holds out the prospect of being recognised and remunerated by publishers and prize operators. Usually "reserved for people with a larger following" ("HOW BOOKTUBERS MAKE MONEY", emmmabooks, 2016), sponsorship constitutes a third possibility to monetise private emotion work. Almost half (153) of my amateur BookTubers mention their mail address for business inquiries and describe their "review policy", such as "I accept and review books on request" (Amanda Jenner, RP), "I accept books written by female authors" (Britta Böhler, RP) or "I do not accept self-published books or e-books for review" (Jen Campbell, RP). 14 BookTubers, six of whom range among the reviewers listed in Table 4.2.2, explicitly state that their video reviews are based on "books that I have been sent by publishers" (YR19, SavidgeReads, 12/01/2017). Eric Karl Anderson (YR17, 08/07/2017) further implies that publishers considerably influence the kind of content that is created around their new releases when he relates that "the good people at Granta Books [...] gave me the idea of making a video about the LGBT books that have made me". Similarly, the "official Man Booker vlogger" Jean from Jean Bookishthoughts (YR16, 22/08/2015) receives "a big box of exciting goodies to unbox for you today from the Man Booker Prize". Such collaborations with publishers, retailers or prize organisers are commonly accompanied

---

25 The number of BookTubers who work with discount codes that, contrary to self-generated affiliate links, indicate contractual relations with retailers is comparatively small. Merely three of the 314 amateur channels "have an agreement" that allows BookTubers such as Russell from Ink and Paper Blog (YR10, 28/02/2019) to "offer my viewers 10% off with the code below".

by BookTubers' assurances that they are "not sponsored" (YR02, The Book Castle, 24/03/2019) or "paid to discuss any of the books" (YR05, Kendra Winchester, 12/01/2019). Understating the commerciality of their trustworthy and "honest review[s]" (YR05, Kendra Winchester, 12/01/2019), the members of the BookTube reading community frequently conceal that publishing and prize operators are "paying us" (YR16, Jen Campbell, 28/08/2015), both in the material form of books and the non-material form of possibilities to enhance their visibility and impact in the digital literary sphere.

Corresponding to the financial opportunities that result from reviewers' public performances of emotion work on BookTube, Amazon and Goodreads run their own programmes that provide their participants with "pre-release or otherwise 'special' content in exchange for posting reviews to their highly active bookish micro-communities" (Murray, 2018, 138). NetGalley, a website that offers free advance reader copies (ARC) in digital format, particularly caters to Goodreads' "readers of influence" who seek to "discover and recommend new books to their audiences" (*NetGalley*). Of my Goodreads reviewers, 99 gained the ARC of one or several of the 20 new Nigerian novels in this fashion and "in exchange for an honest review", as the Goodreads netiquette demands them to express. In addition, 52 Goodreads reviewers allocate their reviews to the "netgalley shelf". NetGalley equally rewards the emotion work publicly performed by 53 of my Amazon reviewers, although the online retailer's Vine Voices programme, which "gives [...] reviewers advance access to not-yet-released products" ("Badges", *Amazon*), proves altogether more popular with the members of the Amazon community, with 186 designating their responses as "Vine Customer Reviews of Free Product". Noting that digital companies "are hazy about the criteria by which one is invited to join", Murray (2018, 138) deems it probable "that favorable coverage of previous or generically similar titles up one's odds for receiving free books and other preferential titbits". In view of the *Observer* article by Vicky Kalpaxis, which discusses "How the Publishing Industry Is Cashing in on Influencer Culture" (2020), one may well add that publishers, retailers and other players of the digital literary economy turn the "personality power" – or, to put it in other words, the social and emotional efforts – of influential amateur reviewers to account.[26]

---

26 Here are a couple of examples that illustrate how amateur marketing on BookTube (and beyond) works: "I've just watched Eric and Anna's predictions and [...] have been quite inspired" (YR10, Anna Baillie-Karas, 27/04/2019); "This [reading challenge] is something that I haven't heard about before and I saw on Jean's channel of Jean Bookishthoughts" (YR04, Your True Shelf, 11/02/2019); "I wanted to read this [*Purple Hibiscus*] last month because it was part of Russell over at Ink and Paper Blog's Reading Around the World book club" (YR05, Chris Bookish Cauldron, 02/04/2018); "If I hadn't heard BookTubers discussing the book [*Freshwater*] before picking it up, I feel like I would have been lost" (GR10); "I finally broke down and bought this book [*Americanah*] when BookTuber [...] Amerie mentioned it" (AR03).

As Hochschild's sociological emotion research demonstrates, the private management and the public performance of emotion continually inform each other, irrespective of the particular economic order that governs social behaviour. Accordingly, Amazon, Goodreads and YouTube and their systems of literary transmission rate as recent manifestation of capitalism only because they exploit the reviewers' affective responses for commercial ends. Like the emotions of the flight attendant who worked for Delta Airlines in the 1980s, the emotions of the reviewers "fall under the sway of large organizations, social engineering and the profit motive" (Hochschild, 2003, 19). In fact, digital corporations may well exceed Delta's scope of power. Hinting at their technological possibilities, Staab and Nachtwey (2016, 469) rightly remark that, with a company such as Amazon, "comprehensive control and regulation of humans by machines are returning to the world of work". While their article focuses on the barcode system governing work in Amazon's warehouses, I claim that algorithmic software not only affects the tastes of but also builds "a new type of labour force" (Staab and Nachtwey, 2016, 468) from the customers and users of Web 2.0 businesses – that is, a type of labour that is not merely contingent but reproductive and underpaid, and therefore points to significant similarities between twenty- and twenty-first-century capitalist endeavours.

Indeed, the primarily female reviewers constituting the affective online communities indicate that women still prove the "more accomplished managers of feeling in private life" and, as a result, show a greater inclination towards "put[ting] emotional labour on the market" (Hochschild, 2003, 11). Notably, they also continue to offer this labour at an absurdly low price. Amazon's Vine Voices and Goodreads's NetGalley collaborators do not produce commissioned reviews in the narrow sense of the term, just as the affiliate links circulating on BookTube do not suggest that the reviewers sell their emotional responses to the novels for contractual wages. Rather than entering into costly contracts with professional reviewers, the Web 2.0 corporations and the various institutions that cooperate with them capitalise on the reviewers' self-fashioning as financially independent amateurs and use the value of their emotional work ethic as marketing tools "at none to negligible costs" (Rauscher, 2018, 310). Digital companies place the reproductive work of caring for literary community into the hands of female amateur reviewers, entrusting them with the task to "report an abuse" (Amazon) or flag other reviews as "inappropriate" (Goodreads) and ensure that prospective customers are warmly welcomed to the affective discussion of aesthetically and politically similar titles.[27] The investment in

---

27 Notably, a similar argument can be made about the predominantly female authors of the Nigerian diaspora who seem bound to rehearse commercially successful narrative structures for a self-enforcing world-literary system. However, and contrary to their female readers, Adichie and her peers do not fashion themselves as amateurs but rather conceptualise authorship as a middle-class profession with a corresponding income.

technologies and server capacities as well as the costs of an occasional ARC stand in marked contrast to the tremendous profits gained from organising the relations of labour in the digital literary sphere. From the perspective of digital companies, the new labour force proves extremely profitable because it generates book sales, advertising revenues and user data, which, in the end, secure the perpetuation of the system.

The reviewers, on the other hand, receive more than a free copy and "the flattering image of [themselves] as bibliophiles" (Murray, 2018, 54). Rather, they appropriate the conferred role as affective caregivers to publicly strengthen their position as emotionally receptive members of a globalising middle-class formation, "replete with its own lingo, rituals and enthusiasms" (Murray 2018, 54). Operating in a digital service network, the reviewers – and specifically "those who are most competent at building [...] relationships following the therapeutic model" (Illouz, 2007, 107) – wield considerable tastemaking power. Systematically built into the algorithmic software of Web 2.0 businesses, their "middle-class preferences [not only] exert enormous influence on the publishing industry" (Aubry, 2011, 12). Working at the forefront of adjusting middlebrow literary culture to the digital age, amateur reviewers will eventually overtake more established mediators.[28] Given their role in defining which books are published and how they are discussed, they represent decidedly more than the "means of production" (Bucher, 2018, 2) of digital literary capitalism.

---

28 The BookTube Prize for Fiction, which was founded by BookTuber Barter Hordes in 2019, is a case in point. According to the website ("About the Prize", *BookTube Prize*), the prize seeks "to bring an award to everyday readers who are active content producers and consumers in the bookish community on YouTube [...]. We start with a field of 48 books in each division and over four rounds of judging by hundreds of readers from more than 40 countries, we identify our favorites."

CHAPTER 5

The Verbal Performance of Affect: Emotion Terms and Patterns

Drawing on my observations about the socio-economic infrastructure of the three communities, this chapter scrutinises the bourgeois emotion ideologies of their reviewers on the level of language. In the first three sections, I implement a variety of corpus-linguistic methods to disclose the recurring verbal, lexico-grammatical and semantic structures of both the emotional expressions of the individual reviewer and the overarching affective norms of online literary discussion. Expanding on the insight that the members of the communities principally express their emotions *through* the characters and authors of the new Nigerian novel, the concluding section employs AntConc to juxtapose the review corpora with several other self-created online corpora to explore the broader communication circuit of the digital literary economy. My application of the corpus analysis toolkit to five selected novels and 284 author videos on YouTube, as well as a range of newspaper reviews and publisher blurbs, not only serves to revisit some of the middlebrow mechanisms of producing and distributing the new Nigerian novel investigated in previous chapters. Moreover, a corpus-assisted discourse analysis of the broader digital sphere enables me to determine the extent to which the results on the linguistic micro-level substantiate my macro-level arguments about the self-enhancing effects of digital literary capitalism.

Keyword Analysis: The Search for "Emotion Hotspots"

In order to determine the idiosyncratic linguistic features of my self-constructed review corpora, I begin by conducting a keyword analysis. AntConc's keyword list tool serves to contrast the three corpora with a reference corpus of "general" English such as the British National Corpus (BNC). Despite the normative assumptions about language use underlying the computer-based definition of keywords, the comparison proves instrumental in locating lexical items that are "statistically significant in terms of frequency" (Bednarek, 2008, 28) and therefore provides preliminary insights into the specific register of the online reviews. Table 5.1 indicates the top 20 key nouns, verbs, adjectives and adverbs of the altogether 15,026 responses, including their absolute frequency (hits) and frequency in proportion to the BNC (keyness).[1]

Emphasising the prevalence of key nouns in the review corpora, the keyword analysis unearths a remarkable frequency of proper Nigerian names, with five author and 12 character names occurring among the top 100 keywords and an additional number of 11 author and 12 character names ranking among the top 200 keywords. At first sight, the high keyness rates of, for instance, *Ifemelu* (17071.44) and *Kambili* (8980.88), the female protagonists of Adichie's *Americanah* and *Purple Hibiscus*, or the many references to their creator – *Adichie* (25883.81), *Chimamanda* (11328.45) and *Ngozi* (6306.54) – appear unobtrusive, as one can reasonably assume that Nigerian names do not prevail in the BNC reference corpus. A similar finding applies to the keyness of *Nigeria* and *Lagos* as well as related nouns and adjectives, such as *Nigerian* and *Igbo*, which reviewers employ to acknowledge that the novels are produced by authors originating from these places or unfold among the country's various ethnic groups. Apart from revealing the mechanisms of Othering that inform the computerised identification of keywords, the keyness of Nigerian proper names points to a central characteristic of the middlebrow reading pattern. Alternately seeking to "become more culturally aware" (AR03) or reinforce that "we are all not so different" (AR05), the ethnically heterogeneous members of the online reading communities constantly stress that the establishment of intimate connections with the characters and authors of the new Nigerian novel does not contradict their pursuit of social distinction. Along these lines, the notable keyness rate of first-person singular pronouns, such as *I* (58261.88) and *me* (7818.56), suggests that individuality and community discourses do not exclude each other but rather perpetuate bourgeois emotion ideologies in equal measure. Since the reviewers' opposing desire to establish both distinction from and connection with others is further addressed with regard to the communities' lexico-grammatical affect patterns, I exclude the proper Nigerian names from Table 5.1 to give more prominence to their discussion in a later section of this chapter.

---

[1] Untagged corpora such as my review corpora require a look at the lexico-grammatical contexts of those keywords whose word class is indeterminable at an isolated glance. AntConc's concordance tool supports the analysis of part of speech (POS) in ambiguous cases. For instance, *read*, *love* or *feel* show both nominal and verbal uses, whereas *Nigerian* or *African* occur as both nouns and adjectives and *reading* or *loved* signify either the continuous and past participle forms of verbs or adjectives. Based on frequency distribution, Table 5.1 further conceals the actual keyness of some items because the software does not differentiate between the singular and plural forms of nouns, the different inflections of verbs or the variant spelling of adjectives.

That the keyness of the items presented in Table 5.1 is preponderantly high can be affirmed by a juxtaposition of the individual review corpora. Allowing for the comparison of several self-constructed corpora, AntConc's keyword list tool proves versatile enough to bypass "general" corpora such as the BNC and the linguistic norms that are commonly ascribed to them. In the context of my material, the software can be used to disclose platform-specific differences in language use – for example, between the written reviews on Amazon and Goodreads and the spoken reviews on YouTube. Figure 5.1 presents a cloud of the top 50 keywords appearing in the corpus of YouTube reviews in relation to the corpora of Amazon and Goodreads reviews. The first striking distinction, which is not recorded in the figure, refers to the use of pronouns. While the comparison between the three review corpora and the BNC reveals that the reviewers prefer the use of first-person singular pronouns, BookTubers choose to address their viewers or fashion themselves as part of a group of readers and thereby conceptualise the act of reviewing as a shared event, as the frequent use of the second-person pronoun *you* (8569.62), as well as the first-person plural pronoun *we* (524.32), highlights. Pursuing a "positive politeness strategy", BookTubers employ pronouns to "claim solidarity" (Brown and Levinson, 1978, 107) and underscore their status as community authorities who guide fellow readers on their way to middlebrow literacy.[2]

A look at the key nouns, verbs, adjectives and adverbs in the YouTube reviews discloses that, in line with the results of the first keyword analysis covering all three review corpora, nouns tend to reach the top keyness rates, although the distance to the other word classes is less conspicuous. The majority of key nouns in the corpus of YouTube reviews refers to the medium (e.g. *channel*, *subscribers*, *video*), the different types of video (e.g. *haul*, *tbr*, *wrap-up*) and the characteristic reading occasions (e.g. *readathon*, *tag*).[3] As the previous chapter indicates, these occasions sporadically inspire the reading of Amazon and Goodreads reviewers as well. However, the keyword analysis substantiates that they occupy an outstanding position in BookTubers' consumption practices, just as the appeal of literary prizes (e.g. *prize*, *shortlist*).

---

2 The term was coined by the anthropological linguists Penelope Brown and Stephen C. Levinson. In their study *Politeness: Some Universals in Language Usage* (1978), they argue that "[p]ositive-politeness utterances are used as a kind of metaphorical extension of intimacy, to imply common ground or sharing of wants [...] even between strangers who perceive themselves, for the purpose of the interaction, as somehow familiar. For the same reason, positive-politeness techniques are usable [...] as a kind of social accelerator, where S [speaker], in using them, indicates that he wants to 'come closer' to H [hearer]" (103).

3 Falling within the first category of the three positive politeness strategies discussed by Brown and Levinson (1978, 103, 102) – that is, strategies of "stressing common ground" – the neologisms created by BookTubers may be read as a means of "[c]laim[ing] in-group membership", just as the associated practices of reading examined in Chapter 4.

Middlebrow 2.0 and the Digital Affect

Figure 5.1 Keywords in YouTube Reviews

The use of the plural noun *books* corresponds to the high keyness rates of *month* or *week*, which, coupled with the many temporal adverbs *now*, *then* or *today*, testify to YouTube reviewers' particularly tight reading schedules and, by implication, their exceptional emotional work ethic explored in Chapter 4. Another notable difference between the written and spoken reviews concerns the use of verbs. Whereas *know* (as in *you know*) and *like*, similar to *okay* and *yeah*, point to the enhanced employment of pragmatic markers and thus underline the function of spoken language to establish contact with others, key verbs such as *see* and *talking* or *watching* frame reviewing on YouTube as an activity that gestures beyond the relatively solitary practice of writing a review on Amazon and Goodreads.

In addition to disclosing platform-specific uses of language, the computational comparison between the three review corpora can reveal similarities. A focus on the shared lexical features of the different social media sites serves to confirm that digital consumption contexts and the resulting reading habits generate "emerging forms of discourse" that are worthy of investigation "on their own terms as complex cultural practices", as Driscoll and Rehberg Sedo (2019, 248) rightly note. In contrast to the keyness numbers indicated in Table 5.1, the juxtaposition of the YouTube corpus with the Amazon and Goodreads corpora displays notably lower rates that rarely pass the three-digit range. Moreover, the comparison between the three review corpora among each other yields the small number of 391 keyword types, whereas the comparison with the BNC reference corpus amounts to almost eight times as many (that is, 3,043) keyword types.

The discrepancies between the results of the two keyword analyses verify that the keywords listed in Table 5.1 apply to the three review corpora in equal parts. Reviewers on Amazon, Goodreads and YouTube employ the same terms to discuss the new Nigerian novels or refer to the act of reading and reviewing them. The absence of these words in Figure 5.1 is not surprising because all of the three self-constructed corpora consist of online reviews. On the other hand, the absence of emotion terms in the word cloud hints at a less evident linguistic property of the digital review genre, which is reinforced by the keywords in Table 5.1. Admittedly, the number of "emotion hotspots" (Driscoll, 2015, 868) appears sparse, especially if compared with the extensive list of emotion terms compiled independently of any reference corpus (Table 5.2). Instead of undermining my argument, however, this observation may just as well signify that the affective lexicon of the online communities intersects to a considerable degree with the corpus of "general" English. Indeed, that similarities across different corpora result in low keyness rates is affirmed by Figure 5.1. The nine emotion hotspots *love* and *loved, enjoyed, feel, felt, feels, heartbreaking, sad* and *emotionally* either do not appear at all or yield negligible keyness figures, emphasising that emotional expressions constitute a common characteristic of the three different review corpora.[4]

Before going into detail about the reviewers' choice and usage of emotion terms, I examine the review-specific register to show how corpus-linguistic approaches serve to strengthen some of the socio-economic insights into the affective online communities presented in Chapter 4. The keyness rates of the nouns *book* and *novel* or the verbs *reading* and *writing*, just as other book-related terms, are unobtrusive as they reference the practices of reading and reviewing, which mostly move on the descriptive level of *character* and *plot*. That reviewing demarcates an evaluative activity is verified by the key noun *stars* and the key verbs *rated* and *recommend*, among others. Illustrating that the authors' national or cultural affiliations, as well as the novels' settings, assume key positions in the reviewers' discussion and evaluation, the frequency of the nouns *Nigeria* and *Biafra* or the adjectives *Nigerian, African* and *Igbo*

---

4 Further emotion hotspots can be located among the top 500 keywords: *enjoyable* (1322.72), *enjoy* (966.44), *excited* (814.36), *emotional* (795.08), *heart-wrenching* (757.64), *emotions* (695.63), *disappointed* (631.77), *loves* (620.36), *glad* (566.75), *hope* (547.83) and *feelings* (460.16).

substantiates that the postcolonial exotic extends into the digital sphere. Key adjectives such as *interesting* or *insightful* evoke the perspective of an outsider who deems *Nigerian* culture (*really, truly, absolutely*, etc.) *fascinating* but, owing to the textual constructions of bourgeois *family life, believable* (1300.68) and *relatable* (1109.87). Offering an occasion to be *educated* (333.45) about "a totally different country and culture" (AR03), the new Nigerian novel's realist techniques of representation also render "the foreign familiar" (GR04) and thereby support the middlebrow objective of obtaining "more global points of view" (AR03) and "car[ing] about the suffering of distant others" (AR04).

As the discussion of the reviewers' identity markers in Chapter 4 highlighted, though, the digital communities not only encompass outsiders to Nigerian culture who "read outside [their] comfort zone" (GR02). Rather, the communities consist of nationally, culturally and ethnically heterogeneous readers who, just as the novels' authors, participate in online literary discussion to publicly fashion themselves as emotionally receptive members of a developing global middle-class formation. Complying with the demographic structures of the communities, the results of the keyword analysis indicate a substantial shift in the power relations of what Huggan (2001, 13) refers to as the "global mode of mass consumption". The keywords in Table 5.1 undoubtedly corroborate that readers who wish to become "more familiar with [...] and understand more about different cultures" (YR05, Kathryn Liquid Grain) alternately exoticise or appropriate the novels. Nonetheless, they equally underscore that cultural difference serves as a prompt to negotiate common *middle-class* (1077.04) aspirations that are not merely reinforced by shared reading contexts, habits and practices but also affirmed by the use of emotion terms and patterns. Nurturing the idea of "a global society" (AR03) that ascribes to the allegedly "universal feelings of hope, longing, understanding and acceptance" (GR17), the reviewers direct their affective energy into overcoming discriminatory practices. The declared "willing[ness] to work at understanding" (AR20) and dissolving perceived differences should, however, not distract from the fact that their emotional efforts emerge from and consolidate material and moral superiority (Aubry, 2011, 183, 188).

This superiority becomes particularly apparent with regard to the reviewers' blurring of evaluative and emotional language use. At first glance, the key emotion words in Table 5.1 contradict the verbal acts of rating and evaluating the new Nigerian novel that are signified by key adjectives such as *great, excellent, well-written* or *brilliant*. Registering the prevalence of evaluative terms in Goodreads reviews, Driscoll and Rehberg Sedo (2019, 251) suggest that "evaluation is implicitly encouraged by the site". The very name of the platform proves that this is certainly an understatement. As my examination of the digital literary economy, my construction of review corpora or my analysis of the platforms' domestic page designs in previous chapters stressed, digital reading sites not only encourage evaluation but also define which emotions can (or cannot) be expressed. Instead of drawing a line between evaluative and emotional language use (Driscoll and Rehberg Sedo, 2019, 251–52), then,

I propose that both the experience and expression of an emotion constitute central criteria of the reviewers' evaluative practices. As Trilbe Wynne (AR16) observes in his review of *The Fishermen*, "[w]hat's important to me is that [...] I always felt something". On the other hand, "a story lacking emotion" or an author who does not "write with heart" (GR08) invariably leaves the reviewers "cold" (AR09) and entails lower star ratings. Exemplifying the degree to which the bourgeois affective norms of the reviewers delineate evaluative practices in the digital sphere, Goodreads reviewer Allison (GR02) takes pleasure in Adebayo's tearjerker *Stay With Me*, which "had me feeling five-star emotions by the end".

Emotion Terms: The Expression of Continuity and Change

What counts as an emotion term? And who decides which emotions can be categorised as "positive" and "negative" or, to use the preferred parlance of my reviewers, "good" and "bad"? A major issue in emotion research concerns "the pronounced tendency to "fix" the feelings by defining and classifying them" (Stedman, 2002, 28). Given that linguists primarily occupy themselves with the meticulous analysis of language as a system, this practice is particularly prevalent in corpus-linguistic approaches. However, countless classificatory emotion schemes indicate that psychologists and sociologists are no less tempted to contain the emotions by arranging them in purportedly objective tables (Ekman, 1984, 319–44; Epstein, 1984, 64–88; Scott, 1980, 35–56; Turner, 2000; Turner and Stets, 2005). As the many illustrations on the subsequent pages and the extensive appendix to this chapter betray, my approach to the online communities' emotion talk by no means manages to resist this temptation. However, making use of scholarly research into historically variable emotion ideologies, my take on emotion terms seeks to go beyond predefined paths.

Complicating my endeavour, emotion studies has mostly failed to put its different disciplinary branches into dialogue. Since the 1980s, when the emotions achieved renewed scholarly recognition, the field has witnessed the steady publication of corpus-linguistic studies covering many genres and methods (Biber and Finegan, 1989, 93–124; Dirven, 1997, 55–86; Johnson-Laird and Oatley, 1989, 81–123; Nöth, 1992, 72–88; Ortony et al., 1987, 341–64; Storm and Storm, 1987, 805–16; Wierzbicka, 1999). Bednarek's *Emotion Talk Across Corpora* (2008), to name a recent example, scrutinises both the frequency and behaviour of more than 1,000 emotion terms in the BRC.[5] While corpus-linguistic approaches to emotion offer an indispensable inspiration on the technical level, I take issue with their missing historical and socio-economic perspectives and the resulting reproduction of bourgeois emotion ideologies.

---

5 The BRC is a sub-corpus of the BNC containing four sample sets of conversation, news reportage, fiction and academic discourses (Bednarek, 2008, 18–24).

In turn, literary and cultural studies scholars with an interest in the shifting socio-economic functions and effects of emotion do not implement computerised linguistic procedures.[6] Starting from Williams's cultural studies definition of "keywords", for example, Stedman (2002, 25–43) traces "The History and Usage of Key Emotion Words" in a plethora of eighteenth- and nineteenth-century dictionaries and encyclopaedia.[7] Comparing the entries for six Victorian emotion terms with her corpus of literary and non-literary material, she examines "the words' most common semantic contexts and semantic shifts in the discourses on emotions" (26).[8] Equally adopting a focus on specific emotion terms, Gohrisch (2005) surveys fictional and non-fictional negotiations of happiness and contentment.[9] Their focus on selected items facilitates the disclosure of lexical continuities across the centuries. Paying special attention to the socio-cultural and literary dimensions of Victorian emotion ideologies, however, the authors do not (and do not seek to) approach their material with the kind of rigorous linguistic accuracy that computational methods allow for (Gohrisch, 2005, 23).

Constituting anything but a disadvantage, their literary and cultural studies perspectives enable Gohrisch and Stedman (2002, 32, 45) to take into account "passages which do not use any of the keywords" or discern and discuss "[e]ntirely metaphorical concepts of the emotions", providing an important reminder that computer-based approaches alone fail to uncover the socio-historical significance of emotion terms. In view of the many promising developments in the digital humanities or the availability of e-books and other online material, it would nevertheless be intriguing to revisit the two monographs and consider the extent to which computational tools enhance the study of nineteenth-century feeling rules and, by implication, transhistorical emotion research. The same applies to

---

6 The work of Driscoll and Rehberg Sedo (2019, 248–59) with SentiStrength constitutes an exception but, as their focus on the "positive" and "negative" emotional experiences of literary festival audiences and Goodreads reviewers implies, tends to echo the shortcomings of much linguistic emotion research.

7 I use inverted commas to indicate that Stedman, just as Moretti (2013a), does not conduct a keyword analysis in the corpus-linguistic sense of the term.

8 In Stedman's study, Victorian does not conceal but consequently refers to historically specific middle-class emotion ideologies. Following her approach, I employ Victorian and nineteenth century synonymously for stylistic reasons.

9 Marked by similar research conceptions and lines of argumentation, Gohrisch and Stedman's studies build on different corpora of primary texts and therefore provide complementary perspectives on the feeling rules of the nineteenth-century middle classes. While Stedman juxtaposes canonical Victorian novels by Brontë and Dickens with lesser known narratives by Geraldine Jewsbury or G.P.R. James's *A Book of the Passions Illustrated with Sixteen Splendid Engravings* (1838–39), Gohrisch reads the highbrow fictions of George Eliot and others alongside Dinah Mulock Craig's commercially successful novel *John Halifax, Gentleman* (1856) and such advice texts as Samuel Smiles's *Self-Help* (1859) or Sarah Stickney Ellis's *Education of the Heart* (1869).

the sociological studies of twentieth- and twenty-first-century emotion ideologies by Hochschild (2003) and Illouz (2003; 2007; 2008). Digital transcriptions of Hochschild's interviews with the flight attendants, selected episodes of Oprah's Book Club or a sample of Oprah's picks may be approached with AntConc to examine the bourgeois affective norms, including the predominant "language of therapy" (Illouz, 2007, 6), of more recent times. Anticipating digital directions for emotion research, this endeavour lies beyond the scope of this book.

Illustrating that corpus-linguistic and socio-historical approaches to emotion are compatible, Moretti (2013a) draws on the Google Books corpus, the Chadwyck-Healey database and the Literary Lab corpus to survey recurring words and word clusters in eighteenth- and nineteenth-century European novels. Moretti's distant reading method uncovers that, "[i]n Victorian times, a large group of adjectives that used to indicate physical traits begin to be widely applied to emotional, ethical, intellectual, or even metaphysical states" (127) and, consequently, start to function as "inconspicuous vehicles" (130) of middle-class norms and values. Suggesting the contribution that the emerging field of digital literary studies can make to emotion studies, his "keywords" include only one term that is immediately relevant to my research: "comfort" (44–51).

Adopting both transhistorical and transdisciplinary perspectives on the affective vocabulary of the online communities, my approach to and definition of emotion terms build on the insights provided by all of the above-mentioned studies. Table 5.2 presents a word list of the three review corpora. Contrary to keyword lists, word lists detail word frequency without reference to some un- or predefined language norm and therefore allow me to bring to bear my expertise about the historical development of affective norms on the selection of emotion terms.[10] Correspondingly, the list displays the productive dynamic between continuity and change (Stedman, 2002, 5) that I see at work in the emotional lexicon of my reviewers.[11]

---

10 This is not to question the utility of keyword analysis. Next to allowing insights into the (bourgeois emotional) norms of "general" reference corpora, keyword lists can pinpoint similarities between self-constructed corpora, especially if the research focus is extended beyond the most frequent keywords (see below).
11 Following Bednarek (2008, 32), I exclude *want* and *like* because, in most cases, they do not express an emotion but are used "to make offers, invitations or demands" or "to make polite demands and express evaluations", respectively. In addition, and as mentioned above, my reviewers frequently use *like* as a pragmatic marker or filler, which is why its categorisation as an emotion term would distort the results. For similar reasons, I exclude terms with non-affect meaning, such as *content* (as a noun), *long* (as an adjective) or *miss* (as a term of address), as well as realisations of *move*, which occur particularly often in the reviews of novels featuring a migration plot, or the emotion noun *luck*, which mostly refers to the protagonist of Abani's *Song for Night*, My Luck. The list is restricted to words with more than 100 raw hits.

By and large, the reviewers do not exhibit a radically new approach to expressing emotion. Moreover, their employment of what various emotion researchers across the disciplines have identified as "primary" or "basic" emotions (Bednarek, 2008, 48; Turner and Stets, 2005, 11), such as *love* and *pleasure*, *happiness* and *sadness* or *anger* and *fear*, shows a tendency towards essentialising conceptions. Jonathan H. Turner and Jan E. Stets's (2005, 11) contention that these emotions "are universal to all humans" comes notably close to the reviewers' confidence that there may be cultural differences "but human emotions are the same" (AR02). Considering that the evolutionary theory of primary emotions goes back to Charles Darwin's exploration of *The Expression of Emotion in Man and Animals* (1872), it is, perhaps, no coincidence that contemporary online discussions feature many similarities with Victorian emotion discourses (Stedman, 2002, 6–7). Dating from a period in British history characterised by a "passion for endless classificatory schemes" (Stedman, 2002, 33), primary emotions evoke nineteenth-century middle-class efforts at legitimising social, economic and cultural authority in a newly developing industrial nation (Gohrisch, 2005, 11, 21–22; Gohrisch, 2011, 49; Stedman, 2002, 5, 24). Instead of taking the common presumption by researchers and reviewers as evidence of "common", "essential", "natural" or "universal" feelings, then, I propose that the members of the online communities adjust the emotional register of the nineteenth-century heterogeneous British middle classes to the socio-economic transformations wrought by the Internet era.

Indeed, most of the terms that are examined by Gohrisch, Moretti and Stedman, such as *emotion* and *feeling* or *happiness* and *comfort*, occupy central positions in the word list of the three review corpora. Looking at their lexical and semantic contexts, one may also conclude that the meaning of some terms has remained notably stable over the course of the last centuries. The "sweet, positive feelings" (GR17) and the "bad feeling[s]" (GR02) of the reviewers prove that digital emotion discourses "are imbued with [the same] morality" (Stedman, 2002, 42) that demarcates nineteenth-century conceptions of *pleasure* and *pain*. Similarly, the reviewers' confirmation that reading the new Nigerian novel "makes me all happy" (YR10, Always Doing) or elicits "the feel of a happy family" (GR05) indicates that the contemporary middle classes are still in search of the "golden path to happiness" (AR03; Gohrisch, 2005, 49–53). The reviewers' uses of *comfort* are broadly in line with the term's semantic shift in the late seventeenth century: "comfort is no longer what returns us to a 'normal' state from adverse circumstances but what takes normality as its starting point and *pursues well-being as an end in itself*, independently of any mishap" (Moretti, 2013a, 46, original emphasis). In fact, "comfort with a character" (AR03) constitutes a prerequisite for reading on, and whenever reviewers stress that they "read outside [their] comfort zone" (GR16), they highlight that it serves their eventual well-being.[12] Moreover, references to *tears* (141 hits) or the *heart*, which continues to be conceptualised "as the [central] seat of the feelings" (Stedman, 2002, 45), reinforce widespread associations of emotion with the body and, in effect, render them "natural" (Stedman, 2002, 6–10), imbuing the responses with a specifically powerful sense of sanctity: "this book grabbed my soul and broke my heart" (AR10); "the characters draw you in and pull at your heart" (AR11); "a formidable examination of the human heart" (GR16); "the writer writes from her heart" (AR17).

However, the affective online communities not only reproduce but also redefine the uses and meanings of Victorian emotion terms, creating a number of linguistic innovations. Judging by the overwhelming occurrence of *feeling* and its different realisations, the term has somewhat obliterated the semantic nuances of the other Victorian emotion words discussed by Stedman (2002, 26). Admittedly, *affection* and *emotion* or *sensibility* and *sentiment* do appear in the digital contexts of bookish emotion talk, albeit less often and semantically shifted. For instance, the sixteenth- and seventeenth-century political connotations of "emotion", latently present in Victorian discourses that warn of "the dangers of unbridled passion" (Stedman, 2002, 31), are entirely absent in the reviews. Synonymous expressions such as "I felt every emotion along with Yejide" (GR02), "I [...] felt every emotion as the story unfolded before me" (AR04) or "you [...] feel every emotion that the characters are feeling" (AR05) demonstrate that, in the new millennium, middle-class emotion ideologies have become so prevalent – indeed, "normal" (Moretti, 2013a, 46) – that they no longer require containment or control. Instead of evoking revolutionary impulses, the present-day use of the term rather signals a kind of "juxtapolitical" complicity with the standards of bourgeois (literary) culture.[13]

The reviewers' employment of another Victorian emotion word, "affection", points in a similar direction. Related to the nineteenth-century meaning of "passion", the term used to function as a synonym of disease or illness,

---

12 The use of the term clarifies reviewers' association of comfort with the middle-class home. Like the eponymous protagonist of Daniel Defoe's *Robinson Crusoe* (1719), who "is clearly identifying comfort with the domestic horizon" (Moretti, 2013a, 46), BookTuber Jasmine (YR02, Jasmine's Reads, 21/11/2017), sharing her "favorite cozy reading accessories", pictures the "ideal reading setup" as "me sitting in a living room in my pajamas or cozy with a cup of tea".

13 The term is borrowed from Berlant (2008, x, original emphasis), who convincingly argues that nineteenth-century literary communities move "in *proximity* to the political, occasionally crossing over in political alliance, even more occasionally doing some politics, but most often not, acting as a critical chorus that sees the expression of emotional response and conceptual recalibration as achievement enough". In a similar vein, the reviewers of the new Nigerian novel "weav[e] a sense of social responsibility into [their] cultural activities" (Driscoll, 2014, 44) without acknowledging that the kind of class privilege that allows for such practices has meanwhile lost its potentially subversive impetus.

including "*the idea of being affected or acted upon* or influenced by someone or something" (Stedman, 2002, 36, original emphasis). Mostly occurring as an adjective with verb realisations of *feel*, such as "I felt deeply affected" (GR02), the semantic shift of "affection" insinuates that the experience of an "*overpowering emotion*" (Stedman, 2002, 38, original emphasis) need not be controlled but, quite the contrary, supports the reviewers' self-construction as emotionally receptive readers.

Put differently, and judging by the emotion terms employed most often by the reviewers, the "capacity for *refined emotion*, delicate sensitiveness of taste [and] readiness to feel compassion" (Stedman, 2002, 40, original emphasis) nowadays exceeds the nineteenth-century meaning of "sensibility" and encompasses a number of terms and clusters that may not immediately indicate the expression of an emotion. Stedman's etymological analysis of the term "feeling" suggests that its semantic redefinition in Victorian discourses prepared the ground for the linguistic development of what Aubry (2011, 3, 11) refers to as the "therapeutic paradigm". Even though its use can be traced back as far as the twelfth century, the word underwent significant changes. Incorporating "the notion of physical sensation or perception through the sense of touch or the general sensibility of the body" at least since the fourteenth century, the "importance of the self, of internal states, and of sensation" among the consolidating British middle classes imbued the word with the kind of "psychological sense" (Stedman, 2002, 35, 34, 35) that persists in the reviewers' therapeutic register.

Enhancing their affective vocabulary, the psychological redefinition of emotion terms serves the reviewers to construct "the interior [as] the staging ground for all the suffering, risk, trouble, and heroism that [...] continue to be perceived as necessary aspects of a meaningful life" (Aubry, 2011, 25). Arguably, their verbal demonstration of "emotional challenges" (AR03), "inner conflict" (GR10), "internal struggle" (AR17) or "psychological stress" (GR08), while amplifying the new Nigerian novel's psychologised or emotionalised representation of national, social and cultural conflict (Jameson, 1986, 71), endows various non-affect terms with affective meaning. Next to these adjective–noun constructions, the reviewers expand their therapeutic lexicon by employing a verbal affect style (Figure 5.2).[14] Underlining their capacity to turn almost any reading impression or textual observation into an emotional

---

14 Figure 5.2 is based on my POS analysis of all occurrences of the terms listed in Table 5.2. Comparing my findings with the results of Bednarek's (2008, 38) POS analysis of the BNC sub-corpora, the online communities' prevalent use of emotion verbs comes closest to conversations that, stressing the social and performative functions of emotion talk, are characterised by "more verbs than adjectives", whereas the notable number of emotion nouns and adjectives brings my review corpora more closely into line with news reportage and fiction that tend towards "a nominal-adjectival affect style". See the next section for my discussion of the varying functional aspects of emotion nouns, verbs and adjectives.

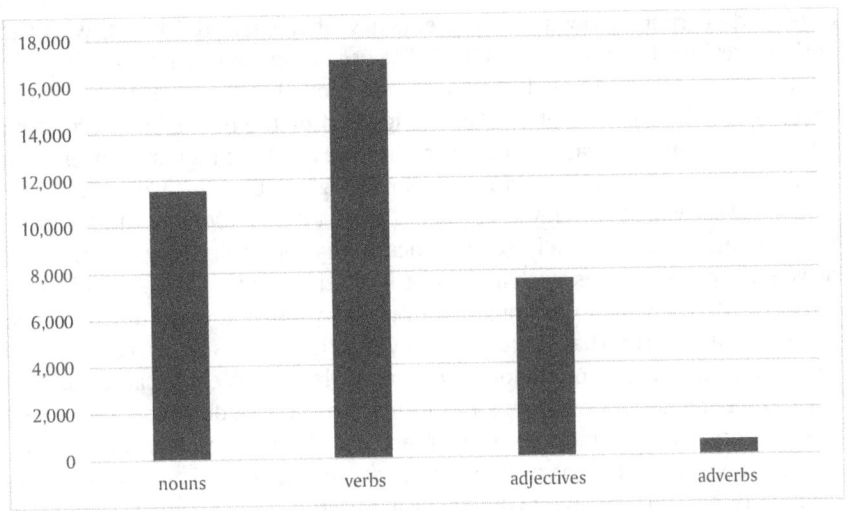

Figure 5.2 POS Distribution of Most Frequent Emotion Terms in Review Corpora

expression, adjective constructions with the emotion verb *feel* predominantly serve to extend the reviewers' therapeutic vocabulary: "I felt really conflicted" (YR10, Eric Karl Anderson, 25/04/2019); "Adichie's aim is to make her readers feel conflicted" (AR03); "I felt confused by so many characters" (AR04); "you feel depressed by the story" (GR16); "I felt lost at times" (GR09); "black girls feel pressured to straighten [...] their hair" (AR03); "that left me feeling troubled" (GR04).

As Chapter 3 demonstrated, the division of online reviews into distinct sub-corpora facilitates a comparative look at the behaviour of top emotion terms across the three platforms and across the responses to the 20 new Nigerian novels. Preparing the juxtaposition of the review corpora with other self-constructed online corpora in the chapter's final section, I select ten of the emotion words listed in Table 5.2 on the basis that they, apart from occurring relatively frequently, represent the communities' oscillation between continuity and change. Figures 5.3 and 5.4 (Tables 5.3 and 5.4) display how the different realisations of the items behave across the three review corpora and across the 20 novel corpora, respectively.[15] Substantiating the results of the keyword analyses, the behaviour of the ten selected terms across Amazon, Goodreads and YouTube indicates merely minor differences. Irrespective of Amazon reviewers' apparent preference for realisations of *love* and *enjoyment*, the Amazon and

---

15 The numbers for some of the selected terms differ from those in Table 5.2. The reason for this is that the figures take into account all realisations, including those with less than 100 raw hits. Figures 5.3 to 5.7 show normalised hits. For my detailed calculations, see the corresponding tables in the appendix.

Goodreads corpora show a similar frequency of the selected items, with the YouTube reviews lagging a little behind. The use of *hope* constitutes an exception to this observation, although it should be noted that its realisations do not necessarily refer to an emotion that is triggered by the novels but more often relate to BookTubers' practices of addressing and involving their audiences, as in "I hope everyone had a wonderful year of reading" (YR02, My Reading Life) or "I hope I will see you soon in my next video" (YR05, Kitty G, 10/08/2018). Moreover, YouTube reviewers continually express uncertainty concerning the pronunciation of Nigerian proper names, such as "I hope I said that right" (YR16, ABookishPair, 24/02/2019), which, quite obviously, does not play a role in written reviews. On the other hand, terms that express a bodily reaction such as *cry* or metaphorical expressions with the emotion noun *heart* may be less prevalent because YouTube videos render emotional reactions visible. Instead of concluding that BookTubers use altogether fewer emotion terms, then, one should keep in mind that the possibilities and limitations of different media influence the choice of emotion terms and the frequency with which they are used.

Constituting a central connection between the reading sites under scrutiny, the reviewers' use of emotion terms also reveals that similar techniques of narration yield similar patterns of reception. The selected terms exhibit a strikingly uniform behaviour across the reviews of the individual novels. Furthermore, the outstanding frequency of terms in the responses to novels that feature a strong romance plot, such as Adebayo's *Stay With Me*, Adichie's *Americanah* or Okparanta's *Under the Udala Trees*, points to a correlation between the reviewers' choice of emotion words and the novels' dominant genre patterns. On the other hand, the frequency peak for a novel such as Evans's *26a* rather illuminates that relatively small sub-corpora can affect comparative measures.

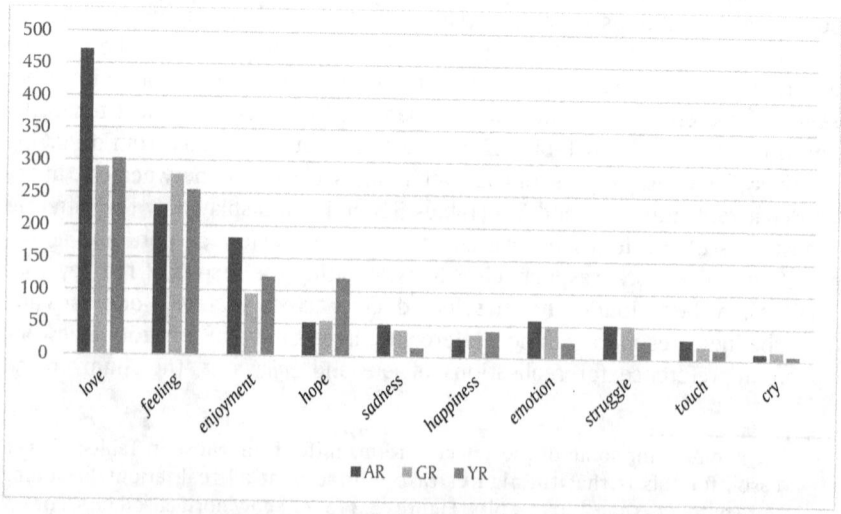

Figure 5.3 Frequency of Emotion Terms across Review Corpora

The Verbal Performance of Affect

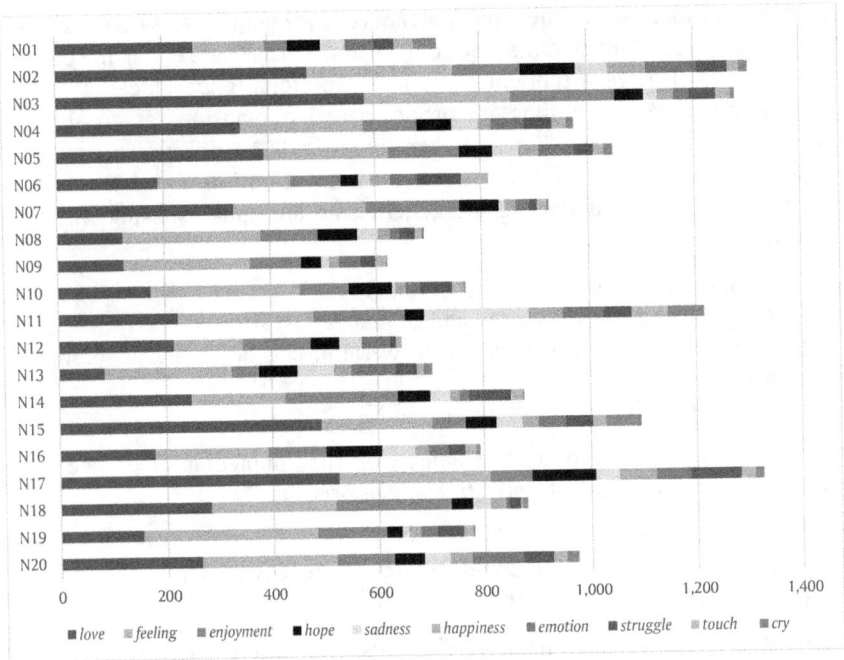

Figure 5.4 Frequency of Emotion Terms across Novel Corpora

Affect Patterns: The Creation of Intimacy with Readers, Characters and Authors

Expanding upon my socio-historically informed definition and discussion of the reviewers' affective lexicon, the present section ventures beyond (the frequency of) the individual item and focuses on the lexico-grammatical patterns of affect in which the emotion terms appear.[16] Since the Amazon, Goodreads and YouTube corpora encompass the specific genre of reviews, it would be fair to assume that the patterns include a reviewer and one of the novels. In addition, and in view of the reviewers' dominant verbal affect style, one may expect the prevalence of subject–verb–object constructions, as numerous examples with the emotion verb *love* suggest: "I love African fiction" (YR16, Poetic Liberty); "I love all the characters" (YR20, Story Nut); "I love Chimamanda Ngozi Adichie" (AR03). That the reviewers realise "emoters" or "triggers" in more complex terms and thus forge intimate connections with other readers, characters or authors (Driscoll and Rehberg Sedo, 2019, 248, 257) is clarified in the subsequent paragraphs.[17]

---

16 I put emphasis on the ten selected terms but, now and again, refer to the other items listed in Table 5.2 as well.
17 Bednarek's (2008, 65–99) syntactic analysis of selected terms in the BRC serves as an inspiration, especially regarding terminology: "emoter" and "trigger" define

My initial approach to the affect patterns of the communities takes account of the reviewers' many nominal uses of emotion words (Figure 5.2). In contrast to verbs, which have a tendency to frame emotional experiences as active negotiation processes, nouns are prone to realise emotion "as an abstract entity" (Bednarek, 2008, 72) and therefore wield the normative power of unambiguous statements. The reviewers employ emotion nouns without an emoter or trigger to underline the generalising and universalising thrust of their feeling rules (1–4).

(1) the importance of love and belief (GR05)
(2) conflicting feelings of hatred and contempt (GR15)
(3) layers of comfort and stability, of warmth, and hope, and assurance (GR01)
(4) a journey with complex emotions (GR17)

This effect is reinforced by the adjectives that immediately precede the emotion nouns, such as *authentic*, *true* and *universal* (5–7).

(5) a more authentic feel (AR03)
(6) insight into true emotions and cultural differences (AR03)
(7) those universal feelings of hope (GR17)

Contrary to the above-named adjectives, the frequent co-occurrence of the emotion nouns with *human* attributes the emotion to an emoter. Realising "authorial (attribution of emotion to self) and non-authorial affect (attribution of emotion to other)" (Bednarek, 2008, 73), the examples in (8–10) do not construct emotional responses as individual or specific. Besides using the novels to define themselves as members of the globalising middle classes – as one Amazon reviewer notes, "it feels good to feel so human" (AR03) – the use of *human* reveals the reviewers' claim to speak for all humanity, which requires the verbal presentation of one's own human qualities.

(8) grounded in real human feeling (GR08)
(9) devoid of any normal human emotion (YR07, My Reading Days, 08/03/2019)
(10) the eternal human struggle between good and evil (GR07)

"the one to whom an emotional response is assigned" and "the cause, reason or target of an emotion" (70). Other approaches to studying genre-specific grammars of affect introduce further categories (Hunston, 2003, 342–58; Galasiński, 2004) that are disregarded because they do not substantially add to the examination of the online reviews. Concerning the means by which emoters and triggers can be realised, Bednarek (2008, 72, 77) distinguishes between unemoted, undirected and directed affect patterns. While the first pattern determines neither emoter nor trigger, the second and third pattern realise an emoter or both an emoter and a trigger. I occasionally use the terms but, by and large, structure my discussion along the distinction between noun, verb and adjective patterns to render it more accessible for the reader without an extensive training in linguistics.

Apart from *human*, the reviewers employ a range of other (but not necessarily more specific) adjectives to assign emotion to self and other. Example (11) illustrates that adjectives occurring in attributive position are used metonymically to construct the emoter as part of a group that the reviewer occasionally identifies with, as in "my African heart" (AR03). The other utterances show that nouns also define emoters if used with pronouns (12–13) or genitive nouns (14–16).

(11) African-American **struggles** (AR03)
(12) we all have our **hopes and dreams** (YR10, Ink and Paper Blog, 28/02/2019)
(13) her **happiness** your **happiness**, her **pain** your **pain** (GR17)
(14) people's **emotions** (AR19)
(15) readers' **enjoyment** (AR13)
(16) an interesting window into Nigeria's emerging **struggles** (GR02)

These three noun patterns function to establish emoter collectives along liberal humanist lines. What enables the reviewers' construction of and identification with these imagined groups emerges from the subsequent utterances in (17–23) that, amplifying the character constructions and constellations of the novels, evoke a lexical pattern linked to middle-class family life. While examples (17–20) follow the structure discussed above, the statements in (21–23) replace the adjectives, pronouns and genitive nouns with prepositional phrases as post-modifiers. Whereas both pre- and post-modification indicate the speaker's attempt at specifying the abstract emotion noun further, post-modification involves more linguistic material but, in turn, attributes less permanent meanings.

(17) the reality of a mother's **love** (AR17)
(18) parents' **hopes and dreams** (YR20, Story Nut)
(19) there is also sisterly **love** (GR04)
(20) an equal measure of brotherly **love and hatred** (GR16)
(21) the enduring **love** of a mother (GR20)
(22) her **desire** for **love** from her father (AR05)
(23) conflicting **emotions** of a family transplanted in culture (AR20)

Reading and discussing the novels as proof of "the universal emotions of *the* human condition" (AR03, my emphasis), the reviewers equally employ the above-described noun patterns to define the affective experiences of both the characters (24–25) and the authors (26–27) as "ordinary" (YR03, diana in color, 05/01/2018) or "everyday" (YR03, BookNympho). Arguably, the new Nigerian novel invites what the African-American BookTuber Marines (YR03, mynameismarines, 20/09/2016) calls "that #MeToo feeling", fostering a sense of sameness among locally and ethnically diverse readers via middle-class emotion ideologies.

(24) their **love** is beautiful (GR03)
(25) Akin's limitless **love and patience** (GR02)
(26) the author's **feelings** (GR08)
(27) Emezi's **struggle** for self-creation (GR10)

The reviewers' prevailing linguistic practice of expressing emotion *through* the characters and authors of the novels also applies to adjective patterns. Although adjective patterns tend to define authorial affect (28–29) or specify triggers (30–31), the utterances in (32–34) emphasise that emotion adjectives also function to construct character-emoters, both in specific (32–33) and metonymic terms (34).

> (28) I am so **sad** (AR04)
> (29) I was **touched**, [...] **horrified**, and filled with **joy** (GR02)
> (30) a **fun, sad, twisted** little novel (AR07)
> (31) really **touching** and interesting story (AR02)
> (32) a **loving** band of brothers (GR16)
> (33) a [...] **confident** and **emotional** woman (AR03)
> (34) a **complex** portrait of a **struggling** nation (GR04)

Whereas the verbal act of attributing emotional experiences to others remains covert in the above-quoted examples (32–34), the reviewers equally employ emotion adjectives to realise two emoters and thereby disclose more clearly the identification practices at work. As the utterances in (35–38) highlight, they combine emotion adjectives with prepositional phrases to stress that their emotional responses correspond to the experiences of the characters and authors and thus affirm their empathic capacity. Realising two imagined emoters, example (38) ascribes this capacity to fellow readers, implying the speaker's assumption that other members of the reading communities apply similar criteria of affective evaluation.

> (35) I was **sad** for Chibundu (GR17)
> (36) I felt so desperately **sad** for Kambili and her brother (AR05)
> (37) I felt **disappointed** for the hawker (AR18)
> (38) you can't help but feel **happy** for her (GR05)

As the communication model of reviews and the communities' middlebrow pattern of literacy indicate, expressions that specify both emoter and trigger predominate in the emotion talk of my reviewers. Mostly realised by emotion verbs (see below), triggers are also specified via emotion nouns and adjectives. Accordingly, noun patterns that define emoters via adjectives, pronouns or genitive nouns, as in (17–20) and (24–27), are often complemented with a prepositional phrase to direct the emotion at a specific target. Other than the above-quoted examples, the utterances in (39–41) do not construct the characters or authors as emoters but frame them as the occasion for the reviewer's emotional expression. While nominal patterns of directed affect corroborate the novels' function to evoke the speaker's emotion, one also finds statements that attribute the emotion-bearing effects of reading to other community members (42) or offer reasons for the perceived emotional constitution of the characters (43–46).

> (39) my **love** for books (YR03, ThroughEllesEyes)
> (40) my **feelings** about this novel (GR03)

(41) my enjoyment of the story (AR08)
(42) your love for African literature (YR02, CHICA)
(43) her feelings for other women (AR17)
(44) their hopes of a reunion between their emotionally estranged parents (GR11)
(45) a young married couple's struggle with infertility (GR02)
(46) her individual struggle with identity (GR10)

Furthermore, the reviewers combine the prepositions following emotion nouns with -ing- and wh-clauses (47–48) or finite (49–50) and non-finite clauses (51) to prove their affective competence of locating, relating to and sympathising with the causes of or reasons for the emotions of others.

(47) the hope of having kids (GR02)
(48) his struggle with what he was taught about God (AR13)
(49) the hope that Kings would find love and honesty (AR14)
(50) you may feel sadness when you read of the Nigerian embassy (GR08)
(51) their struggle to be heard, recognized and loved (AR05)

Applying the terminology of the German linguist Hans-Jörg Schmid (2018), all emotion nouns in (39–51) can be classified as "shell nouns". As he elucidates, shell nouns "open up an inherent semantic gap that must be filled by information from the linguistic context" (111); filled by the successive prepositional phrases or non-finite and finite clauses, these nouns "include, by virtue of their characterizing and encapsulating function, a noticeable symbolic potential" (112). The utterances in (43–51), to put it differently, provide fellow readers with both a key to interpret the characters and the possibility to identify with and adopt the suggested reception pattern. That the interpretation keys encapsulated in shell nouns are limited to emotional responses is substantiated by adjectival realisations of directed affect. Notably, these adjective patterns often conceal the emoter behind a non-referential *it*- or *this*-subject, shifting attention to the trigger and constructing the affective expression that is caused by it as commonly understood, just as the recurring metaphors employed to characterise its effect (57–58). Apart from *book* (52–53), the head nouns that follow the selected emotion adjectives most frequently are *characters*, *read* and *story* (54–56), reinforcing the observation that the novels or their characters and authors function as the prime stimuli of expressing an emotion. Furthermore, employing the adjectives in examples (52–58) in attributive position, reviewers restrict the semantic scope of the triggers to the selected emotion.

(52) this was a lovely book (GR11)
(53) what a lovely book (GR01)
(54) fully imagined and heartfelt characters (GR20)
(55) this is such an emotional read (GR02)
(56) it's a very touching story (YR04, Siyanda Mohutsiwa, 28/06/2013)
(57) I've undergone such a long and emotional journey (GR17)
(58) it is absolutely an emotional rollercoaster (GR02)

The second large group of adjective patterns that realise both emoter and trigger combine emotion adjectives with prepositional phrases (59–60), finite clauses (61–63) or *to*-infinitives (64). In contrast to the utterances in (52–58), these patterns relate in more detail why a specific novel or character triggers an emotion but otherwise resemble the above-quoted examples in serving the performance of intimacy with and attachment to others.

(59) that made me feel deeply emotional about the characters (AR02)
(60) there's something hopeful about watching her do this in a way that felt triumphant (YR10, ONYX Pages)
(61) he doesn't want to make her sad because of what he had been through (GR13)
(62) I'm also hopeful because I believe deeply in the ability of human beings to make and remake themselves for the better (AR03)
(63) it is even more heart-wrenching when you realize the plot is easily the story of so many women (GR20)
(64) it is [...] heart-warming to see a young girl discover that there are other lives (GR05)

Owing to the reviewers' dominant verbal style of affect, emotion verbs in general, and *love*, *feel* and *enjoy* in particular, realise the large majority of directed affect patterns. In notable contrast to the adjective patterns quoted above, the reviewers' verbal patterns, exemplified in (65–70), use *I* as a subject to affirm that they have acquired the kind of emotional sophistication that qualifies for the expressions of non-authorial affect (70).[18]

(65) I absolutely love it (YR05, Lauren and the Books, 27/02/2018)
(66) I love African literature (YR02, CHICA)
(67) I felt a unique connection to her (AR19)
(68) I really enjoy this author's storytelling and writing style (AR03)
(69) I thoroughly enjoyed her descriptions of both the US and Nigeria (AR03)
(70) a modern classic you will love (AR04)

Next to these rather straightforward emoter–emotion–trigger constructions, emotion verbs appear in a range of other patterns, equally determining the trigger via prepositional phrases (71–73), -*ing*- or *wh*-clauses (74–75) or a combination of both (76–77).

(71) I liked Korede and really felt for her (AR07)
(72) you will feel for both husband and wife (AR02)

---

18 Apart from these combinations with *I*-subjects, the linking verb *feel* frequently co-occurs with what the linguist Günter Rohdenburg describes as semantically "unusual subjects" – that is, the occurrence of objects in subject position (Ahrens et al., 1995, 137; König and Gast, 2018, 137). In effect, statements such as the following credit the novels with the capacity to feel: "the second half of the novel feels rushed" (GR17); "the structure of the novel could feel a little repetitive" (GR18); "the conclusion of the novel feel[s] artificial" (AR19).

(73) I wanted to cry for this boy deprived of a childhood (AR01)
(74) I enjoyed diving into Igbo culture (GR15)
(75) I did not enjoy what I considered to be a predictable, sappy, abrupt ending (AR03)
(76) I struggled with what felt like gender normativity (GR20)
(77) I want to care about what I read (GR09)

A third verb pattern splits the trigger in two parts or realises two triggers. In examples (78–83), the emotion verb is followed by two nouns that are divided by a preposition, offering an explanation of why a novel (78–79), a character (80–81) or an author (82–83) may function as a trigger. As Bednarek (2008, 80) notes, here, "the emotion is directed at someone" or something "because of something". Presenting variations of (47–51), these utterances ascribe shell-noun function to the novels, characters and authors that are hence recommended or advertised as promising occasions to voice emotions and thereby strengthen community membership.

(78) I loved this book for the insight it gave me (AR03)
(79) I really loved this novel for the way it weaves Igbo and Yoruba culture throughout the characters, setting and plot (AR16)
(80) I loved Olanna for her complexity (GR04)
(81) I admire Jaja for having the courage to stand up to his father (AR05)
(82) people could [...] admire Emezi for her inventive, edgy story (GR10)
(83) Emezi has surprised me with this wonderful debut novel (GR10)

Like the verb patterns that create two triggers by means of prepositions, finite clauses occasionally split the trigger, with the first trigger realising a non-referential *it*-object that relates to the noun phrase succeeding prepositions such as *because* (84), *that* (85) or *when* (86), although *how* appears most frequently (87). Again, the split of the trigger functions to tout the novels, characters and authors as a prompt to both define and refine the affective norms of the online literary communities.

(84) I enjoyed it because it's a perfect book (GR09)
(85) I love it that the characters are so well etched (GR03)
(86) I love it when a writer takes me out of my world (AR05)
(87) I really enjoyed it how this novel taught me about race (AR03)

The reviewers' complex grammar of affect notably contradicts the repetitive functions it serves. Shifting between the conceptualisation of emotions as private and public states, the realisation of authorial and non-authorial affect or the desire to create distinction from and attachment to others, the reviewers' emotional language use consists of endlessly repeated (and repeatable) verbal acts that strengthen the middle-class emotional structure of the digital literary sphere. Predominantly engaging the novels' readers, characters and authors, the lexico-grammatical patterns show that "belonging online" (Ehret et al., 2018, 160) presupposes and perpetuates the linguistic performance of bourgeois emotion ideologies.

Emotional Language across Corpora: The Mechanisms of a Closed Literary System

The keyness of character and author names as well as their pronounced position among the reviewers' emotional triggers underline the extent to which the new Nigerian novel and its marketing as autobiographical fiction influence the communities' construction and enactment of feeling rules. Based on my definition of online reviews as intertexts that, to a notable degree, register the digital practices of producing and distributing the novels, the final section turns to a range of other self-construed corpora of e-books and author videos, newspaper and publisher blurbs to confirm that keyword analysis exceeds the investigation of online reviews. In addition, the comparison of emotion discourses across various corpora allows for a coherent perspective on the various agents who are present on and/or use Amazon, Goodreads and YouTube and thus serves to disclose how the reviewers' affective norms emerge from the macro- and "micropolitics of all encounters" (Turner and Stets, 2005, 297) in the digital literary sphere.[19]

That literature wields a decisive influence over the definition and mediation of feeling rules has been suggested by a range of emotion researchers across the disciplines (Hogan, 2018; Houen, 2020; Moruzi et al., 2018; Pritzker et al., 2020; Turner and Stets, 2005).[20] Drawing on Ernst Bloch's comparison of literature with a laboratory, Gohrisch's (2011, 49; 2005, 19) approach to the potentially instructive functions of literary texts is particularly helpful to conceptualise the relationship between fiction and its (implied) readers; accordingly, "fiction experiments with feeling rules and emotional dispositions to examine their implications by testing them under extreme conditions. This enables a critical detachment that allows literature to affirm and question them at the same time."[21] Along similar lines, Stedman (2002, 2) employs Ronald de Sousa's notion of "paradigm scenarios"[22] to probe the communi-

---

19 Gohrisch (2005) and Stedman (2002, 16) base their examinations of nineteenth-century emotion discourses on "an enormous array of texts in which different concepts from various genres interpenetrate one another" to take account of the fact that literary texts, including the feeling rules encoded in them, do not appear out of the blue but arise from larger networks of power. As my computerised approach to other agents of the digital literary economy elucidates, a similar observation applies to the online reviews of the new Nigerian novel.

20 Not all of these studies are marked by rather simplistic conceptions of fiction as "deal[ing] with the *description* of human characters, [...] their emotions and emotional reactions" (Bednarek, 2008, 33, my emphasis).

21 Gohrisch (2011, 54) shows how Hardy's *The Mayor of Casterbridge* "simultaneously affirms and abrogates the dominant prescriptions for the middle-class emotional habitus".

22 De Sousa's notion exceeds social constructionist approaches to emotion by stressing the performative aspect of emotional behaviour. According to Bednarek's (2008, 6) typology, the term falls into the category of dramaturgical

cation circuits between fiction and the cultural practices of its consumption; "[a]s readers", she illustrates, "one can learn from these paradigm scenarios which provide examples of emotional behaviour and experience." Significantly, she highlights the constitutive function of literature, arguing that it not only "demonstrate[s] 'feeling rules' explicitly" but moreover "allow[s] the invention of new or different emotion concepts which can later even transcend their textual origin and move out into 'reality'" (2–3, 2).

Building on these literary studies assumptions about the socially and culturally formative effects of fictional texts, the subsequent corpus-linguistic exploration of five selected novels potentially saves the reviewers from reproaches of simply projecting their affective responses onto and thereby turning postcolonial "high" literature into "a *pocket* within commodity culture" (Frow, 1995, 86, original emphasis). Admittedly, the relation between the structures of narration and reception may not always be as straightforward as implied here. In view of the simultaneity of production and consumption in the digital literary sphere, though, one may well conclude that the novels exert an immediate influence over the affective norms of the reviewers – and vice versa. My computational approach to the novels is not exhaustive because it primarily seeks to elucidate how digital methods establish integrated vantage points on the digital literary economy and its self-enforcing effects. Striving to determine whether specific genre patterns foster the use of specific emotion terms by the reviewers, I focus on a selection of five novels in Amazon's Kindle format. While all of them follow the conventions of the *Bildungsroman*, they integrate a handful of features associated with other genres. In addition to Abani's child soldier narrative *Song for Night* (SN01), Adebayo's "modern [...] soap opera romance love story" (YR02, Shellee Stories, 26/11/2017) *Stay With Me* (SN02) and Adichie's migration novel *Americanah* (SN03), I consider Obioma's *The Fishermen* (SN04) and Okparanta's *Under the Udala Trees* (SN05). Representing the coming of age of their protagonists from male and queer viewpoints, respectively, the choice of the latter two novels allows me to gauge the degree to which the gender identities of the authors and/or characters influence the novels' emotional register and their readers' affective responses.[23]

The comparison between the novels and the BNC yields a number of emotion terms that comply with the affective lexicon of the reviewers, suggesting that the literary texts draft the kind of paradigm scenarios that invite readers to

---

emotion theories that "see human behaviour as a scripted on-stage performance". Correspondingly, Stedman (2002, 2) compares the literary text with a stage that allows for the dramatisation and enactment of emotions.

23 The equation of authors and characters corresponds to the online reviewers' repeatedly stated impression that "[i]t's hard to tell where the narrator's voice ends and the writer's begins" (GR09). See Chapter 2 for my discussion of the middlebrow "marketing emphasis on writers' individual biographies and unique expressive lives" (Brouillette and Coleman, 2020, 584) and its considerable facilitation by digital communication technologies.

develop and underline their feeling rules. Significantly, the key emotion terms employed in the five novels do not substantially add to the lexical items that are used most often by the communities of reviewers. With the past tense of the verb *feel* (449 hits) coming in first place, the novels cover all of the primary emotions that cause the reviewers to comprehend their affective reading patterns in universal terms, such as *love* (246), *fear* (113) and *anger* (56), *sadness* (32) and *happiness* (25).[24] The only noteworthy additions to the reviewers' emotional vocabulary are the verbs *smile* (117 hits) and *laugh* (73). A second comparison of the novels with the three review corpora reveals further overlaps between the emotion terms used in the novels and the responses, as only seven of the items listed in Table 5.2 appear among the keywords.[25] This observation also encompasses the therapeutic register so characteristic of the reviews. Like the online reviewers, the characters feel "a conflicted longing" (SN03, 253), experience "inner turmoil" (SN05, 189), fight an "internal battle" (SN04, 98) or worry about their "emotional well-being" (SN03, 303).

Moreover, a closer look at the most frequent emotion terms used in the individual texts substantiates that differences concerning the novels' generic structures or the protagonists' gender identities have little influence on the respective profiles. Apart from the realisations of *love* and *feeling*, which reach top positions and therefore determine the plot designs and character constructions of all selected novels, the overall prevalence of the emotion adjectives *alone* (143 hits) and *lost* (141) indicates that the characters share a range of other traits that point beyond generic boundaries. The child soldier in Abani's fictional biography is as *lost* as the struggling middle-class couple in Adebayo's romance and as *alone* as Ijeoma, the heroine of Okparanta's coming-of-age tale who forges a lesbian identity in the civil war's aftermath. A further comparison of the top emotion terms employed in the individual novels and the respective sub-corpora of reviews (Figure 5.4, Table 5.4) shows that minor generic deviations do not necessarily generate different responses. The only novel that interrupts the reviewers' preference for *love* and *feeling* is Abani's narrative, which is credited with having a *haunting* (15 hits) or *harrowing* (13) effect. In view of the homogeneous profiles of the novels, which also emerge from the direct comparison between the frequency of the ten selected emotion terms (Figure 5.5, Table 5.5), one can well understand the frustration of YouTube reviewer Yeside (YR20, Yeside DS, 26/09/2018), who, after having failed to properly match a number of quotes with three of the novels in her BookTube challenge, asks: "Why did I choose all these books that are quite similar?"

---

24 The numbers in brackets refer to the mentioned items only. See Tables 5.5 to 5.7 for the amount of all realisations of the ten selected emotion terms.

25 Verifying the similarities between the novels' and the reviews' emotional language, the keyness rates of the seven terms and their different realisations mostly rank below the three-digit line: *cried* (146.26), *cry* (66.0) and *cries* (31.79), *alone* (95.12), *wished* (92.35), *afraid* (51.47), *touch* (51.07), *careful* (49.34) and *carefully* (31.36), *feared* (46.87).

The Verbal Performance of Affect

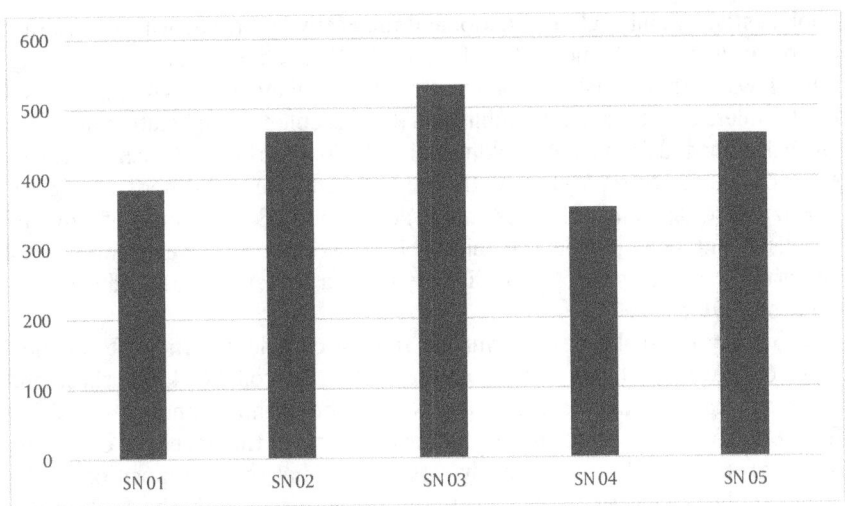

Figure 5.5 Frequency of Emotion Terms across Selected Novels

A comparable conclusion can be drawn from the authors' language use. The researcher with an interest in studying performances of authorship in the World Wide Web would do well to concentrate on YouTube. In contrast to social media platforms such as Facebook and Twitter, or the authors' official websites, YouTube videos have a couple of benefits. Providing the largest amount of coherent text and thus lending themselves to corpus-linguistic procedures,[26] the author videos uploaded on YouTube shine a particularly bright light on the institutional agents who invest in the novels' online marketing. Even though some of the 16 novelists, such as Emezi or Onuzo, run their own channels, most of them appear in the videos of literary and other institutions. The following case study builds on 284 videos featuring the authors of the selected novels that were available at the time of constructing the corpus in September 2019,[27] while the bibliography details the institutions ensuring that Nigerian diasporic writers are "all over YouTube at the moment" (YR04, Kitty G, 23/07/2016). Next to the recordings of major international literary festivals (Ake Arts and

---

26 In notable contrast to the BookTube reviews, the YouTube videos that feature the new Nigerian novelists require little preparation, as most channels provide edited sub-titles, rendering them a worthwhile subject of investigation for those who seek to study the "changes in authorial performance made possible by digital media technology" (Murray, 2018, 26).

27 The distribution of the videos across the authors is as follows: Abani (21 videos, YA01), Adebayo (14, YA02), Adichie (215, YA03), Obioma (18, YA04), Okparanta (16, YA05). In order to avoid any possible bias, I did not exclude videos that focus on more novels by the same author or mention the selected novels only in passing. A comprehensive list of the author videos can be found in the bibliography; the system of citation equals that of the YouTube reviews (see above).

Book Festival, Edinburgh International Book Festival, Hay Festival) and literary award ceremonies (Women's Prize for Fiction, Wellcome Book Prize), one finds interviews with television broadcasters (BBC, Channel 4, FRANCE 24) and book trailers of conglomerate publishers (HarperCollins's 4th Estate, Hachette's Little, Brown and Company).[28] Additionally, the juxtaposition of channels run by *Marie Claire* and *Stylist Magazine* with video content offered by more prestigious magazines (*Granta Magazine*, *The Atlantic*) or UK and US universities affirms the novelists' entanglement in the middlebrow oscillation between commercial and artistic practices that "keeps literary value a contested and fluid concept" (Driscoll, 2014, 151).[29]

Providing middlebrow performance spaces, complete with "soft couches, vases of flowers and mugs on the coffee table" (Driscoll, 2014, 38), these and other institutional agents arguably assist in the authors' smooth transition from one communal structure to the next. In view of the novelists' education in the group workshop, it is hardly astonishing that the juxtaposition of the author videos with the BNC shows a familiar image, with the realisations of *love* and *feeling* occupying top positions and, at least in the first case, exceeding the keyness rate in the corpus of selected novels (1454.21 vs. 124.12). The occurrence of terms denoting primary emotions among the keywords, including *happy* (262 hits) and *angry* (115) or *fear* (76) and *sadness* (23), in turn, implies that the novels and the ways in which their authors speak about them equally function to reinforce middle-class claims to universality. Comparing the corpora of novels and author videos in relation to the frequency with which the terms listed in Table 5.2 appear, moreover, one sees that the authors not only use the same therapeutic language as the reviewers – Adichie and her peers publicly discuss the "psychological need of people" (YA03, Casa África, 20/10/2017), relate that they "suffer from depression" (YA03, The Women's Center) or experience "internal tension" (YA04, TVC News Nigeria) and frequently emphasise that they "feel challenged" (YA03, neafoundation) and "very confused" (YA05, The Center for Fiction, 10/05/2017) – but also use more of the emotion terms and their realisations when discussing as opposed to writing the novels.[30] Irrespective of this observation, Figure 5.6 (Table 5.6)

---

28 Discussing "born-digital marketing innovations", Murray (2018, 63) remarks that "[i]t is no coincidence that book trailers emerged around 2006, at precisely the point when YouTube exploded into popular consciousness". Reinforcing the new Nigerian novel's tendency towards genre fiction, the book trailer represents a key device for marketing children's books and YA novels.

29 As Driscoll (2014, 37) notes in view of the Windham Campbell Prizes, first awarded by Yale University in 2013, "the middlebrow makes use of academia's prestige and authority, but reframes this in a context of accessible, recreational cultural consumption".

30 Normalising the respective raw hits of the terms in Table 5.2, the direct comparison between the review corpora and the corpora of novels and author videos shows that the reviewers (1,542.30) hold a narrow lead over the authors (949.28) and their novels (787.18).

The Verbal Performance of Affect

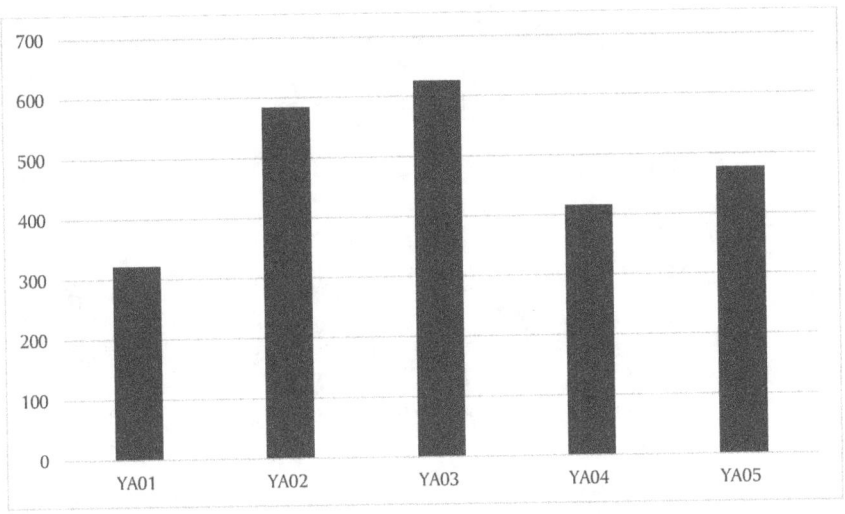

Figure 5.6 Frequency of Emotion Terms across Corpus of Author Videos

shows that the behaviour of the selected emotion terms across the author videos complies with the occurrences across their novels.

Pinpointing a couple of minor deviations, Figure 5.7 (Table 5.7) discloses that authors prioritise realisations of *love, feeling* and *hope*, whereas their novels exhibit a preference for realisations of *touch* and *cry*. If compared with the normalised hits of the ten terms across the corpora of reviews (Figure 5.3, Table 5.3), however, the pattern of behaviour looks similar, although reviewers use most of the terms, such as *love*, altogether more frequently. The use of *feeling* by the authors (195.76) and in the novels (169.48), by contrast, almost parallels the frequency in the reviews, with a norm ranging between 231.40 and 279.27. A comparison with the reviews further indicates that *enjoyment* dominates the experiences of readers, whereas the characters exhibit a stronger penchant for *crying*. Apart from these differences, the comparative analysis of the two corpora with the reviews shows that the novels, as well as their authors' promotional practices, play a crucial role in triggering emotional responses among their readers and that the readers, in turn, play a crucial role in defining the affective norms of the novels and their authors' promotional practices.

I suggest that the strikingly homogeneous sets of feeling rules that emerge from my analysis are ascribable to the mechanisms of the digital literary economy or, more precisely, the creation of closed socio-technical assemblages by the digital companies. Produced, distributed and consumed within these "self-reinforcing and confirmatory" structures, the new Nigerian novel both anticipates and affirms the bourgeois emotion ideologies of an audience that moves "along consumption paths they have already trod" (Murray, 2018, 60). Co-op contracts with publishers and personalised recommendations not only

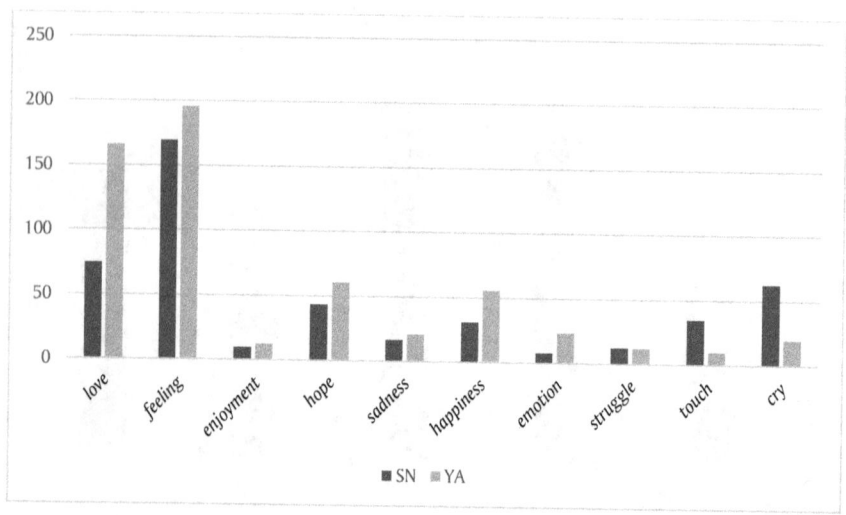

Figure 5.7 Selected Novels vs. Corpus of Author Videos

"give[] the people what they want" (Marcus, 2005, 200) but define what and how readers read and how authors and publishers have to react, removing or at least regulating those agents who potentially disrupt the supremacy of bourgeois literary culture. This finding not only applies to independent publishing houses and bookshops but also encompasses professional reviewers whose influence is reduced to snippets, hardly leaving enough room to express anything but (affective) recommendations.[31]

Correspondingly, my corpus-linguistic analysis of 164 newspaper and 13 publisher blurbs, collected from Amazon and Goodreads for the five selected novels until 30 September 2019, yields a by now familiar profile.[32] The

---

31 Philippa K. Chong's recent study *Inside the Critics' Circle: Book Reviewing in Uncertain Times* (2020) substantiates this argument. Evaluating her "in-depth interviews with forty fiction reviewers" for US-based newspapers and magazines, she finds that amateur online reviewing has turned professional reviewing into a "freelance or single-assignment" occupation (12, 13). Given that most reviewers "work as freelance journalists, creative writing teachers, academics, and – of course – authors", it does not surprise that they tend to "play nice" (13, 68). This tendency is confirmed by the new Nigerian novelists, who discuss the publications of their peers in broadsheet newspapers. The snippets of Evans's review of *Americanah* in *The Times* and Habila's response to *The Fishermen* in *The Guardian*, as featured on the novels' Amazon and Goodreads pages, are included in my corpus of newspaper and publisher blurbs.

32 The distribution across the novels is as follows: SN01 (7 NB, 2 PB), SN02 (21, 2), SN03 (22, 4), SN04 (65, 3), SN05 (49, 2). Detailing which institutions participate in the promotion of the new Nigerian novel, references indicate the particular newspaper or publisher.

comparison of the corpus with the BNC garners a range of key emotion terms that, with the exception of *love* (62 times), shows a strong tendency to occur as adjectives, such as *heartbreaking* (10), *hopeful* (5) or *compassionate* (4). Aside from a few compounds, such as *big-hearted* (3 hits) and *grief-stricken* (3), the emotional lexicon of the professional reviewers mostly complies with the lexical choices of their amateur competitors, including the therapeutic language that is used to praise the authors for their "psychological observations" and emphasise the characters' "familial pressure" (NB02, *Financial Times*) or "heart-tearing struggle for belonging in a fractured world" (NB03, *O, The Oprah Magazine*) and remind the reader that the new Nigerian novel "challenges us to think [...] from all perspectives" (NB02, *Elle*). Significantly, the blurbs use the emotion terms listed in Table 5.2 altogether most frequently (2,192.46), exceeding the norm of all other corpora discussed here. Resulting from the small size of the corpus, this finding may equally be ascribable to the regulating practices of Amazon and Goodreads that also determine the blurbs' dominant pattern of expressing affect.

The POS distribution of the ten most frequent emotion terms in the blurbs discloses a strong preference for emotion nouns (81) and adjectives (34), while the authors and novels' affect style resembles that of the amateur reviewers. In the novels, the top ten terms are employed as verbs (1,193) more than twice as often as nouns (466), while the adjectival and adverbial use of the terms is negligible (if one disregards *alone* and *lost*). A similar distribution characterises the author videos in which verbs (1,710) precede the nominal (584) and adjectival uses (405) of the respective top ten emotion words.[33]

The differences in POS distribution are significant because they signify varying effects on the reviewers' definition and verbal enactment of feeling rules. For although amateur reviewing on social media sites increasingly "[threatens] the relevance and reach of newspaper reviewers" (Driscoll, 2014, 102), Amazon and Goodreads users occasionally point to the blurbs presented on the platforms or printed on the book covers, highlighting that professional reviewers continue to wield affective authority.[34] This finding is reinforced by the blurbs' prevalent use of patterns with emotion nouns that almost always hide the emoter, as in examples (88–90), and recommend the novels on the basis of their "dissection of the universal human experience" (NB03, *The New York Times Book Review*) or their "enormous universal appeal" (PB04, Cassava Republic).

---

33 The words are (in descending order): *love, lost, heart, heartbreaking, hope, impressive, felt, grief, hopeful, affecting* (blurbs); *love, feel, felt, happy, hope, care, laughter, loved, lovely, feeling* (authors); *felt, love, feel, laughed, alone, lost, smile, heart, fear, smiled* (novels).

34 For instance, Goodreads reviewer Ene (GR16) notes that "[i]f you don't believe me, read *The New York Times* review of the book [...] and you will see that *The Fishermen* is a masterpiece of world literature", whereas her fellow community member Mary (GR16) "thought the review in *The Guardian* by Helon Habila was spot on".

(88) a richly told story of love and expectation (PB03, 4th Estate)
(89) a universally salient and timely story of love (NB05, *The Rumpus*)
(90) a layered story of love, sacrifice and hope (NB02, Essence.com)

The pronouns or genitive pronouns preceding the emotion nouns almost exclusively realise non-authorial affect, attributing the emotion either to the characters, such as "their love" (PB05, Houghton Mifflin Harcourt), "their passion" (PB03, Alfred A. Knopf) or "Ijeoma's first love" (NB05, Cleveland.com), or to the readers of the novels, as in the novel "will enrich your heart" (PB05, Granta) or "will grow your sensitivity" (NB02, *Elle*). In marked contrast to the nominal affect patterns of the amateur reviewers, the pre-modifiers never refer to the speaker. The only exception is provided by reviewers who also work as authors, such as Sarah Weinman (NB05, *Publishers Lunch*), who writes that "my heart broke over and over while reading this [...] novel". This finding complies with the noun patterns that are employed by the novelists. Whereas the statements by Adebayo (91) and Adichie (92), which read like exact copies of the phrases taken from their novels in (93) and (94), conceal the emoter, the example in (95) illustrates that authors also use noun patterns to construct (themselves as) the same unspecified *human* who is so frequently evoked by the reviewers, as exemplified in (8–10).

(91) there are things even love cannot do (YA02, Politics and Prose, 28/08/2018)
(92) love is an act of giving (YA03, WellesleyCollege)
(93) even love bends, cracks, comes close to breaking and sometimes does break (SN02, 21)
(94) love was a kind of grief (SN03, 583)
(95) human emotion is complex (YA03, West End Videos)

Especially if compared with the newspaper and publisher blurbs, however, the noun patterns used in the novels and by their authors mostly specify an emoter, following the same grammar rules that the reviewers adhere to. The fact that emotion nouns are frequently preceded by first-person pronouns, as in examples (96–97), results from the novels' preference for first-person narrators, who, except for *Americanah*'s third-person narrator (98), also dominate the five selected novels. First-person narrators, in particular, invite uninhibited identification as their speaking position corresponds to that of the reviewer, who, instead of transposing his or her feelings, rather seeks to align them with the emotional condition of the narrators. Apart from providing readers with the opportunity to practise empathy, the use of genitive pronouns in examples (99–100) emphasises that the narrators and/or characters of the novels equally support the reviewers' negotiation of affective norms in another respect. Proving their sympathy with other characters, they legitimise the verbal practice of ascribing emotion to others.

(96) my feelings are irrational (SN01, 47)
(97) my heart began to race (SN05, 260)

(98) their love was as sparkling as always (SN03, 293)
(99) mother's fear was piqued to curious levels (SN04, 98)
(100) mother's cries had been heard day in and day out (SN05, 228)

The nominal affect patterns in the corpus of author videos underline that the novelists' online presence encourages autobiographical reading modes. Abani, Adichie or Okparanta either attribute an emotion to themselves, as in (101–02), or to their characters (103), providing an affective interpretation of their behaviour. The pronoun *our* in the utterances (104–05) shows that they also venture beyond the story world and ascribe emotion to an unspecified group. Both the use of pronouns and genitive nouns, as in "people's feelings" (YA03, Oswaldo Armendariz) or "people's pain" (YA01, University of Central Florida), are indicative of their emotional or therapeutic competency, which is employed to imagine affective communities beyond the boundaries of the writing workshop.

(101) my love for literature (YA05, The Center for Fiction, 10/05/2017)
(102) my feeling about feminism (YA03, MO nieuwssite)
(103) her desire for another girl (YA05, Barnard Center for Research on Women)
(104) our anxieties about identity (YA03, Kwani Trust, 10/03/2014)
(105) our fears to grow (YA01, Univ. of California, Riverside)

A look at the adjective patterns reinforces that the novels and the blurbs construct feeling rules in different ways. Like Victorian advice texts, "which by definition have to be unambiguous" (Gohrisch, 2011, 45), they use emotion adjectives to modify metonymic triggers – that is, the novels. The attributive position of the adjectives in examples (106–08) reduces the scope of meaning of the *story* or the *book* to an emotion that is, however, not coupled with a prepositional clause and therefore leaves little room for interrogation. The static effect of their affect patterns complies with the finding that blurbs hardly ever use verbs to express an emotion.[35] By contrast, the novelists' adjectival use of emotion terms suggests more dynamic conceptions of emotion. Realising two emoters, the adjective patterns in examples (109–11) point to the necessity to sympathise with others.

(106) a unique and devastatingly hopeful story (NB05, Mia Couto)
(107) a powerfully magnetic and heartbreaking book (NB02, *The New York Times*)
(108) a heartbreaking elegy to Nigeria's lost promise (NB04, Habila, *The Guardian*)

---

35 The only exceptions are provided by the author-reviewer Claire Cameron (NB04), who praises Obioma's debut for reminding her "why I love reading: to be shown what it might be like inside another culture; to slip between someone else's ears; to feel a life that I won't get to live", or her colleague Jami Attenberg (NB05), who admits that she "wept through the final pages of this beautifully written, extremely necessary book" by Okparanta.

(109) I feel sad for a lot of South Africans (YA03, crushing corporate)
(110) I was afraid for him (SN04, 94)
(111) Ifemelu felt frightened for her (SN03, 92)

Moreover, emotion adjectives realising emoter and trigger, mostly via prepositional phrases (112) or finite and non-finite clauses (113–15), explain the cause of a character's emotion and thereby potentially invite reflection and discussion.

(112) I'm just worried about your health, your mental health (SN02, 68)
(113) she was angry [...] that he would drop her off and go home to his other life (SN03, 548)
(114) I was not afraid because I was not alone (SN02, 282)
(115) I leave the armored vehicles [...], afraid to jump into their dark bellies (SN01, 46)

As Gohrisch (2011, 45) notes in view of her corpus of fictional and non-fictional texts, nineteenth-century realist novels by the Brontës, Eliot or Hardy function as laboratories because they allow for a critical rehearsal of emotion ideologies; in contrast to advice texts, "fiction can simultaneously propound the rules of normative feelings, inquire into their feasibility and suggest alternatives". Unlike these Victorian classics, and in spite of their dominant verbal affect style, the new Nigerian novel does not challenge but, like Victorian conduct books, reproduces affective norms. Next to subject–verb–object constructions – "I love the diversity of the world" (YA03, SVT) or "I felt a sharp, unexpected pain" (SN05, 184) – the novelists and characters at times *feel* and *love* in more intricate patterns, using emotion verbs with *ing*-clauses (116), prepositions (117–18) and non-finite (119) or finite clauses (120).

(116) I love writing (YA03, WilliamsCollege)
(117) I care about these subjects (YA02, Ake Arts & Book Festival, 18/04/2018)
(118) I still cared about the pain in his eyes (SN02, 208)
(119) she longed to kiss him (SN03, 550)
(120) I hope that there will be a window for the reader to imagine (YA04, City of Des Moines – DMTV)

And yet, the characters of the new Nigerian novel hardly invite the kind of emotional ambiguity that characterises their nineteenth-century British counterparts on lexical, lexico-grammatical and semantic levels. What is more, their disappointingly static negotiation of feeling rules is reinforced by the novelists' paratextual comments, which, arguably, deprive the novels of any affective ambivalence.

CHAPTER 6

Coda: Revisiting the Digital Affect

I close this book by revisiting its conceptual core. What is the significance of the digital affect? Accounting for the fact that postcolonial literatures and cultures increasingly proliferate online, the digital affect constitutes a most valuable tool to investigate the world-literary system in the Internet era. Building on a specific manifestation of this system – that is, the new Nigerian novel – the notion serves to study how the digital literary economy transforms the socio-economic and emotional relations of its social and institutional agents. Enabling productive shifts between economic macro-, social meso- and linguistic micro-levels of analysis, the digital affect reveals that the socio-technical means of creating and preserving community in the World Wide Web resume and refashion nineteenth-century bourgeois emotion discourses and their underlying relations of ownership and labour. In turn, and since the digital affect fosters a balanced perspective on *"the abstraction of model building and the vividness of individual examples"* (Moretti, 2005, 1–2, original emphasis), the concept contributes to an understanding of the digital literary economy at large, its historical continuities and changes in general, and its promotion of a distinctly middlebrow literacy model and a remarkably closed but gendered bourgeois emotional structure in particular.

Combining the theoretical tenets and methodological measures of various established and emerging fields in the humanities, the digital affect operates as an innovative research tool that opens up new digital paths for analysing the postcolonial and the middlebrow as well as the history of emotions. In postcolonial studies, the concept shifts the focus to global and digitally networked literary cultures. Strengthening the field's historical materialist branch, the digital affect redefines the postcolonial text in socio-economic terms. More than a sign system, it delineates a communicative act and thus a genuinely social process that, in the contemporary milieu of literary transmission, is primarily structured by the diversity policies of the American creative writing workshop as well as by the socio-technical ecosystems and affective algorithms of a US-based new media economy. This redefinition challenges liberal humanist assumptions about the postcolonial reader, who, emerging as an agent with socio-economic interests, contributes to online literary discussion to construct an emotional middle-class identity.

In middlebrow studies, the digital affect heralds a medial, spatial and temporal extension. Specifying the field's approaches to the middlebrow's commercial, emotional and middle-class characteristics, the notion serves to analyse the digital literary economy and its cultural work on three interrelated levels. On the medial level, the digital affect shows that the middlebrow invigorates the systematic study of online reviews. On the spatial level, the concept illustrates that the middlebrow can be productively extended into post/colonial discourses to examine the power relations that structure contemporary cross-border reading formations and practices. On the temporal level, the digital affect highlights that the discipline's critical mode of inquiry can be taken beyond the early twentieth century to position these formations and practices within a larger bourgeois history of emotions.

In digital reception studies, the digital affect proposes how to resolve the practical, methodological and theoretical issues that have hitherto discouraged the comprehensive study of online reading behaviour. Comprising a reproducible method of collecting and evaluating online material, it ventures beyond descriptive approaches to the digital literary sphere and, taking sufficient account of the economic infrastructure of digital literary communities and its significance for the choice of software, exceeds the rehearsal of affective norms. Unlike commercial software applications, my corpus-linguistic methodology integrates the insights of socio-historical emotion research and, exposing the essentialising conceptions of emotion by many a researcher as strategies of bourgeois self-fashioning, envisions the online communities created by and surrounding the new Nigerian novel as recent expressions of a transhistorical middle-class emotional culture.

The application of the concept to a specific case study has produced a number of results on multiple levels. Providing the starting point for my construction of digital review corpora, the repetitive means of narrating the new Nigerian novel suggest that market conditions inscribe themselves into literary texts. This observation applies in particular to the digital milieu of literary transmission, where the chronology of producing, distributing and consuming literature is unhinged and the process of writing is potentially influenced by the algorithmically defined expectations of readers. Putting special emphasis on the novels' repetition and variation of the *Bildungsroman* genre, my literary analysis demonstrates that the texts anticipate their reception in affective online communities, adjusting their ethnically diversified but socially balanced members to the structures of the digital literary economy on the narrative level. More precisely, the new Nigerian novel combines bourgeois realist means of representation with two distinctly Nigerian motifs, the twin and Biafra, to simultaneously create and comply with the emotional needs of their transnational communities of readers.

My economic macro-level analysis of the digital literary sphere confirms that the techniques of narrating the new Nigerian novel are ascribable to the related practices of two key mediators: first, prestigious American universities and their creation of the writing workshop; second, US-based digital companies and their creation of affective online communities. The workshop's communal setting supports the new Nigerian novelists' transition into the digital environments of middlebrow literary production; teaching its participants how to perform an author function in the World Wide Web, the workshop defines the act of writing as an occasion for self-realisation and sociality that feeds backs into authorial online performances and ties in with the companies' marketing of a middlebrow consumption model. Reframing the social interaction with and emotional exchange about books on a hitherto unprecedented scale, Amazon and the like ensure their monopoly position in the digital literary economy by establishing relatively closed and personalised socio-technical systems that function to expand a middle-class affective pattern defining the labour relations and emotional expressions of the novels' online reviewers.

Generated on the basis of accumulated user data, algorithms do not simply govern online purchasing and reading behaviour. Accordingly, my analysis of the socio-economic meso-level of the three online reading formations queries one-dimensional conceptions of corporate power. As the recurring patterns in reader profiles or reading contexts, habits and motivations show, the reviewers benefit from their regular and ritualised contributions to the online discussion of the new Nigerian novel. Crucially, social media platforms define belonging and membership mostly in terms of class and gender. The reviewers' class ambitions manifest themselves in their peculiar mixture of the middlebrow amateur form and the Protestant work ethic, disclosing that the digital literary economy assigns thoroughly reproductive roles to the overwhelmingly female reviewers of my digital review corpora.

Apart from providing significant insights into the socio-economic infrastructure of online reading communities, the digital affect serves to trace the middle-class emotion ideologies of online reviewers on the linguistic micro-level. The use of AntConc facilitates both lexical and lexico-grammatical analyses of the reviews, revealing that the reviewers' affective vocabulary not only resumes but equally refashions nineteenth-century bourgeois emotion discourses in psychological terms. In addition, the syntactic analysis of the reviews' patterns of affect yields that, while framing emotions as public states to raise middle-class claims to universality, the reviewers predominantly express their emotions *through* the new Nigerian novel's characters and authors. A comparison of the reviews with the novels, the appearances of their authors on YouTube and newspaper and publisher blurbs, moreover, substantiates that the reviewers enhance the affective norms of a self-enforcing digital literary economy.

Unlike most middlebrow studies scholars, I do not wish to close this study on a celebratory or defending note, even if the previous pages leave no doubt that, considering its pervasive socio-economic power, middlebrow literary culture deserves to be investigated in its own right. Unlike many a self-proclaimed highbrow cultural commentator of the early twentieth century, I do not wish to end on an evaluative note either. Furthermore, and as a literary and cultural studies scholar, my task does not consist in providing suggestions (if there are any) of how to outwit the ubiquitous algorithms of Web 2.0 companies as a means of diversifying the global literary market. Rather, my task is to offer analytical tools that contribute to an understanding of current transformations in the book world. The Warwick Research Collective (2015, 6) seeks "to resituate the problem of 'world literature' [...] by pursuing the literary-cultural implications of the theory of combined and uneven development". Taking their endeavour into the age of the Internet, this book has found a solution in the concept of the digital affect, which, I hope, inspires further research on a constantly changing digital literary economy and its effects on the postcolonial text and its authors and audiences.

Appendix

Table 2.1 New Nigerian Novelists: Creative Writing

	Training	Teaching
Abani, Chris	BA English and Literary Studies, Imo State University	Professor of Creative Writing, University of California, Riverside, 2007–12
	MA Gender and Culture, University of London	
	MA English, University of Southern California	
	PhD Creative Writing and Literature, University of Southern California	
Adebayo, Ayobami	BA and MA Literature in English, Obafemi Awolowo University	
	MA Creative Writing, University of East Anglia	
	Participant in Lagos writing workshop, designed by Adichie	

	Training	Teaching
Adichie, Chimamanda N.	MA Creative Writing, Johns Hopkins University	Lecturer of Creative Writing, Princeton University, 2005–06
	MA African Studies, Yale University	Creative Director of Farafina Trust Creative Writing Workshop, 2009–16, since 2018: Purple Hibiscus Trust
Atta, Sefi	MA Creative Writing, Antioch University	Mississippi State University
Braithwaite, Oyinkan	Graduate of Creative Writing and Law, Kingston University London	
Cole, Teju	(African) Art History	Professor of Creative Writing, Harvard University, 2018–
Emezi, Akwaeke	Alumna of Adichie's Farafina Trust Creative Writing Workshop	
Evans, Diana	MA Creative Writing, University of East Anglia	Associate Lecturer of Creative Writing, University of London
Habila, Helon	English Language and Literature, University of Jos	Professor of Creative Writing, George Mason University
Iweala, Uzodinma	BA English and American Literature, Harvard College	
	PhD Creative Writing, Harvard University	
Nwaubani, Adaobi T.	Psychology, University of Ibadan	
Obioma, Chigozie	MA Creative Writing, University of Michigan	Professor of Creative Writing, University of Nebraska-Lincoln

	Training	Teaching
Okparanta, Chinelo	MA Creative Writing, Iowa Writers' Workshop	
Onuzo, Chibundu	African History, King's College London	
Oyeyemi, Helen	Social and Political Sciences, Cambridge University	
	Creative Writing, Columbia University	
Selasi, Taiye	BA American Studies, Yale University	
	MA International Relations, Oxford University	

Table 3.1 Review Corpora

Novel	AR			GR			YR		
	Corpus	Reviews	Words	Corpus	Reviews	Words	Corpus	Reviews	Words
N01	AR01	24	4,750	GR01	116	11,454	YR01	0	0
N02	AR02	385	38,558	GR02	256	60,793	YR02	96	70,367
N03	AR03	4,982	388,109	GR03	257	94,716	YR03	118	110,538
N04	AR04	1,653	164,794	GR04	244	77,242	YR04	55	41,045
N05	AR05	1,028	97,429	GR05	204	53,051	YR05	49	41,828
N06	AR06	23	4,133	GR06	83	11,920	YR06	1	1,884
N07	AR07	350	46,072	GR07	246	47,965	YR07	74	62,962
N08	AR08	121	23,448	GR08	283	56,634	YR08	5	6,396
N09	AR09	209	37,199	GR09	272	61,999	YR09	10	11,211
N10	AR10	83	11,510	GR10	294	65,721	YR10	78	60,527
N11	AR11	49	7,825	GR11	118	13,572	YR11	2	491
N12	AR12	9	3,108	GR12	60	6,172	YR12	0	0
N13	AR13	122	21,727	GR13	282	50,383	YR13	10	7,335
N14	AR14	129	16,712	GR14	246	31,332	YR14	2	1,322
N15	AR15	26	4,602	GR15	163	35,841	YR15	13	8,662
N16	AR16	315	34,322	GR16	248	56,538	YR16	36	23,913
N17	AR17	126	17,813	GR17	292	59,985	YR17	44	24,462
N18	AR18	72	5,461	GR18	108	15,939	YR18	9	8,722
N19	AR19	78	14,300	GR19	283	46,655	YR19	6	3,681
N20	AR20	315	33,065	GR20	237	49,106	YR20	27	19,919
		10,099	974,937		4,292	907,018		635	505,265

Table 4.1 Comparison of Reviewer Interaction

Novel	AR		GR		YR	
	Helpful	Comments	Likes	Comments	Views	Comments
N01	40	1	58	17	0	0
N02	430	1	4,827	794	236,438	2,527
N03	4,004	314	8,738	1,400	761,095	3,806
N04	2,640	76	3,483	613	121,254	1,453
N05	1,307	39	2,261	288	87,761	1,004
N06	45	5	105	33	133	10
N07	986	0	9,300	1,165	124,987	1,706
N08	214	46	477	74	2,706	12
N09	1,098	111	1,052	182	13,011	143
N10	218	6	2,536	371	99,759	2,331
N11	163	4	46	18	477	16
N12	37	3	88	9	0	0
N13	344	8	548	84	3,978	126
N14	197	4	267	39	187	11
N15	120	0	1,187	141	23,710	377
N16	610	12	1,630	259	79,247	838
N17	131	24	1,296	120	175,369	1,609
N18	88	3	58	13	1,172	17
N19	249	7	250	33	10,250	115
N20	530	24	734	127	79,634	907
	13,451	688	38,941	5,780	1,821,168	17,008

Table 4.2.1 Top 16 Professional YouTube Channels

Name	Video Corpus		
	Views	Comments	Subscribers
Audiopedia	300	0	192,885
BBC News Africa	9,606	53	213,938
Book Riot	11,842	52	20,560
BritishCouncilPK	165	0	1,190
Burlington Public Library	38	0	41
Catherine Mwangi	60	0	522
Channel 4 News	277	1	787,454
Channels Television	542	0	749,373
Columbia Global Reports	222	0	121
Hatfield Public Library	63	0	44
KingCountyTV	38	0	1,974
Patricia Kay	1,491	3	132
PBS NewsHour	5,928	0	1,370,632
The Palm Print	11,899	21	308
The Wendy Williams Show	18,433	45	2,304,570
Yerba Buena Center for the Arts	63	0	1,474
	60,967	175	5,645,218

Table 4.2.2 Top 16 Amateur YouTube Channels

Name	Video Corpus		Subscribers
	Views	Comments	
A Model Recommends	28,915	142	326,206
Amerie	12,719	123	161,971
Ariel Bissett	31,633	149	155,433
booksandquills	128,302	642	178,825
Eric Karl Anderson	56,874	1,061	8,235
Hannah Witton	45,228	160	582,002
Helly	3,558	35	180,026
Ink and Paper Blog	23,556	569	7,807
Jean Bookishthoughts	54,361	264	65,388
Jen Campbell	97,277	519	49,136
Jouelzy	29,784	298	194,212
Lauren Wade	71,605	517	22,166
MercysBookishMusings	48,355	330	37,572
SavidgeReads	110,457	1,179	16,878
Shirley B. Eniang	330,640	770	752,132
sunbeamsjess	190,168	518	451,465
	1,263,432	7,276	3,189,454

Table 4.3 Types of BookTube Videos

Book(s)	Type	Characteristics	Videos
Single book	Book review	Single-book review, book talk, book chat	207
	Vlog	In-time review of a single book usually filmed over a couple of hours or days	10
Several books	Book haul	Display of books purchased or acquired through publisher sponsorship	56
	TBR	Display of books scheduled to be read soon	78
	Wrap-up	Summary of books read during the previous week or month	187
	Favourites	Display of favourite books of the year or of all times e.g. occasioned by the BookTuber's birthday, etc.	46
	Themed reading	Recommendation of books covering similar themes e.g. African, BAME, female writers, etc.	51
			635

Table 4.4 Demographic Data of YouTube vs. Goodreads Reviewers

	YR		GR	
	n	%	n	%
Gender				
female	293	83.71	210	90.52
male	57	16.29	22	9.48
	350	100.00	232	100.00
Age				
20–40	313	89.43	124	62.31
40–60	25	7.14	49	24.62
60+	12	3.43	26	13.07
	350	100.00	199	100.00
Race				
white	196	56.00	115	65.71
black	110	31.43	36	20.57
mixed	29	8.29	17	9.71
Other	15	4.29	7	4.00
	350	100.00	175	100.00
Location				
US	87	38.16	92	53.80
UK	62	27.19	22	12.87
Other	79	34.65	57	33.33
	228	100.00	171	100.00

Table 5.1 Keywords in Review Corpora

Nouns			Verbs		
Frequency	Keyness	Keyword	Frequency	Keyness	Keyword
22,522	105424.25	book	12,311	53854.60	read
16,356	102123.29	stars	4,212	26152.86	rated
10,067	44187.51	story	4,468	15614.08	reading
5,595	37074.90	Nigeria	3,556	15241.58	liked
6,278	33278.96	novel	5,348	14438.18	love
4,872	24743.59	characters	2,358	8886.99	loved
3,655	16306.34	author	2,766	7281.81	writing
4,357	13929.60	books	1,567	7217.12	recommend
1,858	10008.86	shelves	1,953	6784.18	enjoyed
2,723	8332.92	character	5,165	3332.07	know
869	6264.78	Biafra	2,330	2886.83	feel
927	6230.53	Lagos	4,051	2458.53	think
797	5920.26	blog	2,060	1952.82	felt
1,015	5889.18	narrator	412	1531.37	struggles
1,657	5666.36	reader	1,371	1476.06	makes
2,067	5655.85	race	558	1374.52	writes
2,109	5044.33	America	589	1326.21	feels
3,589	4884.09	family	572	1183.69	tells
1,192	4745.65	plot	395	1100.22	reviewed
4,473	4177.87	life	1,082	969.42	understand

Adjectives			Adverbs		
Frequency	Keyness	Keyword	Frequency	Keyness	Keyword
3,361	23034.69	Nigerian	8,236	21042.08	really
2,450	12835.89	amazing	1,108	5128.16	beautifully
2,173	8014.28	African	6,783	4419.62	very
2,598	7590.00	interesting	6,447	4177.30	just
775	5624.97	Igbo	1,027	3553.01	definitely
622	4443.14	favorite	3,980	1363.75	much
1,748	4308.00	beautiful	592	1346.21	truly
563	4043.59	Biafran	971	1295.56	highly
3,545	3239.07	great	861	1091.03	maybe
1,130	3108.83	wonderful	637	1087.91	absolutely
561	2596.24	compelling	297	1005.54	incredibly
343	2355.80	insightful	444	959.60	basically
489	2244.98	engaging	1,239	786.14	actually
646	2209.67	fascinating	334	675.02	thoroughly
343	2204.16	heart-breaking	203	602.32	emotionally
1,055	2117.65	excellent	411	590.87	deeply
273	2027.83	well-written	229	552.79	honestly
534	2026.76	fantastic	170	533.86	wonderfully
738	1984.15	brilliant	972	523.42	especially
672	1639.28	sad	576	468.19	completely

Table 5.2 Most Frequent Emotion Terms in Review Corpora

1	love *loved* (2,358), *lovely* (277), *loves* (253), *loving* (204), *lover* (170), *lovers* (138)	5,348
2	feel *felt* (2,060), *feeling* (594), *feels* (589), *feelings* (440)	2,330
3	enjoyed *enjoy* (684), *enjoyable* (376), *enjoying* (141)	1,953
4	hope *hoping* (152), *hopes* (145), *hopefully* (135)	944
5	sad *sadness* (113), *sadly* (102)	672
6	heart *heartbreaking* (343), *heart-wrenching* (102)	571
7	happy *happiness* (146)	526
8	emotional *emotions* (329), *emotionally* (203), *emotion* (143)	475
9	lost *loss* (261), *lose* (132)	444
10	wish	429
11	struggles *struggle* (403), *struggling* (175), *struggled* (125)	412
12	care	398
13	glad	392
14	excited *exciting* (159)	354
15	fear *afraid* (145)	332
16	conflict *conflicts* (102)	330
17	disappointed *disappointing* (175)	326
18	expected *expectations* (305), *expect* (269), *expecting* (162), *unexpected* (129)	311
19	pain *painful* (193)	283

20	*appreciate*	270
	appreciated (168)	
21	*surprised*	213
	surprise (149)	
22	*alone*	211
23	*suffering*	202
24	*challenges*	198
	challenge (168), *challenging* (143)	
25	*hate*	196
	hated (118)	
26	*horror*	196
	horrible (138), *horrific* (134), *horrors* (130)	
27	*unfortunately*	195
28	*joy*	177
29	*touching*	175
	touch (152), *touched* (116), *touches* (111)	
30	*tension*	172
31	*trauma*	166
32	*desire*	164
33	*impressed*	162
	impressive (139)	
34	*pressure*	161
35	*angry*	146
	anger (130)	
36	*confusing*	141
	confused (126)	
37	*trouble*	128
38	*affected*	125
39	*shame*	125
40	*pleasure*	124
41	*cry*	123
42	*shocking*	122
43	*uncomfortable*	122
	comfortable (121)	
44	*grief*	120

45	*laugh*	119
46	*satisfying*	116
47	*sensitive*	115
48	*value* *values* (109)	110
49	*empathy*	106
50	*depressing* *depression* (102)	102

Table 5.3 Frequency of Emotion Terms across Review Corpora

	AR		GR		YR	
	raw	norm	raw	norm	raw	norm
love	4,596	471.42	2,633	290.29	1,531	303.01
feeling	2,256	231.40	2,533	279.27	1,289	255.11
enjoyment	1,770	181.55	866	95.48	615	121.72
hope	507	52.00	491	54.13	609	120.53
sadness	476	48.82	374	41.23	70	13.85
happiness	269	27.59	315	34.73	204	40.37
emotion	567	58.16	457	50.38	126	24.94
struggle	510	52.31	462	50.94	143	28.30
touch	300	30.77	183	20.18	80	15.83
cry	103	10.56	128	14.11	38	7.52
	11,354	1,164.59	8,442	930.74	4,705	931.19

Table 5.4 Frequency of Emotion Terms across Novel Corpora

	N01		N02		N03		N04	
	raw	norm	raw	norm	raw	norm	raw	norm
love	42	259.20	804	473.73	3,455	582.27	978	345.48
feeling	22	135.77	468	275.75	1,633	275.21	660	233.15
enjoyment	7	43.20	215	126.68	1,159	195.33	290	102.44
hope	10	61.71	175	103.11	313	52.75	186	65.71
sadness	12	47.06	102	60.10	157	26.46	143	50.52
happiness	0	0.00	121	71.29	187	31.52	68	24.02
emotion	9	55.54	165	97.22	176	29.66	173	61.11
struggle	6	37.03	96	56.56	292	49.21	145	51.22
touch	6	37.03	38	22.39	163	27.47	77	27.20
cry	7	43.20	26	15.32	44	7.42	37	13.07
	121	746.73	2,210	1,302.16	7,579	1,277.30	2,757	973.93

	N05		N06		N07		N08	
	raw	norm	raw	norm	raw	norm	raw	norm
love	751	390.52	34	189.55	519	330.58	106	122.57
feeling	453	235.56	45	250.88	395	251.59	224	259.03
enjoyment	259	134.68	17	94.78	279	177.71	94	108.70
hope	119	61.88	6	33.45	116	73.89	65	75.16
sadness	96	49.92	4	22.30	16	10.19	34	39.32
happiness	70	36.40	7	39.03	34	21.66	21	24.28
emotion	129	67.08	9	50.18	38	24.20	15	17.35
struggle	67	34.84	15	83.63	23	14.65	24	27.75
touch	39	20.28	9	50.18	29	18.47	11	12.72
cry	30	15.60	0	0.00	4	2.55	4	4.63
	2,013	1,046.76	146	813.96	1,453	925.48	598	691.51

	N09		N10		N11		N12	
	raw	norm	raw	norm	raw	norm	raw	norm
love	136	123.18	240	174.22	49	223.87	20	215.52
feeling	263	238.21	386	280.20	56	255.85	12	129.31
enjoyment	107	96.91	128	92.92	38	173.61	12	129.31
hope	42	38.04	114	82.75	8	36.55	5	53.88
sadness	17	15.40	9	6.53	43	196.45	4	43.10
happiness	20	18.11	27	19.60	14	63.96	0	0.00
emotion	46	41.66	37	26.86	17	77.67	5	53.88
struggle	30	27.17	84	60.98	11	50.26	1	10.78
touch	23	20.83	29	21.05	15	68.53	1	10.78
cry	2	1.81	4	2.90	15	68.53	0	0.00
	686	621.33	1,058	768.01	266	1,215.28	60	646.55

Appendix

	N13		N14		N15		N16	
	raw	norm	raw	norm	raw	norm	raw	norm
love	67	84.34	122	247.13	242	492.82	204	177.74
feeling	189	237.90	88	178.26	103	209.75	246	214.34
enjoyment	42	52.87	105	212.70	31	63.13	125	108.91
hope	58	73.01	30	60.77	28	57.02	121	105.43
sadness	55	69.23	19	38.49	24	48.87	72	62.73
happiness	27	33.99	9	18.23	15	30.55	31	27.01
emotion	67	84.34	9	18.23	25	50.91	42	36.59
struggle	31	39.02	38	76.98	25	50.91	36	31.37
touch	10	12.59	11	22.28	12	24.44	25	21.78
cry	13	16.36	1	2.03	32	65.17	7	6.10
	559	703.63	432	875.10	537	1,093.57	909	792.00

Middlebrow 2.0 and the Digital Affect

	N17		N18		N19		N20	
	raw	norm	raw	norm	raw	norm	raw	norm
love	537	525.13	85	282.19	100	154.71	269	263.49
feeling	292	285.55	71	235.71	212	327.99	260	254.68
enjoyment	80	78.23	66	219.11	85	131.51	112	109.71
hope	122	119.30	12	39.84	19	29.40	58	56.81
sadness	45	44.01	10	33.20	8	12.38	50	48.98
happiness	71	69.43	9	29.88	15	23.21	42	41.14
emotion	67	65.52	2	6.64	20	30.94	99	96.97
struggle	97	94.86	6	19.92	32	49.51	56	54.85
touch	28	27.38	1	3.32	11	17.02	25	24.49
cry	15	14.67	3	9.96	2	3.09	23	22.53
	1,354	1,324.08	265	879.76	504	779.75	994	973.65

Appendix

Table 5.5 Frequency of Emotion Terms across Selected Novels

	SN01		SN02		SN03		SN04		SN05	
	raw	norm	raw	norm	raw	norm	raw	norm	raw	norm
love	30	91.68	47	60.87	163	97.44	24	25.72	83	87.20
feeling	42	128.36	140	181.30	375	224.17	66	70.72	168	176.51
enjoyment	7	21.39	9	11.66	12	7.17	3	3.21	13	13.66
hope	10	30.56	40	51.80	88	52.61	28	30.00	36	37.82
sadness	7	21.39	4	5.18	38	22.72	11	11.79	16	16.81
happiness	5	15.28	23	29.79	65	38.86	11	11.79	40	42.03
emotion	0	0.00	7	9.07	22	13.15	1	1.07	5	5.25
struggle	4	12.22	5	6.48	13	7.77	17	18.22	19	19.96
touch	8	24.45	51	66.05	71	42.44	18	19.29	13	13.66
cry	13	39.73	35	45.33	43	25.71	154	165.01	46	48.33
	126	385.07	361	467.50	890	532.04	333	356.80	439	461.23

Table 5.6 Frequency of Emotion Terms across Corpus of Author Videos

	YA01		YA02		YA03		YA04		YA05	
	raw	norm	raw	norm	raw	norm	raw	norm	raw	norm
love	46	97.39	57	140.46	744	179.87	55	143.68	50	151.92
feeling	30	63.52	94	231.63	898	217.10	39	101.88	60	182.30
enjoyment	5	10.59	15	36.96	38	9.19	3	7.84	8	24.31
hope	18	38.11	23	56.68	266	64.31	30	78.37	9	27.35
sadness	7	14.82	3	7.39	100	24.18	6	15.67	2	6.08
happiness	9	19.06	9	22.18	282	68.18	6	15.67	13	39.50
emotion	3	6.35	2	4.93	122	29.49	4	10.45	2	6.08
struggle	10	21.17	7	17.25	41	9.91	4	10.45	7	21.27
touch	3	6.35	21	51.75	26	6.29	2	5.22	3	9.12
cry	21	44.46	6	14.78	71	17.16	10	26.12	3	9.12
	152	321.82	237	584.00	2,588	625.67	159	415.37	157	477.03

Table 5.7 Selected Novels vs. Corpus of Author Videos

	SN		YA	
	raw	norm	raw	norm
love	347	74.35	952	166.25
feeling	791	169.48	1,121	195.76
enjoyment	44	9.43	69	12.05
hope	202	43.28	346	60.42
sadness	76	16.28	118	20.61
happiness	144	30.85	319	55.71
emotion	35	7.50	133	23.23
struggle	58	12.43	69	12.05
touch	161	34.50	55	9.60
cry	291	62.35	111	19.38
	2,149	460.44	3,293	575.05

Bibliography

YouTube Reviews

#Book Draw, "A to Z of LGBT books," 21/05/2017
—, "Femmeuary TBR (by Lauren and the Books)," 01/02/2018
—, "femmuary wrap up," 11/03/2018
#MEiREAD, "Book Review: Stay With Me by Ayọ̀bámi Adébáyọ̀," 24/04/2018
1book1review, "Purple Hibiscus by Chimamanda Ngozi Adichie," 13/02/2015
31 Books, "Stay With Me: review and discussion," 22/09/2017
A Case for Books, "Introducing the Anna & Eric Book Club," 02/07/2017
A Model Recommends, "Top Books for Christmas | A Model Recommends," 22/12/2014
Abisola S, "AFRICAN LITERATURE VLOG | STAY WITH ME – THE BOOK REVIEW," 13/03/2018
Abnormal Growth, "Americanah and Parable of the Sower – Book Review," 27/09/2016
abookeveryotherday, "Library Swap | 12," 27/07/2013
—, "Review | Americanah," 10/09/2013
ABookishPair, "Books From Our To Be Read List! | A Bookish Pair #tbr #tobereadlist," 09/11/2018
—, "A Bookish Pair's Top Reads of 2018," 28/12/2018
—, "Stay with Me by Ayobami Adebayo | Book Review | A Bookish Pair," 25/01/2019
—, "The Fishermen by Chigozie Obioma | Book Review | A Bookish Pair," 24/02/2019
—, "Everything Good Will Come by Sefi Atta | Book Review | A Bookish Pair," 07/06/2019
abookolive, "July 2018 TBR," 29/06/2018
Acacia Ives, "Freshwater || Book Review," 16/02/2018
African and Afro-Diasporan Art Talks, "Book Review: Every Day Is For The Thief by Teju Cole – Narrate Africa," 12/09/2014
—, "5 Things I've Learned About Nigerians," 18/09/2014
Aishyo Joy, "Americanah by Chimamanda Ngozi Adichie – book review," 08/03/2014
Aisling Reina, "5 LGBT+ Novels by Women || the fiction i started the year with," 12/03/2017
Alive as Always, "Reading Diversely Tag | Alive as Always," 12/10/2016
—, "Siblings in Fiction | Alive as Always," 25/11/2017

—, "My Top 10 Books of 2017 | Alive as Always," 24/12/2017
AlleySinai, "Favorite Goodies! Books | Music | Podcasts & More," 14/04/2018
Always Doing, "The BookTube Prize Longlist || Always Doing," 19/01/2019
Alya Eats Books, "Book Review: Americanah by Chimamanda Ngozi Adichie," 04/06/2015
Amanda Elise Carina, "Americanah | Spoiler-Free Book Review [Booktube-a-thon wrap-up]," 28/07/2016
Amanda Jenner, "BOOK REVIEW – HALF OF A YELLOW SUN," 21/06/2016
Amerie, "MAY AKA SPRING BOOK HAUL," 19/05/2015
—, "BOOKTUBEATHON WRAP-UP 2015 | AMERICANAH," 14/08/2015
Ana – bb03aav, "Favourite Books of 2016," 27/12/2016
—, "December 2016 Reads Part I," 04/01/2017
andyreadsbooks, "Half of a Yellow Sun by Chimanda Ngozi Adichie," 13/06/2009
Anna Baillie-Karas, "Women's Prize Longlist Predictions," 27/02/2019
—, "Women's Prize Shortlist Predictions," 27/04/2019
Anomalous Chloe, "2017 Reading Challenge // 6 Month Update | Anomalous Chloe," 01/07/2017
Ariel Bissett, "A UKULELE CHRISTMAS | Book Haul #24," 26/12/2016
ASMR Curls, "ASMR Curl's Book Club," 18/02/2018
Audiopedia, "Americanah," 05/12/2014
Babbling Books, "7 Best Books of 2017 (so far!)," 06/09/2017
Barter Hordes, "Reading Women Month Readathon TBR," 24/05/2018
—, "Friday Reads | February 22, 2019," 22/02/2019
—, "Friday Reads | April 19, 2019," 19/04/2019
BBC News Africa, "Stay With Me by Ayobami Adebayo – BBC Africa Book Club," 18/08/2018
—, "Americanah by Chimamanda Ngozi Adichie – BBC Africa Book Club," 03/11/2018
Becky Ford, "Weekly Wrap Up 9/6/15," 06/09/2015
Belinda's Book Nook, "Book Chat – The Icarus Girl by Helen Oyeyemi," 17/11/2016
Belle Michelle, "BOOK HAUL: THE ALCHEMIST, AMERICANAH, 12 YEARS A SLAVE & MORE," 01/08/2014
Bel's Books, "four book recommendations | what should you read next?" 30/01/2019
BENJAMIN NAMBU, "Purple Hibiscus," 13/12/2018
Benjamina E. Dadzie, "PERSPECTIVES FROM BOOKS | Americanah & The Defining Decade," 13/01/2017
Beth Chats Books, "Goodreads Summer Reading Challenge & Holiday TBR!!! | BethChatsBooks," 04/06/2019
BethanyMegan, "LIFE CHITCHAT + MONTHLY FAVOURITES | JUNE," 11/07/2019
Better Than Dreams, "July 2018 TBR," 25/07/2018
bettyreads, "Update! Books, Book Buying Ban & Bout of Books!" 07/01/2014
bigalbooks, "Try a Chapter Tag (Long Books Edition)," 02/08/2018
—, "POC-a-thon TBR," 11/08/2018
—, "Honourable/Dishonourable Mentions 2018," 05/01/2019
—, "February Wrap Up," 26/03/2019
Bilphena Yahwon, "Ghana Must Go – Season 1," 04/09/2013
Book Club Americanah, "Americanah | Episode 1 | Characters," 27/02/2019
—, "Americanah | Episode 3 | Racism," 09/03/2019
Book Girl Magic, "March 2019 Book Club Pick Announcement: My Sister, The Serial Killer," 18/02/2019

Book Riot, "5 Books to Watch for in April," 02/04/2015
—, "In the Mailbag: April 30, 2015," 30/04/2015
—, "Read Harder: Read a Book by an Author Aged 25 or Younger," 19/06/2015
—, "Read Harder – African Authors," 10/07/2015
—, "New Release Tuesday: August 22, 2017," 22/08/2017
—, "3 International Book Recommendations," 20/06/2018
—, "New Release Tuesday: November 20, 2018," 20/11/2018
—, "Ready, Set, Hold: January 2019," 28/11/2018
—, "New Release Tuesday: January 8, 2019," 08/01/2019
Book Your Imagination, "REVIEW: The Fishermen by Chigozie Obioma," 15/08/2016
—, "Baileys Women's Prize for Fiction | Book Awards Season #13," 13/04/2017
Book.A. Rama, "Half of A Yellow Sun – No spoilers review," 03/03/2017
Bookaxe, "Women's Prize Longlist 2019 | The Week in Books #22," 06/03/2019
—, "Freshwater & Remembered | Women's Prize 2019 Book Reviews," 26/03/2019
—, "Women's Prize Shortlist Predictions 2019," 21/04/2019
BookCave, "Queer Lit Readathon Recommendations," 09/05/2019
Bookie Charm, "Small Booktuber Tag || #smallbooktuber," 02/03/2018
—, "Love Interests to Break Up With || Top 5 Wednesday," 20/02/2019
—, "Book Riot's Read Harder TBR || 2019," 06/03/2019
—, "Queer Lit Readathon TBR || Round 3," 29/05/2019
Bookish Betsy, "Stay with Me | Baileys Prize 2017," 19/05/2017
—, "May Wrap Up | 2017," 01/06/2017
Bookish Realm, "#OwnVoices Recs | #Diverseathon," 25/01/2017
BookNympho, "Americanah by Chimamanda Ngozi Adichie," 28/10/2014
Books and Headscarves, "Best Books of 2018 | Black Women of 2018," 08/01/2019
Books are my Social Life, "WHY YOU SHOULD READ PURPLE HIBISCUS," 03/06/2017
Books on Toast, "BoTcast Episode 28 – Contemporary Female Fiction with Deepanjana Pal," 09/05/2018
—, "BoTcast Episode 32 – Books & Mental Health with Nikhil Taneja," 25/07/2018
booksandquills, "Book Haul | Penguin Bloggers Evening," 26/04/2013
—, "The Reading Diversely Tag | Books from Six Continents," 19/11/2014
—, "On My Shelf III," 03/10/2015
—, "What We're Reading w/ Rosianna | Booksandquills," 20/08/2016
—, "October Book Haul | Booksandquills," 27/11/2016
—, "August Book Haul | Booksandquills," 11/09/2017
BooksbyNature, "Americanah Book Talk," 30/07/2016
BookWhimsy, "End of the Year TBR 2018," 28/11/2018
—, "November 2018 Wrap Up," 18/12/2018
—, "Top 10 Books of 2018," 28/12/2018
Bookworm In Gh, "Top Five Tuesday: Contemporary African Women Writers," 18/07/2017
—, "Stay With Me by Ayobami Adebayo – Book Review," 31/01/2018
—, "January Wrap-up 2018," 05/02/2018
—, "February 2018 Wrap-up," 05/04/2018
—, "November 2018 Wrap Up!" 03/12/2018
Botlhale GH, "Reading 'Ghana Must Go' as an epic poem," 18/05/2019
bravelittlebooks, "Brave Little Books – Open City," 15/04/2012
BritishCouncilPK, "Friday Five: Humans of Karachi founder, Khaula Jamil recommends five inspirational female authors," 10/03/2018

Britta Böhler, "BooksWeekly: New Voices – Devoted Debuts," 30/10/2016
—, "BooksWeekly: Mixed Feelings," 06/11/2016
—, "BooksWeekly: Onwards!" 13/11/2016
—, "BooksWeekly: Last, but not least!" 31/12/2016
—, "Books Weekly: Moral Grounds," 04/06/2017
—, "BookTube Prize Quarterfinals," 09/06/2019
—, "RecentReads: Deadly Encounters," 16/06/2019
Brooke Lee, "Americanah by Chimamanda Ngozi Adichie," 13/09/2013
—, "Christmas Reading Vlog #1," 24/12/2018
Brown Girl Reading, "Book Review – Americanah," 07/03/2014
—, "Book Review – Ghana Must Go," 27/04/2014
—, "April 2014 Wrap up," 13/05/2014
—, "Book Haul 5–18–14," 18/05/2014
—, "#FridayReads 11 13 15," 13/11/2015
—, "26a – Diana Evans Readalong," 02/10/2018
btwnbookcovers, "Not a review, not a discussion: Ghana Must Go. Also, Book Giveaway Winner!" 18/02/2014
Burlington Public Library, "'Americanah' by Chimamanda Ngozi Adichie – A Book Review from Marnie," 14/03/2016
Cali Bourne, "WHAT I'VE BEEN READING | Cali Bourne," 09/07/2018
Catherine Martinez, "Book Talk: Purple Hibiscus," 03/01/2019
Catherine Mwangi, "Reviewing 'Stay With Me' by Ayobami Adebayo – Part 1," 20/12/2018
—, "Reviewing 'Stay With Me' by Ayobami Adebayo – Part 2," 20/12/2018
Catriona Reads, "Purple Hibiscus | Book Review (CC)," 19/02/2017
Chadel Mathurin, "5 HOT 'Summer' Reads | Reading Black Girl | #OutsideTheHairBox," 15/06/2018
Channel 4 News, "C4 News Alternative Booker: Jon Snow on Americanah," 16/10/2013
Channels Television, "Irede Reviews Chibundu Onuzo's The Spider King's Daughter Pt 1," 24/12/2015
—, "Irede Reviews Chibundu Onuzo's The Spider King's Daughter Pt 2," 24/12/2015
—, "Irede Reviews Chibundu Onuzo's The Spider King's Daughter Pt 3," 24/12/2015
—, "Channels Book Club: Reviewing 'The Spider King's Daughter' By Chibundu Onuzo Pt 1," 27/06/2017
—, "Channels Book Club: Reviewing 'The Spider King's Daughter' By Chibundu Onuzo Pt 2," 27/06/2017
Chapter32, "Book Review: Stay With Me," 13/09/2017
Charles Heathcote, "Currently Reading 24.01.2017," 24/01/2017
—, "Those Books What I Read in February," 06/03/2019
—, "Those Books What I Read in March | 2019," 07/04/2019
CHICA, "Book Chat With Lebza – Stay With Me by Ayobami Adebayo," 10/04/2018
Chris Bookish Cauldron, "#Bookbusters Wrap Up and Reviews," 07/10/2017
—, "A Quick Book Haul (October 2017)," 11/11/2017
—, "A Catch Up & Currently Reading 02Apr2018," 02/04/2018
—, "March 2019 Wrap Up," 04/04/2019
Claire Reads Books, "Reading Wrap Up | December 2018," 17/12/2018
Classic Movies Remastered 4K, "My Sister The Serial Killer by Oyinkan Braithwaite [Book Review]," 19/02/2019
Coffee Bookshelves, "My Sister the Serial Killer by Oyinkan Braithwaite," 04/07/2019

Columbia Global Reports, "'Americanah' and the Rise of Migrant Literature," 20/04/2017
Comfycozyup, "August Wrap-Up | September TBR," 31/08/2017
—, "Reading Vlog | An Orchestra of Minorities," 08/03/2019
Courtney Marie Presents, "Americanah Book Talk & Review," 27/04/2017
CreatingColleen, "Half of a Yellow Sun | 90 Second Book Review," 08/08/2015
Crispin Dude, "Americanah Vlog #2," 26/03/2016
Dancing Lawn, "April Reading Wrap Up | 2019 | Dancing Lawn," 06/05/2019
Daniel Daudu, "Three-views: Stay With Me Book Review," 05/02/2018
—, "Three-views: I Do Not Come To You By Chance," 12/02/2018
Danika Leigh Ellis, "Book Haul & TBR!" 20/09/2015
—, "October Wrap Up!" 01/11/2015
Deanna Buley, "Americanah Video Blog," 10/04/2015
diana in colour, "Black Writers Corner | Discussion | Americanah – Chimamanda Ngozi Adichie," 05/01/2018
—, "Reading Wrap Up | Pocathon," 25/08/2018
—, "Most Anticipated Books of 2019!" 02/01/2019
Dinh G, "The Fishermen Book Review," 14/07/2016
Distinguished Diva, "Stay with Me Book Review," 21/04/2017
doz, "12 Books for Black Women," 24/07/2018
Duvan Viafara, "Americanah book review," 27/06/2016
Dyslexic Muggle, "Winter Biannual Bibliothon TBR & Plans for #strikebackvideoathon," 19/01/2018
earnestalexreads, "February 2019 | Wrap Up Part One," 21/02/2019
Ellen, "Stay With Me By Ayobami Adebayo | 2 Minute Review (SF)," 11/11/2017
Eric Karl Anderson, "Best Books of 2016 so far & Book Giveaway," 06/07/2016
—, "The Best Books of 2016," 31/12/2016
—, "Reading Wrap Up / March 2017," 17/03/2017
—, "Baileys Prize Shortlist Predictions with Anna from A Case for Books," 27/03/2017
—, "Reading Wrap Up / June 2017 Part 1," 16/06/2017
—, "Best Books of 2017 so far & Book Giveaway," 01/07/2017
—, "The LGBT Books That Made Me," 08/07/2017
—, "10 Exciting Debut Novels from 2017," 14/12/2017
—, "November Book Haul," 07/11/2018
—, "Reading Wrap Up / November 2018," 02/12/2018
—, "Women's Prize for Fiction Longlist 2019 – Reaction!" 04/03/2019
—, "Women's Prize 2019 shortlist predictions with Anna," 25/04/2019
—, "Women's Prize for Fiction Shortlist 2019 – Reaction with Anna!" 29/04/2019
—, "100 Best Books for Summer," 07/07/2019
—, "The 2019 Booker Prize Longlist – Reaction!" 24/07/2019
erica garner, "Every Day Is for the Thief," 09/07/2017
erin go read, "March 2019 mid-month wrap-up," 20/03/2019
Erin Megan, "My Sister, The Serial Killer Book Review," 01/06/2019
ethnique185, "Americanah book review," 25/12/2013
—, "Ghana Must Go book review," 01/01/2014
eudaimonliving, "Stay With Me by Ayobami Adebayo | Pakistani Youtuber," 19/09/2017
Eve's Alexandria, "Winter TBR 2016," 10/11/2016
—, "Booktuber Meet-Up Book Haul," 02/04/2019
—, "April Reading Wrap Up," 12/05/2019
Faith Masengo, "Americanah Book Review," 01/06/2017

FollyFlo, "*95* A Must Read: 'Spider Kings Daughter' Book," 01/11/2012
ForTheLoveOfRyan, "READ WITH ME: An Update (Libra and Americanah)," 01/08/2016
Fred Weasley Died Laughing, "Weekly Wrap Up || April 23rd 2017," 23/04/2017
—, "Weekly Wrap Up || January 20th 2019," 21/01/2019
FredeReads, "My Favourite Women Writers and Books Written by Women [CC]," 08/03/2018
—, "September TBR Update [CC]," 10/10/2018
FreeFormLady, "Book Talk: Purple Hibiscus," 04/10/2016
frizzgirljane, "Chimamanda Ngozi Adichie – AMERICANAH Book Review!" 18/12/2013
From Beginning to Bookend, "2017 Baileys Review – Part 3 | Essex Serpent | First Love | Little Deaths | Stay With Me," 17/05/2017
Gathoni Kimaru, "Episode 20: What I Read | February 2019," 17/02/2019
Georgiana Gligor, "FIRST BOOK CHAT: Half of A Yellow Sun by Chimamanda Ngozi Adichie," 25/04/2018
gerard thebookworm, "Booktube Vlog 62: An Orchestra of Minorities and The Girls They Left Behind," 04/02/2019
Girl About Library, "MY SISTER THE SERIAL KILLER BY OYINKAN BRAITHWAITE // 60(ISH) SECOND BOOK REVIEW," 30/04/2019
Hannah Lincoln, "Book Review: Half a Yellow Sun," 07/01/2018
Hannah Morris, "October Wrap Up Part 2," 18/11/2016
Hannah Witton, "Summer 2019 Favourites | Books, Netflix & Podcasts | Hannah Witton," 23/07/2019
Hardcover Hearts, "Week of Reading April 12th, 2019," 13/04/2019
—, "Week of Reading April 19th, 2019," 20/04/2019
Harriet Rosie, "Books I Did Not Finish," 30/04/2019
Hatfield Public Library, "Unboxing #20: Adult Fiction and Nonfiction," 06/03/2018
Hello Shaha, "Book Review | Half of a Yellow Sun by Chimamanda Ngozie Adichie," 22/06/2019
Helly, "Purple Hibiscus by Chimamanda Ngozi Adichie | Reading Vlogs with Helly," 14/01/2018
HeyHeyBooks, "Literary Acquisitions (AKA Book Haul)," 25/03/2018
HollaAtFola, "On My Bookshelf," 10/05/2014
Holly Dunn Design, "August Wrap Up Part I," 16/08/2015
—, "4 Man Booker Longlist Reviews #ManBooker2015," 03/09/2015
—, "A Novel Christmas Guide," 09/12/2015
—, "February Book Haul Part II | Design Books, Graphic Novels," 09/03/2016
—, "April Wrap Up 2016," 15/05/2016
—, "March Wrap-Up 2017," 12/04/2017
—, "Favourite Books of 2017 So Far," 24/07/2017
—, "My Top 10 Books of 2017 | Holly Dunn Design," 30/12/2017
Hungry Bookworm, "AUDIOBOOK REVIEW | MY SISTER THE SERIAL KILLER | #AUDIOBABBLE," 10/07/2019
IdaraJoy, "My Current Favorite Books // Spirituality, Sex, & Finding Purpose," 21/11/2017
Indie Book Show Africa, "Americanah review | Jemila Pratt | 5* rating | Positivecreativeenergy.com," 06/10/2016
—, "Under The Udala Trees | Chinelo Okparanta | 5* review," 31/03/2018
Ink and Paper Blog, "My Top 10(ish) Books of 2017 – So Far!" 22/06/2017
—, "Immigrant Fiction & My Winners!" 28/06/2017
—, "UK Pride Video – A Granta Book Haul," 08/07/2017

—, "My Top 11 Books of the Year (Published in 2017)," 03/01/2018
—, "5 Books People Have Recommend To Me," 10/02/2018
—, "Around the World in 1000 Pages Book Club #2," 01/03/2018
—, "Around the World in 1000 Pages Book Club #3," 31/03/2018
—, "March Wrap Up – 2018," 03/04/2018
—, "April Wrap Up – 2018," 08/05/2018
—, "November 2018 Wrap Up: Part 2," 12/12/2018
—, "Women's Prize 2019: Long List Predictions," 28/02/2019
insert book pun here, "recent reads | march & april 2019," 17/05/2019
—, "Reading and Walking Vlog | Stay With Me by Ayobami Adebayo," 24/05/2019
Insert Literary Pun Here, "Stay With Me | Baileys 2017 Review," 20/05/2017
—, "Travel TBR," 09/08/2017
—, "(Nonfiction) November TBR," 31/10/2017
—, "Contemporary Women Writers | Haul Introduction," 28/01/2018
Jacob Paul, "Jacob and Jadyn talk tailgating: AMERICANAH," 09/06/2016
Janill Briones-Lopez, "Blackathon! Books I will be reading for Black History Month," 03/02/2019
Jasmine's Reads, "The Fall Book Tag," 21/11/2017
—, "BAME | 5 Book Recommendations," 21/02/2018
—, "Book Haul | Man Booker 50, Poetry, Middle Grade, Classics and more," 06/06/2018
—, "Literary Fiction | 5 Book Recommendations," 09/01/2019
—, "2019 Proofs/Pre-Releases Book Haul!" 16/01/2019
—, "Women's Prize for Fiction 2019 Longlist!" 10/03/2019
—, "5 Star Predictions!" 11/04/2019
—, "Women's Prize Longlist 2019 Reviews + GIVEAWAY | CLOSED," 17/04/2019
Jay Shay, "#74 Freshwater | Book Review," 12/07/2018
Jean Bookishthoughts, "Man Booker Longlist 2015 Unboxing | #ManBookerVloggers," 22/08/2015
—, "Celebrating Women Writers | Discussion & Recommendations | ad," 10/05/2017
—, "The Best Books I've Read in 2017 So Far!" 17/06/2017
—, "My Most Anticipated 2019 Book Releases!" 19/12/2018
—, "Huge Book Haul | May 2019," 17/05/2019
Jen Campbell, "February Wrap Up 2015," 05/03/2015
—, "Man Booker Prize 2015 | Unboxing #ManBookerVloggers," 19/08/2015
—, "The Fishermen by Chigozie Obioma | #ManBookerVloggers," 28/08/2015
—, "August Wrap Up 2015 | Part 2," 02/09/2015
—, "Fairy Tale Retellings: Where to Start," 18/01/2016
—, "Baileys Prize Shortlist Reviews | May Wrap Up, Part 2 | AD," 06/06/2017
—, "My Favourite Books of 2017 So Far," 10/07/2017
—, "My Favourite Books of 2017 | Honourable Mentions," 02/01/2018
—, "December Book Haul 2018 | GIVEAWAY," 05/12/2018
—, "Book Haul | January 2019," 21/01/2019
Jennifer Meltzer, "Kotula's review of Purple Hibiscus," 25/09/2017
Jessi Tarbet, "March Book Haul 2018," 03/04/2018
Jimi Can Read, "Freshwater by Akwaeke Emezi and Convenience Store Woman by Sayaka Murata | Review & Discussion," 25/12/2018
JoansBookReviews, "Joan Mackenzie reviews Americanah by Chimamanda Ngozi Adichie," 25/03/2013
Joel Swagman, "Americanah by Chimamanda Ngozi Adichie: Book Review," 06/10/2018

John534, "americanah book review (Chimamanda Gnozi Adichie)," 02/07/2018
JoInRealLife, "Hello, It's Jo: Americanah," 07/03/2017
jojo reads books, "March TBR," 10/03/2019
Jonathan H. LATER, "My Sister, The Serial Killer Review (Spoiler)," 07/12/2018
jortizi27, "Americanah Lecture Chapters 1–4," 13/11/2015
—, "Prep for Americanah by Chimamanda Ngozi Adichie Lecture," 13/11/2015
Jouelzy, "A Book Review: Americanah by Chimamanda Ngozi Adichie | Jouelzy," 05/06/2014
Juan Pablo Giraldo, "Americana's Themes," 08/07/2016
Julian Bartholomee, "Open City Book Discussion," 16/01/2015
Just CHI-CHI, "Book Recommendations," 06/04/2017
Kacha's Space, "AMERICANAH | Book Review | Kacha," 04/05/2018
Katadactyl, "May Wrap-Up | Part 2 | 2018," 06/06/2018
Kathleen Ann, "Thoughts on Purple Hibiscus," 25/11/2014
Kathryn Liquid Grain, "Purple Hibiscus Book Review," 10/06/2018
Kay T, "Book Review – Stay With Me," 12/11/2017
—, "Book Review: My Sister the Serial Killer," 04/03/2019
Kendra Winchester, "August Wrap Up Pt. 1 | 2017 | Kendra Winchester," 16/08/2017
—, "Christmas Book Haul!! | 2018 | Kendra Winchester," 17/01/2018
—, "Five-Star Reads: Round Three!! | 2018 | Kendra Winchester," 17/02/2018
—, "#FridayReads | 2018 | Kendra Winchester," 03/03/2018
—, "March Book Haul Pt. 2 | 2018 | Kendra Winchester," 24/03/2018
—, "April Wrap Up Pt. 1 | 2018 | Kendra Winchester," 14/04/2018
—, "Favorite Books of 2018!! (So Far) | 2018 | Kendra Winchester," 14/07/2018
—, "FAVORITE BOOKS OF 2018!! | Kendra Winchester," 12/01/2019
—, "APRIL BOOK HAUL | 2019 | Kendra Winchester," 13/04/2019
—, "June Wrap Up Pt. 1 | 2019 | Kendra Winchester," 15/07/2019
KidStoryTime With Iffy, "THE SPIDER KING'S DAUGHTER | AFRICAN READ | BOOK TALK," 30/01/2018
Kim M. Watt, "My Sister the Serial Killer by Oyinkan Braithwaite – elegant, different, immersive & individual," 22/03/2019
KingCountyTV, "King County Reads – Emily's Pick," 06/02/2019
Kitty G, "Half of A Yellow Sun | Book Review," 23/07/2016
—, "Americanah | True Things About Me | Reviews," 20/02/2018
—, "Almost Love | Purple Hibiscus | Sweet Black Waves | Book Reviews," 10/08/2018
KnightHunter Books, "Book Haul | May 2017," 21/07/2017
—, "Wrap Up | August 2017," 07/09/2017
ktxx22, "Book Burst – Americanah by Chimamanda Ngozi Adichie," 12/03/2019
Kylah Sadè, "My Sister The Serial Killer | Quick Book Review," 30/05/2019
Laura Heninger, "Purple Hibiscus – Reflection Sample," 06/02/2014
Lauren and the Books, "What Makes a 5* Book? | Lauren and the Books," 12/10/2016
—, "GIRL POWER | International Women's Day | Lauren and the Books," 08/03/2017
—, "Femmeuary TBR | Lauren and the Books," 28/01/2018
—, "Currently Reading Femmeuary | Lauren and the Books," 11/02/2018
—, "Femmeuary Wrap Up | Lauren and the Books," 27/02/2018
—, "Women's Prize Long List Plans | Lauren and the Books," 08/03/2019
Lauren Wade, "Reading Wrap Up | October 2015 PART 1," 01/11/2015
—, "Upcoming Reads | October – December 2016," 06/10/2016
—, "Reading Wrap Up | October 2016 Part 2," 06/11/2016

—, "Super Massive Book Haul II," 20/04/2017
—, "Reading Wrap Up | April 2017," 01/05/2017
—, "Reading Wrap Up | May 2017 + Baileys Prize Shortlist Chat! Ad," 21/05/2017
—, "Baileys Women's Prize for Fiction Shortlist Discussion w/ Jen Campbell | Ad," 06/06/2017
—, "My Top Reads of 2017!" 04/01/2018
—, "3 Books to Take on Holiday This Summer!" 10/07/2018
—, "My All Time Favourite Books," 18/05/2019
—, "Reading Wrap Up | May 2019," 10/06/2019
Leanne Rose, "SO MANY BOOKS! | Book Haul," 21/06/2018
—, February TBR | #ThrillerAThon," 15/02/2019
—, "Women's Prize 2019 Thoughts & Predictions," 31/05/2019
LEFT ON READ, "SEPTEMBER TBR READING LIST + WRAP UP," 07/09/2018
Lesley Rickman, "Americanah | Chimamanda Ngozi Adichie," 22/06/2014
Lily Eleanor Reads, "PRIDE MONTH TBR!" 28/05/2018
LindaReads, "Book Review | Teju Cole | Open City," 09/07/2017
Lindsey's Book Life, "Reading Wrap Up | Books 65–70 | July 2018," 03/07/2018
Liv J Hooper, "May Catch Up | The Book Nook," 14/05/2017
Lizzie Reads, "A Belated March Wrap Up," 20/04/2018
lucyrutherford, "March Reads | 2019," 02/04/2019
LumosLeviosa2777, "December Book Haul 2014," 12/12/2014
lyndsayreads, "STAY WITH ME | book review," 22/01/2018
Makida Danielsbooks, "A column of fire and more," 12/11/2017
Malinka Reads, "Half of a Yellow Sun by Chimamanda Ngozi Adichie Book Review," 07/03/2014
Marc Nash, "Emezi, Crumey," 18/04/2019
Mariana's Study Corner, "What I Read in April // May Bookclub Update," 01/05/2019
Masked Fox Creations, "From Fox's Bookshelves – Under the Udala Trees," 09/02/2017
Matthew Sciarappa, "Under The Udala Trees | Review | #AnnaAndEric," 27/09/2017
—, "Freshwater | Vlog," 15/12/2018
Mayah Reads, "My Favourite Audiobooks! || Best Audiobooks 2018," 20/01/2019
MCS-books, "#POCathon | Wrap Up," 23/08/2018
—, "5 Adult Reads for YA Readers | Recommendations," 12/06/2019
Me, Simone & I, "June TBR // Buddy Reads & YOU DECIDE!!" 31/05/2019
meaghan kelling, "everyday is for the thief vlog," 01/06/2018
Meera Nair, "My Sister, the Serial Killer by Oyinkan Braithwaite | Book Review," 26/07/2019
MercysBookishMusings, "Americanah by Chimamanda Ngozi Adichie | Book Review," 14/06/2015
—, "Book Haul March 2017 | Part 1 of 2," 31/03/2017
—, "Stay With Me & The Dark Circle | Book Reviews | VEDA Day 18," 20/04/2017
—, "Christmas Book Haul | Part 2 of 2," 08/01/2019
—, "My Favourite Books (since I've been on Booktube)," 22/01/2019
—, "Women's Prize Reviews | 2019 Longlist," 25/03/2019
MH Books, "Part 2 Book Haul: Recommendations and Prize Winners," 02/09/2018
—, "Friday reads – the one with the bleeps," 29/03/2019
Mia Moreno, "Book Review/Discussion: Stay With Me by Ayobami Adebayo," 21/02/2018
Mickey's Booktube Experiment, "Book Raves for Americanah and Who Fears Death," 04/06/2015
—, "Mini Reviews: Purple Hibiscus, The Awakening, and The Grownup," 30/03/2016

modernmrshuxtable, "More Hair Books & My Love for Reading," 09/12/2013
molliesoldtheworld, "March Reading Wrap Up // molliesoldtheworld," 07/04/2016
Moments With M, "Black Girls Book Club – Part I," 03/11/2016
Morgane Krauth, "March 2019 Wrap-Up | 8 books," 14/04/2019
most mambo, "Half of a yellow sun – review – Chimamanda Ngozi Adichie," 03/05/2016
MrChasingRainbows, "Brooke's Book Nook: Purple Hibiscus," 30/09/2013
Musical Tati, "Purple Hibiscus Review (Spoiler Free)," 28/03/2016
—, "Review: My Sister: The Serial Killer (Spoiler-Free)," 28/08/2018
My Reading Days, "My Sister, the Serial Killer by Oyinkan Braithwaite [READING VLOG]," 08/03/2019
—, "Freshwater by Akwaeke Emezi [READING VLOG]," 12/04/2019
My Reading Life, "Top Ten Fiction Books of 2017," 02/01/2018
mynameismarines, "americanah and ... natural hair? (review and discussion)," 20/09/2016
—, "books #41–45 (2016): ACOMAF, Americanah, Blood of Elves + More!" 20/12/2016
—, "buying myself books for Christmas: a haul," 30/12/2018
Narrate Africa, "Final Thoughts," 22/09/2013
Natassa Karamouzis, "Black History Month TBR," 08/02/2019
—, "VLOG | Reading My Sister, the Serial Killer and barely touching Invisible Man," 13/02/2019
NATHALY CADENA TAMAYO, "Americanah Review," 25/06/2016
Naturally Unbothered, "Read With Me Half Of A Yellow Sun – Chimamanda Ngozi Adichie | Naturally Unbothered Daily Vlogs #15," 16/06/2018
Ndabenhle Ntshangase, "Stay With Me by Ayobami Adebayo. Paying Respect," 20/08/2018
Neeru chopra, "Xmas Book Reviews And Haul 2017," 14/12/2017
nerdintranslation, "Review | Beasts of No Nation + Authentic Writer's Discussion," 31/08/2012
—, "Reading Wrap Up | August 2012," 05/09/2012
Nfinite Pages, "The Fishermen by Chigozie Obioma (High 5)," 13/11/2015
—, "Review | Americanah by Chimamanda Ngozi Adichie," 01/04/2016
NHDgirls, "Nancy Pearl NPR – Purple Hibiscus by Chimamanda Adichie," 26/05/2011
Noria Reads, "Top 5 Books of 2018," 29/12/2018
—, "Books That Saved My Life: Americanah, Dealing with Sexual Assault," 17/02/2019
Official Longidi, "Chigozie Obioma Book Review | The Fishermen," 06/01/2017
OhSheReads, "The May of Adichie Read-a-Long!" 30/04/2015
—, "A SEAT AT THE TABLE BOOK CLUB JANUARY LIVE SHOW | My Sister the Serial Killer by Oyinkan Braithwaite," 11/02/2019
Old Blue's Chapter and Verse, "Winter Wrap-Up and Spring TBR," 30/03/2019
ONYX Pages, "100. Review of Freshwater, by Akwaeke Emezi (Also: This may be my 2018 best read!!! Find out why)," 09/12/2018
Oona Abrams, "Book Talk on Americanah by Chimamanda Ngozi Adichie," 30/07/2017
outofthebex, "My Sister, the Serial Killer | Book Review," 19/10/2018
Patricia Kay, "Book Review: Americanah by Chimamanda Ngozi Adichie," 28/05/2013
PBS NewsHour, "Great books to fall for now that summer's over," 23/09/2017
Philly Aime, "Purple Hibiscus by Chimamanda Ngozi Adichie | Book Review | PhillyAime," 30/01/2019
PippityBop, "September Book Haul!" 01/09/2015
Poetic Liberty, "The Fishermen – Chigozie Obioma (Review)," 31/08/2017

Portal in the Pages, "My Sister The Serial Killer Review," 06/02/2019
—, "Easter Weekend Reading Vlog," 22/04/2019
—, "April Wrap Up," 05/05/2019
Possibly Literate, "BOOK REVIEW: HALF OF A YELLOW SUN," 05/02/2017
—, "OCTOBER READING WRAP UP || 2017," 08/11/2017
—, "GIFT GUIDE: BOOKS FOR 'HARD TO SHOP FOR' PEOPLE || 2017," 12/12/2017
—, "FAVORITE BOOKS OF 2017," 09/01/2018
POUNDEDYAMZ, "AMERICANAH BY CHIMAMANDA NGOZI ADICHIE | NO SPOILER BOOK REVIEW," 17/07/2017
ProblemsofaBookNerd, "JUNE TBR | PRIDE AND EMOJIATHON," 02/06/2017
—, "Top 20 Queer TBR!" 04/11/2018
Pull Down The Moon, "VLOG: Visiting 4 bookshops in Glasgow & a book haul | Pull Down The Moon," 11/04/2019
Rachel Rae', "My Sister the Serial Killer by Oyinkan Braithwaite – Book Review," 30/01/2019
Raja Sharma, "Americanah (Brief Summary)," 13/04/2018
Rashmika Likes Books, "shithole countries tag," 30/11/2018
RatherBeReading, "December Wrap Up | 2018 [CC]," 02/01/2019
Read It Forward, "The Great American Read | Six Picks," 13/09/2018
Readers' Room Consulting, "Under the Udala Trees," 07/03/2018
READING in the DARK, "TBR | February (feat. Phillip the TBR Dog)," 01/02/2019
Reading. Writing. Coffee, "7 Lesbian Books I Wanna Read | TBR," 14/03/2019
rebeccadhilly, "Americanah Video Essay," 06/04/2015
RedheadReading, "Book Chat #24: Becky Chambers, Alison Weir, Chigozie Obioma & Ann Bausum," 28/06/2018
Rene Pierre, "Recent Reads | January TBR," 08/01/2019
Retired Book Nerd, "Americanah-Book Review (6/15/15)," 15/06/2015
rincey reads, "January Book Haul," 28/01/2014
—, "February Wrap Up," 28/02/2014
—, "March Book Haul," 25/03/2014
—, "April Wrap Up & Book Haul," 29/04/2014
—, "Read Diversely Tag," 04/11/2014
—, "Purple Hibiscus by Chimamanda Ngozi Adichie | Book Review," 08/12/2015
—, "February Wrap Up," 29/02/2016
—, "24 in 48 & Diverseathon TBR," 20/01/2017
—, "Friday Reads | May 25, 2018," 25/05/2018
—, "May Wrap Up Part 2," 01/06/2018
Robin Blue, "Book Review: Americanah," 13/01/2017
Rosianna Halse Rojas, "THE END GAMES, MADNESS UNDERNEATH, GHANA MUST GO, PICTURE ME GONE and A WORKING THEORY OF LOVE," 10/06/2013
—, "Chimamanda Ngozi Adichie's Books | New Covers!" 08/09/2016
Runwright Reads, "FEBRUARY HAUL," 24/02/2017
—, "Christmas Book Haul," 28/12/2017
—, "Why I Got These Books | Book Haul," 29/07/2018
—, "On the Shelf | Black History Month | Runwright Reads," 07/02/2019
SADE ON THE RUN, "Winter Book Haul," 23/12/2018
Sam D, "Americanah Summary and Review," 20/06/2016
SamuelDaram, "Booker Prize 2019 Longlist – Reaction (NEW)," 26/07/2019
Sankofa Reviews, "Half of A Yellow Sun (Review)," 21/06/2016

179

Sarahn Says, "Americanah | Book Review," 29/07/2017
Sarai Talks Books, "Book Review | Americanah by Chimamanda Ngozi Adichie," 26/01/2015
—, "Sunday Reads | Currently Reading Aug. 16, 2015," 16/08/2015
SavidgeReads, "January Book Haul | Part 1 | 2017," 12/01/2017
—, "Some #OwnVoices Reading Recommendations," 27/01/2017
—, "Baileys Women's Prize for Fiction Longlist | 2017," 12/03/2017
—, "April Wrap Up | Part One | 2017," 27/04/2017
—, "Baileys Prize for Women's Fiction Shortlist & Prediction | 2017," 06/06/2017
—, "My Books of the Year So Far | 2017," 20/07/2017
—, "My Very Favourite Books of 2017," 31/12/2017
—, "The Wellcome Book Prize Shortlist 2018," 20/03/2018
—, "April Book Haul | Part Two | 2018," 29/04/2018
—, "October Book Haul | Part Two | 2018," 03/11/2018
—, "January Book Haul | Part One | 2019," 16/01/2019
—, "January Wrap Up | Part One | 2019," 19/01/2019
—, "The Books I Love The Most | 2019," 14/02/2019
—, "Guessing the Women's Prize Longlist | 2019," 24/02/2019
—, "The Women's Prize for Fiction Longlist | 2019," 04/03/2019
—, "Some of My Favourite Women Writers | March 2019," 08/03/2019
—, "February Wrap Up | Part Two | 2019," 10/03/2019
—, "Crime Time With Pip & Simon #7: The Seven Deaths of Evelyn Hardcastle & More | March 2019," 14/03/2019
—, "Women's Prize Longlist 2019 | Halfway Chat," 28/03/2019
—, "Women's Prize Longlist Thoughts & Shortlist Possibilities with My Mum | 2019," 28/04/2019
—, "A Women's Prize Project | ft. All The Previous Winners | 2019," 11/06/2019
—, "Books of the Year (So Far!) | 2019," 07/07/2019
SCSReads, "What I Read | December 2015 and January 2016," 02/02/2016
—, "Book Haul 05," 16/02/2016
Shaelin Writes, "Recent Reads #13," 30/11/2018
—, "Recent Reads #16," 09/04/2019
Shamina Yuki Crawford, "June TBR (Japanese Lit + LGBTQ + Reads)," 04/06/2017
—, "Favorite Reads of 2017 | Part 2," 08/01/2018
—, "African Writers TBR | Tag [CC]," 04/03/2018
Shawn the Book Maniac, "THE SHITHOLE COUNTRIES TAG," 21/01/2018
—, "FRIDAY READS: BE-BE-BE-WITCH WAY IS UP? SOME ENTRANCEMENTS," 16/02/2018
—, "FRIDAY READS: MORTAL BRUSHES; ALWAYS UNDER-BUTT; THE STINK OF KNOWLEDGE," 24/02/2018
—, "REVIEW: FRESHWATER – AKWAEKE EMEZI," 02/03/2018
—, "FEBRUARY WRAP UP (INCLUDING BAILS)," 05/03/2018
—, "Book Postscript 2018 (Vlogmas, Day 17)," 17/12/2018
—, "African Writers Tag," 07/03/2019
Shellee Stories, "Book Review: Stay with Me by Ayobami Adebayo," 26/11/2017
—, "Book Review: Purple Hibiscus," 16/04/2018
—, "Book Review: Freshwater by Akwaeke Emezi," 11/11/2018
Shirley B. Eniang, "AUTUMN (FALL) HAUL!!! | Books, Zara, Other Stories, ASOS, Hair, Makeup & More! | SHOPPING," 08/09/2014

shoutame, "Reading Wrap-Up | February 2017," 04/03/2017
Siani Reads, "Book Haul," 15/03/2019
—, "Friday Reads – a little haul and what I'm reading," 19/04/2019
Siwe Magadla, "Book Review Purple Hibiscus," 31/08/2016
—, "Book Unboxing | Freshwater by Akwaeke Emezi & The January Children by Safia Elhillo," 15/06/2018
—, "Book Review | Freshwater by Akwaeke Emezi [CC]," 16/09/2018
Siyanda Mohutsiwa, "Book Review | Half of a Yellow Sun by Chimamanda Ngozi Adichie," 28/06/2013
—, "8 of The Best Books I've Read This Year | Open City, Room, End of Men, Letters From Botswana ... etc," 07/12/2013
SomdahSaysSo, "July 2016 Book Haul," 17/07/2016
Story Nut, "Ghana Must Go | Book Review (CC)," 25/08/2016
sugarbanana, "june faves 2016! | @sugarbananaa," 01/07/2016
suhani aggarwal, "The Icarus Girl Review," 17/01/2019
sunbeamsjess, "AUGUST BOOKS | sunbeamsjess," 28/09/2016
—, "SEPTEMBER AND OCTOBER BOOKS | sunbeamsjess," 19/11/2017
Super Pao, "May + Asian Readathon Wrap Up," 06/06/2019
Supposedly Fun, "Recent Reads from June 2019 Part 1," 12/06/2019
Susan Gamboa stumpf, "Americanah Book Review," 11/02/2019
sweetmarsha, "Book Review | Americanah by Chimamanda Ngozi Adichie," 08/09/2014
SweetPea Reads, "Emojiathon Round 2 | TBR," 06/06/2017
tbgreads, "Stay With Me by Ayobami Adebayo | Wisdom Wednesday | tbgreads | book talk," 20/02/2019
That's So Poe, "TBR | Black History Month 2019," 03/02/2019
That's What She Reads, "Casual Friday Reads," 25/05/2018
The Artisan Geek, "My Sister the Serial Killer | Book Review," 25/11/2018
the audiobook aficionado, "2016 books #161–165," 10/12/2016
The Black Curriculum, "Americanah by Chimamanda Ngozi Adichie," 21/11/2017
The Book Castle, "May Wrap Up | The Book Castle," 01/06/2016
—, "Best Books of 2016 | The Book Castle," 08/01/2017
—, "February Wrap Up Part I | The Book Castle," 16/02/2017
—, "February Wrap Up Part II | The Book Castle," 02/03/2017
—, "Reading the World: Round I | The Book Castle," 12/03/2017
—, "May Book Haul | The Book Castle," 28/05/2017
—, "5 Summer Book Recommendations | The Book Castle," 25/06/2017
—, "Reading the World: Round II | The Book Castle," 23/11/2017
—, "Best Books of 2017: Fiction & Poetry | The Book Castle," 07/01/2018
—, "10 Fiction Books I Want To Read In 2018 | The Book Castle," 08/01/2018
—, "My Favorite Literary Quotes | The Book Castle | 2018," 20/05/2018
—, "Reading the World: Round III | The Book Castle | 2018," 14/06/2018
—, "Women's Prize for Fiction 2019: Books I've Read + Want To Read | The Book Castle | 2019," 10/03/2019
—, "3 Books Set in Nigeria | The Book Castle | 2019," 24/03/2019
—, "My Favorite Books From The Last 5 Years | The Book Castle | 2019," 13/06/2019
The Book Rookie, "#Novellathon TBR | Spring 2017," 05/05/2017
The Book Wanderer, "AUTUMN WRAP UP | Glass Castle, Americanah, Girlboss & More," 04/12/2014
The Bookish Bulletin, "My Top 5 Favourite Reads of 2018 | Recommendations," 13/12/2018

The Bookish Land, "My Top 10 Books of 2017 | The Bookish Land," 19/12/2017

—, "MY SISTER THE SERIAL KILLER | PRAISE SONG FOR THE BUTTERFLIES | Women's Prize Dual Review 2019," 30/04/2019

—, "THE SILENCE OF THE GIRLS | ORDINARY PEOPLE | FRESHWATER | Women's Prize Triple Review," 01/06/2019

The Literary Life, "BOOKS I READ RECENTLY #1," 09/08/2018

The Maddie Hatter, "Book Review || Purple Hibiscus, by Chimamanda Ngozi Adichie #continentreads," 05/02/2015

the modisher, "Last wrap up of 2015," 30/12/2015

The Palm Print, "The Living Room Ep. 1 – Conversations on 'Half of a Yellow Sun' by Chimamanda Ngozi Adichie," 28/09/2013

—, "Episode 2: War. Conversations," 28/09/2013

—, "Episode 3: Colonialism. Conversations," 28/09/2013

—, "Episode 4: Culture. Conversations," 28/09/2013

—, "Episode 5: Love. Conversations," 28/09/2013

—, "Episode 6: Perspectives. Conversations," 01/10/2013

—, "Episode 7: Conversations on 'Half of a Yellow Sun'," 02/10/2013

—, "Series 2. The Living Room – The Lives of Children Intro," 17/01/2014

—, "The Lives Of Children – Protection," 25/01/2014

—, "The Lives Of Children – Protection (continued)," 25/01/2014

—, "A Different Kind Of Black," 06/02/2015

The Pool Of English, "Americannah summary Chimamanda Ngozi Adichie," 04/09/2017

The Reader's Athenaeum, "My 10 Favourite Books of 2017," 28/12/2017

The Storyscape, "Americanah [Book Review]," 25/02/2014

—, "TIA Talks LIVE: Americanah with FrenchieDee," 08/03/2014

—, "To know how it would feel to be free [Book Review]," 26/10/2017

The Wendy Williams Show, "Americanah," 28/09/2015

The Yacker Reviews, "Americanah – Book Review," 21/07/2017

The Zurich Review, "Recent Reads Wrapup – And By the Way, I'm Back!" 13/06/2018

TheCurlyBookworm, "WHY I LOVED PURPLE HIBISCUS || Book Review (spoiler-free!)," 29/01/2018

TheThriftyReader, "Review | Half of a Yellow Sun," 20/06/2014

ThisAfropolitanLife, "Book Review: Every Day Is For The Thief by Teju Cole," 04/03/2016

ThroughEllesEyes, "What am I reading | ThroughEllesEyes | South African YouTuber," 28/02/2018

Tochi Danny, "Book Review Episode 1 – Americanah," 25/12/2017

Todd the Librarian, "'STAY WITH ME' BOOK REVIEW! Did a Buddy Read with Peta (ComfyCozyup)," 27/01/2018

Toyin Afolabi-Ogunbiyi, "Half of a Yellow Sun by Chimamanda Ngozi Adichie," 08/03/2019

—, "Purple Hibiscus," 20/05/2019

Toyin Unboxed, "STAY WITH ME by Ayobami Adebayo Book Chat ft Shewa Vlogs + Our message to Nollywood," 05/06/2019

Trace This Space, "Book Review: Half of A Yellow Sun," 18/08/2017

Tunrayo, "Book review: Purple Hibiscus by Chimamanda Adichie," 22/04/2016

—, "Reading Wrap Up | July 2017," 03/08/2017

Tyler McClelland, "My Two Cents: Americanah," 10/10/2015

unmanaged mischief, "Book Review | The Fishermen #ManBookering," 21/08/2015

Unveiled Stories Online Counselling with Nicole Hind, "Unveiled Stories Book Club: Americanah and how it can help you bravely follow your desires," 10/10/2016
VelmaVlogs, "January Wrap Up," 09/02/2017
—, "A Mindless June Wrap Up," 07/07/2017
Videl Blind – The Blind Reader, "My Sister, the Serial Killer by Oyinkan Braithwaite Review," 09/07/2019
vuvu vena reads, "PURPLE HIBISCUS | REVIEW," 21/12/2018
Vynexa, "A TOO LONG FEBRUARY 2019 WRAP UP || Vynexa," 05/03/2019
Waffle'sVeryHappy, "My Favourite Books 2017," 29/01/2018
Wandering Reader, "'Stay With Me' by Ayobami Adebayo | Book Review," 17/05/2017
Weird Book Book Club, "WBBC Reviews: Convenience Store Woman by Sayaka Murata," 12/02/2019
WhatKamilReads, "Americanah (2013) by Chimamanda Ngozi Adichie | Book Talk #6," 24/07/2014
—, "Adichie, Atwood, Walton | Mini Reviews," 11/12/2014
—, "The Fishermen (2015) by Chigozie Obioma #ManBooker2015 (spoilers free)," 30/07/2015
—, "New Books Releases – January and February of 2016," 24/01/2016
Wilde Reads, "Six more books to look out for in March | Wilde Reads," 28/02/2018
Worth The Read, "Book Review: My Sister The Serial Killer," 29/04/2019
Writers Bone, "Friday Morning Coffee: The Best Novels of 2015," 11/12/2015
Yaiza Canopoli, "5 books about death | Halloween recs!" 16/10/2018
Yerba Buena Center for the Arts, "YBCA: You Summer Book Club: July, w/Andi Mudd & Isaac Fitzgerald," 18/06/2013
Yeside DS, "THOUGHTS ON 'GHANA MUST GO' BY TAIYE SELASI," 14/02/2018
—, "SISTER TAG BOOKTUBE CHALLENGE," 26/09/2018
—, "THOUGHTS ON 'AMERICANAH' BY CHIMAMANDA NGOZI ADICHIE," 11/02/2019
yogi with a book, "FEB WRAP-UP + MAR TBR | Contemporaryathon, #ReadingBlackout & more [CC]," 03/03/2018
—, "O.W.L.s RECOMMENDATIONS | Care of Magical Creatures, DADA, Divination, Potions, Transfigurations," 31/03/2018
You Know Now, "THE ICARUS GIRL Helen Oyeyemi | SUMMARY – THEME – PLOT REVIEW Multicultural Literature," 15/02/2017
Youngiftedandblack, "Favorite books of 2018 (the physical ones, i realised that i didn't check my tablet)," 13/01/2019
Your True Shelf, "The Reading Women Challenge 2019 | Your True Shelf," 11/02/2019
—, "The 2019 Wellcome Book Prize Longlist | Your True Shelf," 18/02/2019
—, "March Wrap Up 2019 | Your True Shelf," 08/04/2019

Author Videos on YouTube

2nacheki, "African Writer Chimamanda React to Racist Question 'Does Nigeria Have Bookstores?'," 30/01/2018
—, "African Writer Chimamanda Honest Reactions to Trump and Racism," 08/02/2018
—, "Nigerian Writer Chimamanda Speech on Sexual Harassment by African Men," 13/05/2018
—, "Acclaimed Nigerian Author Chimamanda Calls Melania Trump a Racist," 23/10/2018

4th Estate Books, "Chimamanda Ngozi Adichie talks to Fourth Estate.mp4," 17/03/2011

5x15 Stories, "Ayòbámi Adébáyò @ 5x15 – Stay With Me – Wellcome Book Prize 2018," 03/05/2018

AALBC.com, "Chimamanda Ngozi Adichie with Zadie Smith," 21/03/2014

Action Against Hunger USA, "Chimamanda Adichie, Action Against Hunger 2018 Humanitarian Awardee," 06/11/2018

Adri Lazarus, "Chimamanda Ngozi Adichie | Baltimore Book Festival 2017," 24/09/2017

AFP news agency, "Nigeria's Adichie says bestseller helped recall painful past," 11/10/2013

AfriQtalk Media, "Chimamanda Adichie – Nigerian Award Winning Author," 03/07/2013

Afro Buzz UK, "AFROBUZZ: It's the Half of a Yellow Sun Premiere #VOXAFRICA," 16/04/2014

Ake Arts & Book Festival, "#AkeFest16 Bookchat: Panashe Chigumadzi and Chinelo Okparanta," 27/04/2017

—, "#AkeFest17: Ouida Book Launch," 09/04/2018

—, "Book Chat: Dami Ajayi, Ayobami Adebayo and Yvonne Owuor," 18/04/2018

Al Jazeera English, "The Stream – In conversation with Chimamanda Ngozi Adichie," 01/09/2016

American University, "Chimamanda Ngozi Adichie Commencement Address for American University College of Arts & Sciences," 12/05/2019

AriseEntertainment 360, "Award-Winning Author Chimamanda Ngozi Adichie Part I," 14/03/2014

—, "Award-Winning Author Chimamanda Ngozi Adichie Part II," 14/03/2014

AriseNewsChannel, "CHIGOZIE OBIOMA," 14/10/2015

askanews, "Chimamanda Adichie: le storie delle donne sono storie per tutti," 09/10/2018

AtlanticLIVE, "Chimamanda Ngozi Adichie / Washington Ideas Forum 2014," 27/03/2015

Atprick B, "Between the Lines: Chimamanda Ngozi Adichie with Zadie Smith," 26/12/2014

Atria Kennisinstitute, "We should all be feminists | Chimamanda Ngozi Adichie – Atria," 15/10/2016

—, "A short impression of the visit of Chimamanda Ngozi Adichie at Atria," 22/11/2016

Ayebia Clarke, "Ayebia Clarke Publishing @ SOAS, University of London, Chimamanda Ngozi Adichie Lecture, July 2012," 13/07/2012

BabsonCollegeTV, "Author Chris Abani," 10/12/2014

Barnard Center for Research on Women, "Chinelo Okparanta and Akwaeke Emezi: Reading and Conversation," 20/05/2019

Barnard College, "Chimamanda Adichie says 'Eat Real Food'," 19/05/2016

BBC Afrique, "*** – BBC Afrique: Chimamanda Ngozi Adichie en 5 phrases," 22/10/2018

BBC Newsnight, "Is Donald Trump racist? Chimamanda Ngozi Adichie v R Emmett Tyrrell – BBC Newsnight," 12/11/2016

—, "Chimamanda Ngozi Adichie and R Emmett Tyrrell: Full debate – BBC Newsnight," 16/11/2016

Bhumika Regmi, "Chimamanda Ngozi Adichie on Religion and Feminism," 15/04/2017

BLM WORLDWIDE, "Chimamanda Ngozi Adichie on race in America 'Race is America's original sin'," 10/08/2016

Bonnier, "Chimamanda Ngozi Adichie: Even Though We Didn't Have a Children's Driver (from GRID11)," 24/10/2017

bookarmy, "Chimamanda Ngozi Adichie talks to 5th Estate," 27/10/2009

Boots UK, "Introducing Chimamanda Ngozi Adichie," 31/10/2016

Bibliography

Boshemia Magazine, "Chimamanda Ngozi Adichie Responds to Her Transphobic Comments," 17/03/2017

Brainwash, "Waarom censuur van binnenuit komt – Schrijver Chimamanda Ngozi Adichie," 19/03/2018

BREAKING NEWS TODAY, "BREAKING! Chimamanda Ngozi Adichie wins PEN Pinter Prize," 12/06/2018

Bree Rolfe, "Chris Abani Background Video," 11/01/2016

Brittlepaper, "Purple Hibiscus Literary Evening with Chimamanda," 20/07/2019

BrooklynBookFestival, "Brooklyn Book Festival – 2015 – The Transgressive Writer: Sexuality, Politics, History," 23/09/2015

buchmesse, "Eröffnungs-PK der Buchmesse 2018 – Chimamanda Ngozi Adichie," 09/10/2018

Bustle, "Chimamanda Ngozi Adichie Discusses Her New Feminist Manifesto, Dear Ijeawele," 09/03/2017

Casa África, "Enrevista a Chigozie Obioma," 05/05/2016

—, "Entrevista a Chimamanda Ngozi Adichie," 20/10/2017

—, "Conversación con Chimamanda Ngozi Adichie / CCCB," 16/01/2018

CelebratingProgress, "Chimamanda Adichie: Powerful words (2)," 03/08/2009

—, "Chimamanda Ngozi Adichie: Powerful words (1)," 20/08/2009

—, "Chimamanda Ngozi Adichie: Powerful words (3)," 20/08/2009

Chanel AverageMarcos, "Chimamanda Ngozi Adichie: 'Can people please stop telling me feminism is hot?'," 04/03/2017

Channel 4 News, "Author Chimamanda Ngozi Adichie on love, race and hair," 10/04/2013

—, "Chimamanda Ngozi Adichie: 'Hair is political'," 10/04/2013

—, "Chimimanda Ngozi Adichie: Black Lives Matter is doing something really important," 08/08/2016

—, "Chimamanda Ngozi Adichie Interview," 11/03/2017

Channels Television, "Chimamanda Adichie On Chinua Achebe," 26/03/2013

—, "Buy Books Instead Of Recharge Cards – Chimamanda Ngozi Adichie," 27/04/2013

—, "I Have Fallen In Love With My Hair – Chimamanda Ngozi Adichie," 27/04/2013

—, "Channels Book Club Features Chinelo Okparanta Author Of 'Under The Udala Trees' Pt. 1," 22/11/2016

—, "Channels Book Club Features Chinelo Okparanta Author Of 'Under The Udala Trees' Pt. 2," 22/11/2016

Chatham House, "London Conference 2018 – Dinner Keynote Speech: Chimamanda Ngozi Adichie," 22/06/2018

—, "Chimamanda Ngozi Adichie on Storytelling – Chatham House 2018," 25/06/2018

Chicago Humanities Festival, "Chris Abani, Global Igbo," 14/11/2015

Christian Dior, "Chimamanda Ngozi Adichie on the Dior Autumn–Winter 2019–2020 Haute Couture Show," 05/07/2019

City of Asylum, "The Writer's Block: A Video Q&A with Chris Abani," 01/07/2013

City of Des Moines – DMTV, "Chigozie Obioma – Authors Visiting in Des Moines (Avid)," 29/04/2019

CNN, "Capturing the African voice," 14/10/2009

—, "Amanpour interviews Chimamanda Ngozi Adichie," 17/04/2017

—, "Chimamanda Ngozi Adichie talks feminism, #MeToo movement," 20/04/2018

Commonwealth Foundation, "Chimamanda Ngozi Adichie: Commonwealth Lecture 2012," 16/03/2012

Commonwealth Writers, "Chimamanda Ngozi Adichie," 10/10/2011

Congo Vision TV, "Chimamanda Ngozi Adichie in interview during the introductions of Americanah book," 26/05/2013

Craig Rintoul, "Chimamanda Ngozi Adichie – Half of a Yellow Sun," 24/01/2007

—, "Chimamanda Ngozi Adichie – The Thing Around Your Neck – Bookbits author interview," 10/09/2009

Creative Writing at Penn State, "Chinelo Okparanta Interview," 21/06/2016

Critical Thinkers, "The real problem of Africa | Chimamanda Ngozi Adichie," 09/03/2019

crushing corporate, "Trevor Noah and Chimamanda Ngozi Adichie interviewed at PEN America," 09/05/2017

Daily Mail, "Nigerian author says Meghan Markle should be Commonwealth head – Daily Mail," 19/04/2018

dailyemerald, "Chimamanda Adichie Speaks at the University of Oregon," 04/04/2013

Det Kgl. Bibliotek, "Chimamanda Ngozi Adichie – 'Americanah' – International Authors' Stage," 20/05/2014

—, "Chimamanda Ngozi Adichie: 'If Michelle Obama had natural hair, Barack Obama would not have won'," 28/05/2014

edbookfest, "Chimamanda Ngozi Adichie with Nicola Sturgeon at the Edinburgh International Book Festival," 04/09/2017

Emmanuel Ikhapoh, "HARDtalk Chimamanda Ngozi Adichie Author b045In9h default," 05/06/2014

English Speeches, "ENGLISH SPEECHES | CHIMAMANDA NGOZI ADICHIE: Be Courageous (English Subtitles)," 16/03/2019

englishpen1921, "Chimamanda Ngozi Adichie – Pen Pinter Prize 2018," 10/10/2018

Esquire UK, "Chimamanda Ngozi Adichie talks Trump, race and the future of #MeToo," 24/10/2018

Exclusive Books, "Africa's Lit Volume 12: Ayòbámi Adébáyò," 28/09/2017

Expresso Show, "Nigerian Author, Ayobami Adebayo – Debut Novel Stay With Me | 6 September 2017," 07/09/2017

FIFDH Genève, "Meet Chimamanda Ngozi Adichie," 21/03/2018

—, "Discussion with Chimamanda Ngozi Adichie – English," 29/03/2018

figmentdotcom, "Girls Write Now CHAPTERS – Interview with Chimamanda Ngozi Adichie," 21/03/2011

Financial Times, "Emerging Voices awards | FT World," 06/10/2015

Flip – Festa Literária Internacional de Paraty, Flip 2019 – 'Angico', com Ayòbámi Adébáyò (trecho)," 12/07/2019

FORA.tv, "Chinelo Okparanta: 'I Belong Wherever I Am'," 12/01/2015

—, "Chimamanda Ngozi Adichie: Refugees, Race, and Americanah," 29/09/2016

Foyles, "Ayòbámi Adébáyò: Stay With Me | Her debut novel, women in Nigeria and the Baileys Prize," 13/03/2017

FRANCE 24 English, "Nigeria's literary star Chimamanda Ngozi Adichie speaks to FRANCE 24," 23/01/2015

—, "Meet Nigeria's latest literary star Chigozie Obioma," 30/06/2016

—, "Homosexuality, war and religion in Nigeria," 04/09/2018

—, "Chimamanda Ngozi Adichie on social media, Donald Trump and feminism," 04/02/2019

—, "Chimamanda Ngozi Adichie: 'It's in the US that I thought that being black was a value-free idea'," 06/02/2019

—, "Chimamanda Ngozi Adichie: 'There's a new idea that it's OK to be racist' under Trump," 06/02/2019

France in the US, "Chimamanda Ngozi Adichie: Night of Ideas keynote speech," 04/02/2019
Free Word, "Writers Bloc: Chimamanda Ngozi Adichie | Free Word," 31/01/2012
FT Life, "My fashion nationalism, by Chimamanda Ngozi Adichie," 20/10/2017
gbgfilmfestival, "A conversation with Chimamanda Ngozi Adichie," 27/01/2014
—, "GIFF2014 Live: Studio Draken, CHIMAMANDA NGOZI ADICHIE | STUDION," 27/01/2014
GirlsWriteNow, "Behind the Scenes at Girls Write Now's June CHAPTERS reading," 29/09/2010
—, "Chimamanda Ngozi Adichie 2015 Girls Write Now Awards Speech," 20/05/2015
—, "Chimamanda Ngozi Adichie 2015 Girls Write Now Interview," 20/05/2015
Go On Girl Book Club, "Chimamanda Ngozi Adichie's Go On Girl! Book Club Award Presentation," 05/08/2017
GoldMyneTV, "Culture Space Icon – Writer Chimamanda Ngozi Adichie," 18/02/2014
Google Zeitgeist, "Why Do Women Always Have to Be Nice? | Chimamanda Ngozi Adichie & Mary Beard | Google Zeitgeist," 21/05/2018
Granta Magazine, "Chinelo Okparanta | Granta's Best of Young American Novelists," 30/06/2017
Hall Center, "Chris Abani Conversation 11/01/2009," 14/04/2017
—, "'Stories of Struggle, Stories of Hope, Art, Politics and Human Rights', Chris Abani, 2009," 14/04/2017
Harvard University, "Author Chimamanda Ngozi Adichie addresses Harvard's Class of 2018," 23/05/2018
Hay Festival, "Chimamanda Ngozi Adichie on feminism," 15/02/2019
hessischerrundfunk, "Die nigerianische Autorin Chimamanda Ngozi Adichie auf der #FBM18," 09/10/2018
hitlist n cruzin, "SHOOTING FOR CHIMAMANDA ADICHIE'S AMERICANAH TO BEGIN IN 2019," 19/10/2018
IgboBiafran, "Igbo Author, Chimamanda Ngozi Adichie 'If Michelle Obama had natural hair'," 08/11/2015
IgboConference, "'Igbo bu Igbo' by Chimamanda Ngozi Adichie – Keynote Speaker: 7th Igbo Conference," 20/05/2018
—, "Chimamanda Adichie in Conversation at City, University of London," 20/08/2018
INBOUND, "Chimamanda Ngozi Adichie | INBOUND 2018 Keynote," 11/09/2018
—, "Chimamanda Ngozi Adichie | The INBOUND Studio," 22/04/2019
InterKontinental Literary Agency, "Chris Abani and Mukoma wa Ngugi in Berlin for WRITING IN MIGRATION | African Book Festival," 20/05/2018
—, "Olumide Popoola and Chris Abani | African Book Festival 2018," 28/02/2019
jc2670, "PEN WORLD VOICES: Chris Abani," 17/04/2007
JHSPH Student Life, "Chimamanda Ngozi Adichie || Faces of Africa 2018 at Johns Hopkins," 13/07/2018
Jide Salu, "Chimamanda Ngozi Adichie NPR Interview," 20/03/2014
—, "Chimamanda Ngozi Adichie with Jide Salu," 10/04/2014
Jim Foster: Conversations On The Coast, "Chimamanda Ngozi Adichie, The Thing Around Your Neck," 12/12/2016
Kalamazoo College, "2009 Commencement Address at Kalamazoo College, Chimamanda Ngozi Adichie," 01/07/2009
Kleopatra Jones, "Chimamanda Adichie at Middlesex University Dubai 1," 06/03/2009
—, "Chimamanda Adichie at Middlesex University Dubai 2," 07/03/2009
—, "Chimamanda Adichie at Middlesex University Dubai 3," 07/03/2009

—, "Chimamanda Adichie at Middlesex University Dubai 4," 07/03/2009
—, "Chimamanda Adichie at Middlesex University Dubai 9," 07/03/2009
—, "Chimamanda Adichie at Middlesex University Dubai 6," 08/03/2009
—, "Chimamanda Adichie at Middlesex University Dubai 7," 08/03/2009
Krull magazine, "Krull magazine. Chimamanda Ngozi Adichie at Kulturhuset, Stockholm," 27/11/2018
KTN News Kenya, "Book review: Americanah by Chimamanda Ngozi," 04/12/2013
KU EGARC, "Stories About Migration: Chris Abani," 07/06/2016
Kwani Trust, "#Kwaniat10 Book Party: Chimamanda Adichie & Yvonne Owuor," 21/12/2013
—, "#Kwaniat10 Lecture III: Chimamanda Ngozi Adichie," 10/03/2014
labforculture, "Chimamanda Ngozi Adichie.flv," 29/04/2011
Lannan Foundation, "Kwame Dawes with Chris Abani, 29 September 2010," 24/02/2011
—, "Chimamanda Ngozi Adichie with Binyavanga Wainaina, 28 Sept 2011," 02/10/2011
Lawrence Green, "Chimamanda Adichie speaks at the 2014 New African Film Festival," 17/03/2014
Leisha Camden, "Chimamanda Ngozi Adichie 1:4," 25/11/2009
—, "Chimamanda Ngozi Adichie 3:4," 29/11/2009
librairie mollat, "Chimamanda Ngozi Adichie – Americanah," 10/02/2015
Library of Congress, "Conversations with African Poets and Writers: Chinelo Okparanta," 07/04/2015
LifeWithGladys, "Chimamanda Ngozi Adichie on feminism, addressing recent transgender video, book signing, etc," 17/03/2017
Little, Brown and Company, "An Orchestra of Minorities by Chigozie Obioma," 31/01/2019
Louisiana Channel, "Chimamanda Ngozi Adichie Interview: The Right to Tell Your Story," 02/09/2013
—, "Chimamanda Ngozi Adichie Interview: Beauty Does Not Solve Problems," 27/06/2014
—, "Chigozie Obioma Interview: Everything We Do is Preordained," 16/03/2017
—, "Chigozie Obioma: Reading from 'The Fishermen'," 01/05/2017
Marie Claire Brasil, "Chimamanda Ngozi Adichie é a estrela da edicao de aniversário de Marie Claire," 10/04/2019
Melissa Adams, "The Family: A Talk with Chimamanda Ngozi Adichie," 27/09/2017
—, "Violence and Silence: A Talk with Chimamanda Ngozi Adichie," 27/09/2017
—, "Writing Advice: A Talk with Chimamanda Ngozi Adichie," 27/09/2017
—, "Writing Purple Hibiscus: A Talk with Chimamanda Ngozi Adichie," 27/09/2017
Mkenya Ujerumani, "Chimamanda Ngozi Adichie answers questions on Americanah in Cologne Germany," 25/05/2014
—, "Chimamanda Ngozi Adichie on the Complexities of Migration," 25/05/2014
MO nieuwssite, "MO*lezing Chimamanda Ngozi Adichie op Mind The Book 2014," 27/02/2014
neafoundation, "Chimamanda Ngozi Adichie's Closing Story," 10/10/2018
New America, "In Conversation: Chimamanda Ngozi Adichie and Anne Marie Slaughter," 22/05/2017
New York State Writers Institute, "Chimamanda Ngozi Adichie at the NYS Writers Institute in 2007," 09/04/2009
newdawnvideos, "Chimamanda Ngozi Adichie," 03/08/2017
News24, "Novel by Nigerian author sparks gay rights conversation in Africa," 01/06/2016

Bibliography

NTA2Lagos, "CHIMAMANDA – 16 THINGS YOU NEED TO KNOW ABOUT HER – NTA 2 Lagos," 01/05/2013

—, "CHIMAMANDA, CHILD ABUSE BY PRIESTS – NTA 2 Lagos," 01/05/2013

—, "CHIMAMANDA ... NIGERIA WAS NOT SET UP TO SUCCEED – NTA 2 Lagos," 01/05/2013

—, "CHIMAMANDA – NIGERIAN ATTITUDE TO RAPE – NTA 2 Lagos," 01/05/2013

NUHumanitiesCenter, "NU Humanities Center Presents: Chimamanda Ngozi Adichie Q&A 1," 13/09/2012

—, "NU Humanities Center Presents: Chimamanda Ngozi Adichie Q&A 2," 13/09/2012

NYC Mayor's Office, "AMERICANAH is the winner of the One Book, One New York in 2017 #OneBookNY," 04/10/2018

Oi Futuro, "Chimamanda Ngozi Adichie no WISE 2017," 17/11/2017

omolola15, "Chimamanda Q&A at Half of a Yellow Sun screening pt 1," 19/03/2014

—, "Chimamanda Ngozi Adichie Half of a Yellow Sun screening pt 2," 19/03/2014

Open Book Festival, "Yewande Omotoso in Conversation with Ayòbámi Adébáyò," 24/09/2017

Oswaldo Armendariz, "Night Waves .- Chimamanda Ngozi Adichie .- Americanah," 22/11/2015

PBS Books, "Chimamanda Ngozi Adichie on 'We Should All Be Feminists' at the 2017 AWP Book Fair," 11/02/2017

—, "Chris Abani on 'The Secret History of Las Vegas' at the 2018 AWP Book Fair," 10/03/2018

PEN America, "Conversation: Chris Abani & Walter Mosley," 05/02/2010

—, "2018 #FreedomToWrite Lecture: Hillary Rodham Clinton with Chimamanda Ngozi Adichie (Low-Res)," 23/04/2018

PENfaulkner, "Chimamanda Ngozi Adichie Writers in Schools visit to Cardozo," 02/03/2017

Penguin Random House Canada, "Chimamanda Ngozi Adichie, author of The Thing Around Your Neck," 29/06/2009

PHOENIX Magazine, "Meet Ayobami Adebayo, Author of 'Stay With Me'," 29/03/2018

Plus TV Africa, "'Merit, Not Gender, Should Earn You an Appointment Anywhere' – Chimamanda Adichie," 11/10/2018

—, "'Some Men Have Become Better Fathers by Listening to Me' – Chimamanda Adichie," 11/10/2018

poetsandwriters, "Chimamanda Ngozi Adichie Remarks: Annual Dinner 2018," 07/05/2018

Politics and Prose, "Chimamanda Ngozi Adichie, 'Dear Ijeawele' (with Audie Cornish)," 25/03/2017

—, "Ayòbámi Adébáyò, Stay With Me," 28/08/2018

PreviewNaija, "Part 1 Author Chimamanda Ngozi Adichie Speaking at Harvard," 21/10/2008

—, "Part 2 Author Chimamanda Ngozi Adichie Speaking at Harvard," 21/10/2008

Pulse Nigeria, "Chimamanda Adichie, Mo Abudu, Omotola Jalade-Ekeinde Won Variety Magazine Awards," 12/03/2018

Purple Feminists Group, "Chimamanda Ngozi Adichie Messages to Her Translator Nandar & Myanmar Audiences," 28/05/2019

Queen Hunter, "Chatting with Chimamanda at the 2018 Abantu Book Festival," 22/12/2018

robmaitra, "The Boys' Club of New York Presents Chris Abani," 18/02/2008

Rollins College, "Winter With the Writers: Chimamanda Adichie," 14/02/2013
SABC Digital News, "Ayobami Adebayo on her debut novel 'Stay With Me'," 09/12/2017
SaharaTV, "Chimamanda Ngozi Adichie: A Conversation About AMERICANAH In New York City," 25/05/2013
saison15, "Chris Abani lectures Buffalo," 17/04/2011
Sharai Robin, "Chimamanda Ngozi Adichie on her writing and editing process," 20/02/2019
Silverbird Television, "The Movie 'Half Of A Yellow Sun' Gets Censors Board Approval," 09/07/2014
SOAS University of London, "Chimamanda Ngozi Adichie receives Honorary Doctorate from SOAS University of London," 30/07/2018
South African Book Fair, "NBW Broadcast Coverage – SABC Trendz with Ayobami Adebayo – 9 Sep," 23/02/2018
Southbank Centre, "WOW 2017 – Chimamanda Ngozi Adiche in conversation," 13/03/2017
Spotlite by Literandra, "Chigozie Obioma on Nigeria, Nostalgia, Cyprus and 'An Orchestra of Minorities'," 21/07/2019
—, "Chigozie Obioma on the Importance of Igbo Culture in 'An Orchestra of Minorities'," 21/07/2019
—, "Igbo Cosmology in 'An Orchestra of Minorities'," 27/07/2019
—, "Chigozie Obioma on Gbolahan Obisesan's adaptation of 'The Fishermen'," 30/07/2019
—, "The story and inspiration behind Chigozie Obioma's 'The Fishermen'," 31/07/2019
—, "Chigozie Obioma on finding his voice through his siblings," 02/08/2019
Stadsbiblioteket Göteorg, "Chigozie Obioma – Internationell författarscen Göteborg 2019," 07/05/2019
Stories234, "Chimamanda Adichie's Shocking Story About Being Sexually Assaulted By A Big Media Guy At Age 17," 19/04/2018
Stylist Magazine, "How To Become A Published Author; Advice From Chimamanda Ngozi Adichie," 10/06/2014
SVT, "Chimamanda Ngozi Adichie i BABEL: SVT," 06/11/2013
Swedish Institute, "Key note speech – Chimamanda Ngozi Adichie – Congress hall A," 20/04/2018
Sweet Briar College, "Chimamanda Adichie at Sweet Briar College," 02/11/2018
TED, "Chris Abani denkt über Menschlichkeit nach (Chris Abani on the stories of Africa)," 09/08/2007
—, "Chris Abani über die Erzählungen Afrikas (Chris Abani: On humanity)," 22/07/2008
—, "Chimamanda Adichie: Die Gefahr einer einzigen Geschichte," 07/10/2009
TEDx Talks, "Wir sollten alle Feministen sein | Chimamanda Ngozi Adichie | TEDxEuston," 12/04/2013
tehelkatv, "In Conversation with Chimamanda Ngozi Adichie," 04/03/2011
Tenement Museum, "Chimamanda Ngozi Adichie: Tenement Talk from March 12, 2014," 09/04/2014
The Aspen Institute, "Chimamanda Ngozi Adichie in conversation with Damian Woetzel," 11/03/2014
—, "An Interview with 'Americanah' Author Chimamanda Ngozi Adichie," 04/11/2014
The Atlantic, "Chimamanda Adichie on What Americans Get Wrong About Africa," 21/02/2017
The Center for Fiction, "CHAPTER: Chimamanda Ngozi Adichie (1/1)," 28/10/2010
—, "PEN World Voices: Viet Thanh Nguyen and Chinelo Okparanta," 10/05/2017

The Daily Show with Trevor Noah, "Chimamanda Ngozi Adichie – Dear Ijeawele & Raising a Child to Be a Feminist | The Daily Show," 09/06/2018
The GamaPhile, "Chimamanda Ngozi Adichie on Her Admiration of Michelle Obama, Hillary Clinton and Trans Comments," 05/09/2019
The Met, "A Conversation on Africa's Heritage," 07/03/2012
The Monthly Video, "Chimamanda Ngozi Adichie in conversation with Ramona Koval," 03/05/2013
—, "Chimamanda Ngozi Adichie in conversation with Ramona Koval (p2)," 03/05/2013
The New York Public Library, "Wole Soyinka on the odd complexity of Nigeria, with Chris Abani | LIVE from the NYPL," 10/11/2016
The New Yorker, "Chimamanda Ngozi Adichie on Liberal Cannibalism | The New Yorker Festival," 09/10/2017
The Palm Print, "Conversations with Chinelo Okparanta – Beyond the Skin," 05/10/2014
—, "Conversations with Chinelo Okparanta – Influences. Culture and Society," 05/10/2014
—, "Conversations with Chinelo Okparanta – Voiceless Women," 05/10/2014
The RSA, "Humanising History – Chimamanda Ngozi Adichie," 15/05/2013
The Tea, "WE SHOULD ALL BE FEMINISTS – Get2Know – AUTHOR Chimamanda Ngozi Adichie," 12/10/2017
The University of Edinburgh, "Acclaimed Nigerian author Chimamanda Ngozi Adichie receives honorary degree," 28/08/2017
The White, "Interview with Americanah author C. Adichie (French subtitles)," 10/01/2018
The Women's Center, "Chimamanda Ngozi Adichie – Be The Change," 07/05/2018
TIFF Originals, "FROM STORY TO SCREEN | TIFF Industry Conference 2013," 16/05/2014
TimesTalks, "TimesTalks: Chimamanda Ngozi Adichie," 05/05/2017
todaynewscnn, "BBC Culture Writer Chimamanda Ngozi Adichie discusses her career," 24/12/2013
toxnaija, "Nigeria Chimamanda Adichie," 09/05/2013
TVC News Nigeria, "The Platform Episode 89: Big Talk with Chigozie Obioma," 06/04/2019
Uncensored, "Funke Akindele, MO Abudu, Ayobami Adebayo, Yagazie Eguare @ The Future Awards Africa," 11/12/2017
Ungdoms Web TV, "BURT Web TV: A talk with Chigozie Obioma," 26/08/2016
UNICEF Innocenti, "Talking children, women and Africa with author Chimamanda Adichie," 30/05/2014
United Nations, "Chimamanda Ngozi Adichie – World Humanitarian Day 2016," 22/08/2016
Univ. of California, Riverside, "Christopher Abani – UCR CHASS Group 2 Commencement – June 16, 2012," 05/07/2012
University of Central Florida, "On the Issues – Author Chris Abani," 28/01/2009
USC Annenberg, "Chimamanda Ngozi Adichie on fake news," 09/03/2019
—, "Chimamanda Ngozi Adichie Receives USC Everett M. Rogers Award," 26/09/2019
Vagner Junior, "Milêno Escritora militante feminista tem livro lido por toda Nova York Assista online no GloboNe," 13/09/2017
Viewers Zone, "Chimamanda Ngozi Adichie speaks at the 7th International Annual Igbo Congress II #ViewersZone," 02/08/2019
voicesinwartime, "Chris Abani in Voices in Wartime," 20/07/2008

WellesleyCollege, "Chimamanda Ngozi Adichie: 2015 Wellesley College Commencement Speaker," 29/05/2015
West End Videos, "Keynote Chimamanda Ngozi Adichie," 05/07/2019
WGBHForum, "Ayòbámi Adébáyò reads from Stay With Me," 23/07/2018
WilliamsCollege, "Williams 2017: Chimamanda Ngozi Adichie," 05/06/2017
WISE Channel, "Why literature is key in 21st century education – Chimamanda Adichie," 20/03/2018
Women in the World, "Chimamanda Ngozi Adichie deconstructs masculinity," 06/04/2017
—, "Chimamanda Ngozi Adichie – What Is Feminism Light?" 06/04/2017
—, "Chimamanda Ngozi Adichie – Women in power in Nigeria," 06/04/2017
—, "WITW TOYOTA SOLUTIONS STUDIO 2017: Chimamanda Ngozi Adichie," 06/04/2017
Women's Prize for Fiction, "Chimamanda Ngozi Adichie interview," 04/11/2015
—, "Chimamanda Ngozi Adichie on winning the Best of the Best," 04/11/2015
Wondiya Usa, "Chimamanda Ngozi Adichie in San Francisco 2014," 04/10/2014
YaleUniversity, "Chimamanda Adichie, 2019 Yale Class Day Speaker," 21/05/2019
YAPTV, "Chimamanda Adichie and Uzo Iweala discussion I.mpg," 17/04/2010
YITV Young Immigrant TV, "Chimamanda Ngozi Adichie and Nkechi Mariel Sand Nwosu in Oslo," 24/03/2014
YNaija, "Chinelo Okparanta, Toni Kan, Kolade Arogundade, Kiru Taye … #AkeFest16," 22/11/2016
ZEE Jaipur Literature Festival, "JLF at Boulder 2018: An Orchestra of Stories #JLFatBoulder #SiblingStories #CreativeWriting," 02/12/2018
ZeitgeistMinds, "Woman, Power & Modern Feminism – Chimamanda Ngozi Adichie & Professor Mary Beard," 21/05/2018

Additional Primary Sources

Abani, Chris. *GraceLand*. Farrar, Straus and Giroux, 2004.
—. *Becoming Abigail*. Akashic Books, 2006.
—. *The Virgin of Flames*. Penguin, 2007.
Abraham, Tola Rotimi. *Black Sunday*. Catapult, 2020.
Achebe, Chinua. *Things Fall Apart*. 1958. Penguin Classics, 2001.
—. "Mango Seedling." 1968. *The New York Review*, 22 May 1969. https://www.nybooks.com/articles/1969/05/22/mango-seedling/. Accessed 30 April 2022.
Adeyemi, Tomi. *Children of Blood and Bone*. Henry Holt & Company, 2018.
—. *Children of Virtue and Vengeance*. Henry Holt & Company, 2019.
Adichie, Chimamanda N. *We Should All Be Feminists*. 4th Estate, 2014.
—. *Dear Ijeawele: A Feminist Manifesto in Fifteen Suggestions*. 4th Estate, 2017.
—. *Notes on Grief*. Alfred A. Knopf, 2021.
Atta, Sefi. *Swallow*. Interlink Books, 2010.
—. *A Bit of Difference*. 2013. 4th Estate, 2015.
Beasts of No Nation. Directed by Cary Fukunaga, performances by Abraham Attah and Idris Elba, Netflix, 2015.
Braithwaite, Oyinkan. *The Baby Is Mine*. Atlantic Books, 2021.
Emecheta, Buchi. *The Joys of Motherhood*. 1979. Heinemann, 1994.
—. *Destination Biafra*. 1982. Heinemann, 1994.

Emezi, Akwaeke. *Pet*. Knopf, 2019.
—. *The Death of Vivek Oji*. Riverhead Books, 2020.
—. *Dear Senthuran: A Black Spirit Memoir*. Riverhead Books, 2021.
Evans, Diana. *The Wonder*. Vintage, 2009.
—. *Ordinary People*. Chatto & Windus, 2018.
Habila, Helon. *Oil on Water*. W.W. Norton & Company, 2010.
—. *Travelers*. W.W. Norton & Company, 2019.
Iweala, Uzodinma. *Speak No Evil*. Harper Perennial, 2018.
Ndibe, Okey. *Foreign Gods, Inc*. Soho Press, 2014.
Nwaubani, Adaobi T. *Buried Beneath the Baobab Tree*. Katherine Tegen Books, 2018.
Okigbo, Christopher. "A Shrub Among Poplars." 1971. *Labyrinths, with Path of Thunder*, Africa World Press, 2008.
Okri, Ben. *The Famished Road*. 1991. Vintage, 1992.
Onuzo, Chibundu. *Welcome to Lagos*. Faber and Faber, 2017.
—. *Sankofa*. Catapult, 2021.
Oyeyemi, Helen. *The Opposite House*. 2007. Anchor Books, 2008.
—. *Boy, Snow, Bird*. Picador, 2014.
—. *Peaces*. Riverhead Books, 2021.
Papillon, Buki. *An Ordinary Wonder*. Dialogue Books, 2021.
Saro-Wiwa, Ken. *Sozaboy: A Novel in Rotten English*. 1985. Longman, 1994.
Soyinka, Wole. "Abiku." 1961. *The Penguin Book of Modern African Poetry*, edited by Gerald Moore and Ulli Beier, Penguin, 1984, p. 187.
Unigwe, Chika. *On Black Sisters' Street*. Vintage, 2010.
—. *Night Dancer*. Jonathan Cape, 2012.

Electronic Sources

"About Goodreads." *Goodreads*, www.goodreads.com/about/us. Accessed 2 July 2021.
"About the Prize." *BookTube Prize*, www.booktubeprize.org/about.html. Accessed 12 April 2021.
"About Us." *The Cut*, www.thecut.com/about-us/. Accessed 15 May 2021.
"About Us." *The Middlebrow Network*, www.middlebrow-network.com/About.aspx. Accessed 18 June 2021.
Adichie, Chimamanda N. "To Instruct and Delight: A Case for Realist Literature." *Commonwealth Foundation*, 15 March 2012, https://commonwealthfoundation.com/resource/commonwealth-lecture-2012-2/. Accessed 15 April 2021.
"AdSense Help." *Google*, www.support.google.com/adsense/?hl=en#topic=3373519. Accessed 12 April 2021.
"All You Need to Do to Get Started with Affiliate Marketing." *Influencer Marketing Hub*, 21 May 2021, www.influencermarketinghub.com/affiliate-marketing/. Accessed 28 April 2022.
Anthony, Laurence. AntConc (Version 3.5.8) [Computer Software]. Waseda University, www.laurenceanthony.net/software. Accessed 30 April 2022.
"Badges." *Amazon*, https://www.amazon.de/-/en/gp/help/customer/display.html?nodeId=GED7RL944YMQ8CE3&language=en_GB. Accessed 12 April 2021.
Boot, Peter. "The Desirability of a Corpus of Online Book Responses." *ACL Anthology*, 14 June 2013, www.aclweb.org/anthology/W13-1405.pdf. Accessed 16 March 2021.

Brown, Erica. "Introduction." *Working Papers on the Web*, vol. 11, 2008, https://extra.shu.ac.uk/wpw/middlebrow/Brown.html. Accessed 18 June 2021.

"Community Guidelines." *Amazon*, https://www.amazon.de/-/en/gp/help/customer/display.html?nodeId=GLHXEX85MENUE4XF. Accessed 2 July 2021.

"Community Guidelines." *Goodreads*, www.goodreads.com/community/guidelines. Accessed 2 July 2021.

"Community Guidelines." *YouTube*, www.youtube.com/intl/en_us/howyoutubeworks/policies/community-guidelines/. Accessed 2 July 2021.

Emezi, Akwaeke. "Transition." *The Cut*, 19 January 2018, https://www.thecut.com/2018/01/writer-and-artist-akwaeke-emezi-gender-transition-and-ogbanje.html. Accessed 15 May 2021.

Fenza, David. "A Letter from the AWP's Director." *AWP Director's Handbook: A Compendium of Guidelines and Information for Directors of Creative Writing Programs*, 2006, www.awpwriter.org/membership/dh_2.htm. Accessed 1 May 2021.

Finn, Ed. "Revenge of the Nerd: Junot Díaz and the Networks of American Literary Imagination." *Digital Humanities Quarterly*, vol. 7, no. 1, 2013, http://www.digitalhumanities.org/dhq/vol/7/1/000148/000148.html. Accessed 16 March 2021.

Fister, Barbara. "Platforms and the Shape of Reader Participation." *Digital Reading Network*, 26 June 2014, www.barbarafister.wordpress.com/2014/07/01/platforms-and-the-shape-of-reader-participation/. Accessed 26 February 2022.

Flood, Alison. "'It is obscene': Chimamanda Ngozi Adichie Pens Blistering Essay against Social Media Sanctimony." *The Guardian*, 16 June 2021, https://www.theguardian.com/books/2021/jun/16/chimamanda-ngozi-adichie-social-media-sanctimony. Accessed 28 January 2023.

Geyser, Werner. "YouTube Money Calculator: Calculate How Much You Can Make." *Influencer Marketing Hub*, 14 June 2021, www.influencermarketinghub.com/youtube-money-calculator/. Accessed 12 April 2021.

"Google AdSense." *Google*, www.google.com/intl/en_uk/adsense/start/. Accessed 12 April 2021.

"Graduate Programs in Liberal Arts & Sciences." *Iowa Graduate Admissions*, https://grad.admissions.uiowa.edu/cost/graduate-programs-liberal-arts-sciences-estimated-costs-domestic. Accessed 18 June 2021.

"Highlights of the 2017 Author Tour with Chimamanda Ngozi Adichie." *Maryland Humanities*, 4 October 2017, www.mdhumanities.org/2017/10/highlights-of-the-2017-author-tour-with-chimamanda-ngozi-adichie/. Accessed 29 April 2022.

"Home." *The Middlebrow Network*, https://middlebrownetwork.com/. Accessed 18 June 2021.

"HOW BOOKTUBERS MAKE MONEY." *YouTube*, uploaded by emmmabooks, 19 November 2016, www.youtube.com/watch?v=OYa8bJkad-w. Accessed 12 April 2021.

"Ifemelu's Blog." *Chimamanda Adichie*, 27 August 2014, https://www.chimamanda.com/ifem-ceiling/. Accessed 15 April 2021.

Jameson, Fredric. "Dirty Little Secret." *London Review of Books*, 22 November 2012, www.lrb.co.uk/the-paper/v34/n22/fredric-jameson/dirty-little-secret. Accessed 1 May 2021.

Kalpaxis, Vicky. "How the Publishing Industry Is Cashing in on Influencer Culture." *Observer*, 2 September 2020, www.observer.com/2020/02/booktube-influencer-culture-publishing-industry-bookstagram/. Accessed 2 July 2021.

Lobash, Lynn. "One Book, One New York Winner Announced." *The New York Public*

Library, 16 March 2017, www.nypl.org/blog/2017/03/16/one-book-one-new-york. Accessed 29 April 2022.

Moody, Rick. "Writers and Mentors." *The Atlantic*, 1 August 2005, https://www.theatlantic.com/magazine/archive/2005/08/writers-and-mentors/304101/. Accessed 1 May 2021.

NetGalley, www.netgalley.com. Accessed 12 April 2021.

"Oprah's Book Club 2.0 Launches Online June 4 with *Wild* by Cheryl Strayed." *Oprah.com*, 1 June 2012, www.oprah.com/pressroom/oprahs-book-club-20-launches-online-monday-june-4. Accessed 30 April 2022.

"Our Mission." *TED*, www.ted.com/about/our-organization. Accessed 15 May 2021.

Packer, George. "Cheap Words." *The New Yorker*, 9 February 2014, https://www.newyorker.com/magazine/2014/02/17/cheap-words. Accessed 9 March 2022.

"Philosophy." *Iowa Writers' Workshop*, www.writersworkshop.uiowa.edu/about/about-workshop/philosophy. Accessed 18 June 2021.

Richard and Judy Book Club, www.richardandjudy.co.uk/. Accessed 30 April 2022.

Selasi, Taiye. "Bye-Bye Babar." *The Lip Magazine*, 3 March 2005, https://thelip.robertsharp.co.uk/2005/03/03/bye-bye-barbar/. Accessed 18 June 2021.

Sethi, Anita. "'I didn't know I was writing a novel.'" *The Guardian*, 10 January 2005, www.theguardian.com/books/2005/jan/10/fiction.features11>. Accessed 15 May 2021.

So, Richard Jean and Andrew Piper. "How Has the MFA Changed the Contemporary Novel?" *The Atlantic*, 6 March 2016, https://www.theatlantic.com/entertainment/archive/2016/03/mfa-creative-writing/462483/. Accessed 18 June 2021.

Stedman, Gesa. "Global Pudding – Review of Zadie Smith's New Novel Swing Time." *Literary Field Kaleidoscope*, 5 April 2017, http://literaryfield.org/review-zs-swingtime/. Accessed 28 April 2022.

Tveit, Marta. "The Afropolitan Must Go." *Africa Is a Country*, 28 November 2013, www.africasacountry.com/2013/11/the-afropolitan-must-go/. Accessed 18 June 2021.

Secondary Sources

Ablow, Rachel, editor. *The Feeling of Reading: Affective Experience & Victorian Literature*. The University of Michigan Press, 2010.

Adenekan, Shola. *African Literature in the Digital Age: Class and Sexual Politics in New Writing from Nigeria and Kenya*. James Currey, 2021.

Adenekan, Shola and Helen Cousins. "Class Online: Representations of African Middle-Class Identity." *Postcolonial Text*, vol. 9, no. 3, 2014, pp. 1–15.

Adesanmi, Pius and Chris Dunton. "Nigeria's Third Generation Writing: Historiography and Preliminary Theoretical Considerations." *English in Africa*, vol. 32, no. 1, 2005, pp. 7–19.

—. "Everything Good Is Raining: Provisional Notes on the Nigerian Novel of the Third Generation." *Research in African Literatures*, vol. 39, no. 2, 2008, pp. vii–xii.

Adichie, Chimamanda N. "African 'Authenticity' and the Biafran Experience." *Transition*, no. 99, 2008, pp. 42–53.

Ahmad, Aijaz. "The Politics of Literary Postcoloniality." *Contemporary Postcolonial Theory: A Reader*, edited by Padmini Mongia, Routledge, 1996, pp. 276–93.

Ahrens, Rüdiger, Wolf-Dietrich Bald and Werner Hüllen, editors. *Handbuch Englisch als Fremdsprache*. Erich Schmidt Verlag, 1995.

Aldridge, John W. "The New American Assembly-Line Fiction: An Empty Blue Center." *The American Scholar*, vol. 59, no. 1, 1990, pp. 17–38.

Allington, Daniel. "'Power to the Reader' or 'Degradation of Literary Taste'? Professional Critics and Amazon Customers as Reviewers of *The Inheritance of Loss*." *Language and Literature: International Journal of Stylistics*, vol. 25, no. 3, 2016, pp. 254–78.

Anderson, Benedict. *Imagined Communities: Reflections on the Origin and Spread of Nationalism*. 1983. Revised edition, Verso, 2006.

Andrade, Susan Z. "Adichie's Genealogies: National and Feminine Novels." *Research in African Literatures*, vol. 42, no. 2, 2011, pp. 91–101.

Anyokwu, Christopher. "Inheritance of Loss: Narrative and History in Helon Habila's *Measuring Time*." *California Linguistic Notes*, vol. 33, no. 2, 2008, pp. 1–27.

Arthur, John A., Joseph Takougang and Thomas Owusu. "Searching for Promised Lands: Conceptualization of the African Diaspora in Migration." *Africans in Global Migration: Searching for Promised Lands*, edited by John A. Arthur, Joseph Takougang and Thomas Owusu, Lexington Books, 2012, pp. 1–8.

Ashcroft, Bill, Gareth Griffiths and Helen Tiffin. *Post-Colonial Studies: The Key Concepts*. 2000. Second edition, Routledge, 2007.

Atia, Nadia and Kate Houlden. "Introduction." *Popular Postcolonialisms: Discourses of Empire and Popular Culture*, edited by Nadia Atia and Kate Houlden, Routledge, 2019, pp. 1–23.

Aubry, Timothy. *Reading as Therapy: What Contemporary Fiction Does for Middle-Class Americans*. University of Iowa Press, 2011.

Baker, Paul. "'Unnatural Acts': Discourses of Homosexuality within the House of Lords Debates on Gay Male Law Reform." *Journal of Sociolinguistics*, vol. 8, no. 1, 2004, pp. 88–106.

—. *Using Corpora in Discourse Analysis*. Continuum, 2006.

Baker, Paul and Tony McEnery. "A Corpus-Based Approach to Discourses of Refugees and Asylum Seekers in UN and Newspaper Texts." *Journal of Language and Politics*, vol. 4, no. 2, 2005, pp. 197–226.

Banaji, Shakuntala. *Reading 'Bollywood': The Young Audience and Hindi Films*. Palgrave Macmillan, 2006.

Barber, Karin. *Africa's Hidden Histories: Everyday Literacy and Making the Self*. Indiana University Press, 2006.

Barber, Karin, editor. *Readings in African Popular Culture*. The International African Institute in Association with James Currey and Indiana University Press, 1997.

Barker, Chris. *The Sage Dictionary of Cultural Studies*. Sage, 2004.

Barker-Benfield, G.J. *The Culture of Sensibility: Sex and Society in Eighteenth-Century Britain*. Chicago University Press, 1992.

Beauman, Nicola. *A Very Great Profession: The Woman's Novel 1914–39*. Virago, 1983.

Bednarek, Monika. *Emotion Talk Across Corpora*. Palgrave Macmillan, 2008.

Beer, David and Roger Burrows. "Consumption, Prosumption and Participatory Web Cultures: An Introduction." *Journal of Consumer Culture*, vol. 10, no. 1, 2010, pp. 3–12.

Bell, Alice. *The Possible Worlds of Hypertext Fiction*. Palgrave Macmillan, 2010.

Benwell, Bethan, James Procter and Gemma Robinson. "Introduction." *Postcolonial Audiences: Readers, Viewers and Reception*, edited by Bethan Benwell, James Procter and Gemma Robinson, Routledge, 2012, pp. 1–23.

Berlant, Lauren. *The Female Complaint: The Unfinished Business of Sentimentality in American Culture*. Duke University Press, 2008.

Berndt, Katrin. "West Africa." *English Literatures across the Globe: A Companion*, edited by Lars Eckstein, Fink, 2007, pp. 61–85.

Biber, Douglas and Edward Finegan. "Styles of Stance in English: Lexical and Grammatical Marking of Evidentiality and Affect." *Text*, vol. 9, no. 1, 1989, pp. 93–124.

Bode, Katherine and Robert Dixon. *Resourceful Reading: The New Empiricism, eResearch, and Australian Literary Culture*. Sydney University Press, 2009.

Boehmer, Elleke. "Achebe and His Influence in Some Contemporary African Writing." *Interventions: International Journal of Postcolonial Studies*, vol. 11, no. 2, 2009, pp. 141–53.

—. *The Future of the Postcolonial Past: Beyond Representation*. Leiden University Press, 2017.

Boehmer, Elleke and Alex Tickell. "The 1990s: An Increasingly Postcolonial Decade." *The Journal of Commonwealth Literature*, vol. 50, no. 3, 2015, pp. 315–52.

Bongie, Chris. *Friends and Enemies: The Scribal Politics of Post/Colonial Literature* [Postcolonialism across the Disciplines, 3]. Liverpool University Press, 2008.

—. "Exiles on Main Stream: Valuing the Popularity of Postcolonial Literature." *Bourdieu and Postcolonial Studies* [Postcolonialism across the Disciplines, 19], edited by Raphael Dalleo, Liverpool University Press, 2016, pp. 53–79.

Bosch Santana, Stephanie. "From Nation to Network: Blog and Facebook Fiction from Southern Africa." *Research in African Literatures*, vol. 49, no. 1, 2018, pp. 187–208.

Botshon, Lisa and Meredith Goldsmith. "Introduction." *Middlebrow Moderns: Popular American Women Writers of the 1920s*, edited by Lisa Botshon and Meredith Goldsmith, Northeastern University Press, 2003, pp. 3–21.

Bourdieu, Pierre. *The Logic of Practice*. Translated by Richard Nice, Polity Press, 1990.

—. *The Field of Cultural Production: Essays on Art and Literature*. Translated by Randal Johnson, Polity Press, 1993.

—. *The Rules of Art: Genesis and Structure of the Literary Field*. Translated by Susan Emanuel, Stanford University Press, 1996.

Boxall, Peter. *Twenty-First-Century Fiction: A Critical Introduction*. Cambridge University Press, 2013.

Brouillette, Sarah. *Postcolonial Writers in the Global Literary Marketplace*. Palgrave Macmillan, 2007.

—. "Postcolonial Authorship Revisited." *Bourdieu and Postcolonial Studies* [Postcolonialism across the Disciplines, 19], edited by Raphael Dalleo, Liverpool University Press, 2016, pp. 80–101.

Brouillette, Sarah and John R. Coleman. "Prizing Otherness: Black and Asian British Writing in the Global Marketplace." *The Cambridge History of Black and Asian British Writing*, edited by Susheila Nasta and Mark U. Stein, Cambridge University Press, 2020, pp. 584–97.

Brown, Erica and Mary Grover, editors. *Middlebrow Literary Cultures: The Battle of the Brows, 1920–1960*. Palgrave Macmillan, 2012.

Brown, Penelope and Stephen C. Levinson. *Politeness: Some Universals in Language Usage*. Cambridge University Press, 1978.

Bryce, Jane. "'Half and Half Children': Third-Generation Women Writers and the New Nigerian Novel." *Research in African Literatures*, vol. 39, no. 2, 2008, pp. 49–67.

Bucher, Taina. *If... Then: Algorithmic Power and Politics*. Oxford University Press, 2018.

Carter, David. "Tasteless Subjects: Postcolonial Literary Criticism, Realism and the Subject of Taste." *Southern Review*, vol. 25, no. 3, 1992, pp. 292–303.

Chibber, Vivek. *Postcolonial Theory and the Specter of Capital*. Verso, 2013.

Chong, Phillipa K. *Inside the Critics' Circle: Book Reviewing in Uncertain Times*. Princeton University Press, 2020.

Coetzee, Carli. "Contemporary Conversations. Afropolitanism: Reboot. Introduction." *Journal of African Cultural Studies*, vol. 28, no. 1, 2016, pp. 101–03.

Cohen, William A. *Embodied: Victorian Literature and the Senses*. University of Minnesota Press, 2009.
Cooper, Brenda. "Diaspora, Gender and Identity: Twinning in Three Diasporic Novels." *English Academy Review: Southern African Journal of English Studies*, vol. 25, no. 1, 2008, pp. 51–65.
Cooppan, Vilashini. *Worlds Within: National Narratives and Global Connections in Postcolonial Writing*. Stanford University Press, 2009.
Cousins, Helen. "A Good Authentic Read: Exoticism in the Postcolonial Novels of the Richard & Judy Book Club." *The Richard & Judy Book Club Reader: Popular Texts and the Practices of Reading*, edited by Jenni Ramone and Helen Cousins, Ashgate, 2011, pp. 137–53.
Cruz-Gutiérrez, Cristina. "Hair Politics in the Blogosphere: Safe Spaces and the Politics of Self-Representation in Chimamanda Adichie's *Americanah*." *Journal of Postcolonial Writing*, vol. 55, no. 1, 2019, pp. 66–79.
Cuddon, J.A. *A Dictionary of Literary Terms and Literary Theory*. 1977. Fifth edition, Wiley-Blackwell, 2013.
Cuder-Domínguez, Pilar. "Double Consciousness in the Work of Helen Oyeyemi and Diana Evans." *Women: A Cultural Review*, vol. 20, no. 3, 2009, pp. 277–86.
Cumpsty, Rebekah, "Sacralizing the Streets: Pedestrian Mapping and Urban Imaginaries in Teju Cole's *Open City* and Phaswane Mpe's *Welcome to Our Hillbrow*." *The Journal of Commonwealth Literature*, vol. 54, no. 3, 2019, pp. 305–18.
Dalleo, Raphael, editor. *Bourdieu and Postcolonial Studies* [Postcolonialism across the Disciplines, 19]. Liverpool University Press, 2016.
Dalley, Hamish. "The Idea of 'Third Generation Nigerian Literature': Conceptualizing Historical Change and Territorial Affiliation in the Contemporary Nigerian Novel." *Research in African Literatures*, vol. 44, no. 4, 2013, pp. 15–34.
—. *The Postcolonial Historical Novel: Realism, Allegory, and the Representation of Contested Pasts*. Palgrave Macmillan, 2014.
Damrosch, David. *How to Read World Literature*. Wiley Blackwell, 2008.
—. *Comparing the Literatures: Literary Studies in a Global Age*. Princeton University Press, 2020.
Darroch, Fiona. "Journeys of Becoming: Hair, the Blogosphere and Theopoetics in Chimamanda Ngozi Adichie's *Americanah*." *Text Matters*, vol. 10, 2020, pp. 135–50.
Dean, Jodi. *Blog Theory: Feedback and Capture in the Circuits of Drive*. Polity Press, 2010.
Debray, Régis. *Media Manifestos: On the Technological Transmission of Cultural Forms*. Translated by Eric Rauth, Verso, 1996.
—. "What is Mediology?" Translated by Martin Irvine, *Le Monde Diplomatique*, 1999, pp. 1–4.
Denger, Marijke. *Caring for Community: Towards a New Ethics of Responsibility in Contemporary Postcolonial Novels*. Routledge, 2019.
Desan, Mathieu Hikaru. "Bourdieu, Marx, and Capital: A Critique of the Extension Model." *Sociological Theory*, vol. 31, no. 4, 2013, pp. 318–42.
Dirven, René. "Emotions as Cause and the Cause of Emotions." *The Language of Emotions: Conceptualization, Expression, and Theoretical Foundation*, edited by Susanne Niemeier and René Dirven, Benjamins, 1997, pp. 55–86.
Dolata, Ulrich. "Volatile Monopole: Konzentration, Konkurrenz und Innovationsstrategien der Internetkonzerne." *Berliner Journal für Soziologie*, vol. 4, 2015, pp. 505–29.

Domsch, Sebastian. "Critical Genres: Generic Changes of Literary Criticism in Computer-Mediated Communication." *Genres in the Internet: Issues in the Theory of Genre*, edited by Janet Giltrow and Dieter Stein, John Benjamins, 2009, pp. 221–38.

Driscoll, Beth. "How Oprah's Book Club Reinvented the Woman Reader." *Popular Narrative Media*, vol. 1, no. 2, 2008, pp. 139–50.

—. *The New Literary Middlebrow: Tastemakers and Reading in the Twenty-First Century*. Palgrave Macmillan, 2014.

—. "Sentiment Analysis and the Literary Festival Audience." *Continuum: Journal of Media & Cultural Studies*, vol. 29, no. 6, 2015, pp. 861–73.

Driscoll, Beth and DeNel Rehberg Sedo. "Faraway, So Close: Seeing the Intimacy in Goodreads Reviews." *Qualitative Inquiry*, vol. 25, no. 3, 2019, pp. 248–59.

Dunton, Chris. "'Wherever the Bus Is Headed': Recent Developments in the African Novel." *Research in African Literatures*, vol. 50, no. 4, 2019, pp. 1–20.

Durán-Almarza, Emilia María, Ananya Kabir and Carla Rodríguez González. "Introduction: Debating the Afropolitan." *European Journal of English Studies*, vol. 21, no. 2, 2017, pp. 107–14.

Edmondson, Belinda. *Caribbean Middlebrow: Leisure Culture and the Middle Class*. Cornell University Press, 2009.

Ehland, Christoph and Jana Gohrisch, editors. *Imperial Middlebrow*. Brill, 2020.

Ehland, Christoph and Jana Gohrisch. "Introduction: Cross-Colonial Encounters and Expressions of Power in Middlebrow Literature and Culture, 1890–1940 and the Present." *Imperial Middlebrow*, edited by Christoph Ehland and Jana Gohrisch, Brill, 2020, pp. 1–21.

Ehland, Christoph and Cornelia Wächter, editors. *Middlebrow and Gender, 1890–1945*. Brill, 2016.

Ehret, Christian, Jacy Boegel and Roya Manuel-Nekouei. "The Role of Affect in Adolescents' Online Literacies: Participatory Pressures in BookTube Culture." *Journal of Adolescent & Adult Literacy*, vol. 62, no. 2, 2018, pp. 151–61.

Ekman, Paul. "Expression and the Nature of Emotion." *Approaches to Emotion*, edited by Klaus R. Scherer and Paul Ekman, Psychology Press, 1984, pp. 319–44.

Emenyonu, Ernest N. "Introduction." *A Companion to Chimamanda Ngozi Adichie*, edited by Ernest N. Emenyonu, James Currey, 2017, pp. 1–13.

Epstein, Seymour. "Controversial Issues in Emotion Theory." *Review of Personality and Social Psychology*, edited by Philip Shaver, Sage, 1984, pp. 64–88.

Esplin, Marlene. "The Right Not to Translate: The Linguistic Stakes of Immigration in Chimamanda Ngozi Adichie's *Americanah*." *Research in African Literatures*, vol. 49, no. 2, 2018, pp. 73–86.

Evans, Geoffrey and James Tilley. *The New Politics of Class: The Political Exclusion of the British Working Class*. Oxford University Press, 2017.

Evaristo, Bernardine. "Diana Evans in Conversation." *Wasafiri*, vol. 20, no. 45, 2005, pp. 31–35.

Farr, Cecilia Konchar. *Reading Oprah: How Oprah's Book Club Changed the Way America Reads*. SUNY Press, 2005.

Featherstone, Simon. *Postcolonial Cultures*. Edinburgh University Press, 2005.

Feldner, Maximilian. *Narrating the New African Diaspora: 21st Century Nigerian Literature in Context*. Palgrave Macmillan, 2019.

Foucault, Michel. "What Is an Author?" 1969. *Textual Strategies*, edited by Josué V. Harari, Cornell University Press, 1979, pp. 141–60.

Frow, John. *Cultural Studies and Cultural Value*. Oxford University Press, 1995.

Fuller, Danielle and DeNel Rehberg Sedo. *Reading Beyond the Book: The Social Practices of Contemporary Literary Culture*. Routledge, 2013.
Galasiński, Dariusz. *Men and the Language of Emotions*. Palgrave Macmillan, 2004.
Gehrmann, Susanne. "Re-Writing War in Contemporary Nigerian Fiction: From Biafra to Present Times." *Listening to Africa: Anglophone African Literatures and Cultures*, edited by Jana Gohrisch and Ellen Grünkemeier, Universitätsverlag Winter, 2012, pp. 209–38.
—. "Cosmopolitanism with African Roots: Afropolitanism's Ambivalent Mobilities." *Journal of African Cultural Studies*, vol. 28, no. 1, 2016, pp. 61–72.
Gibbons, Alison and Sara Whiteley. *Contemporary Stylistics: Language, Cognition, Interpretation*. Edinburgh University Press, 2018.
Gilbert, Sandra M. and Susan Gubar. *The Madwoman in the Attic: The Woman Writer and the Nineteenth-Century Literary Imagination*. 1979. Second edition, Yale University Press, 2000.
Gillespie, Tarleton. "Algorithm." *Digital Keywords: A Vocabulary of Information Society and Culture*, edited by Benjamin Peters, Princeton University Press, 2016, pp. 18–30.
Giorgi, Liana. "A Celebration of the Word and a Stage for Political Debate: Literature Festivals in Europe Today." *European Arts Festivals: Strengthening Cultural Diversity*, European Commission, 2011, pp. 11–23.
Gohrisch, Jana. *Bürgerliche Gefühlsdispositionen in der englischen Prosa des 19. Jahrhunderts*. Universitätsverlag Winter, 2005.
—. "Negotiating the Emotional Habitus of the Middle Classes in *The Mayor of Casterbridge*." *The Thomas Hardy Journal*, vol. 28, 2011, pp. 44–67.
—. "Imagining the British West Indies in Middlebrow Fiction." *Imperial Middlebrow*, edited by Christoph Ehland and Jana Gohrisch, Brill, 2020, pp. 103–23.
—. "Review of *The Cambridge History of Black and Asian British Writing*, edited by Susheila Nasta and Mark U. Stein." *Anglia: Journal of English Philology*, vol. 139, no. 2, 2021, pp. 463–67.
Gohrisch, Jana and Ellen Grünkemeier, editors. *Postcolonial Studies across the Disciplines* [ASNEL Papers, 18], Rodopi, 2013.
Goldstone, Andrew and Ted Underwood. "The Quiet Transformations of Literary Studies: What Thirteen Thousand Scholars Could Tell Us." *New Literary History*, vol. 45, no. 3, 2014, pp. 359–84.
Griswold, Wendy. *Bearing Witness: Readers, Writers, and the Novel in Nigeria*. Princeton University Press, 2000.
Gruzd, Anatoliy and DeNel Rehberg Sedo. "#1b1t: Investigating Reading Practices at the Turn of the Twenty-First Century." *Mémoires du Livre/Studies in Book Culture*, vol. 3, no. 2, 2012, pp. 1–25.
Guarracino, Serena. "Writing 'So Raw and True': Blogging in Chimamanda Ngozi Adichie's *Americanah*." *Between*, vol. 4, no. 8, 2014, pp. 1–27.
Gunning, Dave. "Dissociation, Spirit Possession, and the Languages of Trauma in Some Recent African-British Novels." *Research in African Literatures*, vol. 46, no. 4, 2015, pp. 119–32.
Habermas, Jürgen. *The Structural Transformation of the Public Sphere: An Inquiry into a Category of Bourgeois Society*. 1962. Translated by Thomas Burger, The MIT Press, 1989.
Halliday, Michael A.K. *An Introduction to Functional Grammar*. Edward Arnold, 1985.
Harris, Ashleigh. "Awkward Form and Writing the African Present." *The Johannesburg Salon*, vol. 7, 2014, pp. 3–8.
Hartwiger, Alexander Greer. "The Postcolonial Flâneur: *Open City* and the Urban Palimpsest." *Postcolonial Text*, vol. 11, no. 1, 2016, pp. 1–17.

Hawley, John C. "Biafra as Heritage and Symbol: Adichie, Mbachu, and Iweala." *Research in African Literatures*, vol. 39, no. 2, 2008, pp. 15–26.

Hayles, Katherine N. *Electronic Literature: New Horizons for the Literary*. University of Notre Dame Press, 2008.

Hochschild, Arlie Russell. *The Managed Heart: Commercialization of Human Feeling*. 1983. Twentieth anniversary edition, University of California Press, 2003.

Hogan, Patrick Colm. *Literature and Emotion*. Routledge, 2018.

Houen, Alex, editor. *Affect and Literature*. Cambridge University Press, 2020.

Hron, Madelaine. "*Ora na-azu nwa*: The Figure of the Child in Third-Generation Nigerian Novels." *Research in African Literatures*, vol. 39, no. 2, 2008, pp. 27–48.

Hu, Tung-Hui. *A Prehistory of the Cloud*. The MIT Press, 2015.

Huck, Christian. *Digitalschatten: Das Netz und die Dinge*. Textem Verlag, 2020.

—. "How Cultural Studies Came to Germany, or, Rather, the Events and Circumstances that Led to the Foundation of the German Association for the Study of British Cultures." *JSBC: Journal for the Study of British Cultures*, vol. 28, no. 1, 2021, pp. 13–111.

Huggan, Graham. *The Postcolonial Exotic: Marketing the Margins*. Routledge, 2001.

—. *Interdisciplinary Measures: Literature and the Future of Postcolonial Studies* [Postcolonialism across the Disciplines, 1]. Liverpool University Press, 2008.

Hughes, John. *Affective Worlds: Writing, Feeling & Nineteenth-Century Literature*. Sussex Academic Press, 2011.

Humble, Nicola. *The Feminine Middlebrow Novel, 1920s to 1950s: Class, Domesticity, and Bohemianism*. Oxford University Press, 2001.

—. "Sitting Forward or Sitting Back: Highbrow v. Middlebrow Reading." *Modernist Cultures*, vol. 6, no. 1, 2011, pp. 41–59.

—. "The Feminine Middlebrow Novel." *The History of British Women's Writing, 1920–1945*, edited by Maroula Joannou, Palgrave Macmillan, 2013, pp. 97–111.

Hunston, Susan. "Frame, Phrase or Function: A Comparison of Frame Semantics and Local Grammars." *Proceedings of the Corpus Linguistics 2003 Conference* [URCEL Technical Papers, 16], edited by Dawn Archer, Paul Rayson, Andrew Wilson and Tony McEnery, URCEL, 2003, pp. 342–58.

Illouz, Eva. *Oprah Winfrey and the Glamour of Misery: An Essay on Popular Culture*. Columbia University Press, 2003.

—. *Cold Intimacies: The Making of Emotional Capitalism*. Polity Press, 2007.

—. *Saving the Modern Soul: Therapy, Emotions, and the Culture of Self-Help*. University of California Press, 2008.

Innes, C.L. *The Cambridge Introduction to Postcolonial Literatures in English*. Cambridge University Press, 2007.

Jameson, Fredric. "Postmodernism, or, The Cultural Logic of Late Capitalism." *New Left Review*, vol. 146, 1984, pp. 53–92.

—. "Third-World Literature in the Era of Multinational Capitalism." *Social Text*, no. 15, 1986, pp. 65–88.

Jenkins, Henry. *Convergence Culture: Where Old and New Media Collide*. New York University Press, 2006.

Jockers, Matthew L. *Macroanalysis: Digital Methods and Literary History*. University of Illinois Press, 2013.

Johanson, Katya and Robin Freeman. "The Reader as Audience: The Appeal of the Writers' Festival to the Contemporary Audience." *Continuum: Journal of Media & Cultural Studies*, vol. 26, no. 2, 2012, pp. 303–14.

Johnson-Laird, P.N. and Keith Oatley. "The Language of Emotions: An Analysis of a Sematic Field." *Cognition and Emotion*, vol. 3, no. 2, 1989, pp. 81–123.

Keen, Andrew. *The Cult of the Amateur: How Blogs, MySpace, YouTube, and the Rest of Today's User-Generated Media Are Destroying Our Economy, Our Culture, and Our Values.* Doubleday, 2007.

Kirschenbaum, Matthew G. *Mechanisms: New Media and the Forensic Imagination.* The MIT Press, 2008.

Klaniecki, Beniamin. "Affirmation and Contestation: Negotiating and Contextualizing African Masculinity in Chigozie Obioma's *The Fishermen.*" *Journal of Postcolonial Writing*, vol. 56, no. 3, 2020, pp. 397–410.

Knudsen, Eva Rask and Ulla Rahbek. *In Search of the Afropolitan: Encounters, Conversations, and Contemporary Diasporic African Literature.* Rowman & Littlefield, 2016.

—. "An Afropolitan Literary Aesthetics? Afropolitan Style and Tropes in Recent Diasporic African Fiction." *European Journal of English Studies*, vol. 21, no. 2, 2017, pp. 115–28.

Koegler, Caroline. *Critical Branding: Postcolonial Studies and the Market.* Routledge, 2018.

König, Ekkehard and Volker Gast. *Understanding English–German Contrasts.* Fourth edition, Erich Schmidt Verlag, 2018.

Krishnamurthy, Ramesh. "Ethnic, Racial and Tribal: The Language of Racism?" *Texts and Practices: Readings in Critical Discourse Analysis*, edited by Carmen Rosa Caldas-Coulthard and Malcom Coulthard, Routledge, 1996, pp. 129–49.

Krishnan, Madhu. "Biafra and the Aesthetics of Closure in the Third Generation Nigerian Novel." *Rupkatha Journal on Interdisciplinary Studies in Humanities*, vol. 2, no. 2, 2010, pp. 185–95.

—. "On National Culture and the Projective Past: Mythology, Nationalism, and the Heritage of Biafra in Contemporary Nigerian Narrative." *CLIO: A Journal of Literature, History, and the Philosophy of History*, vol. 42, no. 2, 2013, pp. 187–208.

—. "The Storyteller Function in Contemporary Nigerian Narrative." *The Journal of Commonwealth Literature*, vol. 49, no. 1, 2014, pp. 29–45.

Latour, Bruno. *Reassembling the Social: An Introduction to Actor-Network Theory.* Oxford University Press, 2005.

Leavis, Q.D. *Fiction and the Reading Public.* 1932. Chatto & Windus, 1965.

Light, Alison. *Forever England: Femininity, Literature and Conservatism Between the Wars.* Routledge, 1991.

Llewellyn, Matthew P. and John Gleaves. "A Universal Dilemma: The British *Sporting Life* and the Complex, Contested, and Contradictory State of Amateurism." *Journal of Sport History*, vol. 41, no. 1, 2014, pp. 95–116.

Long, Elizabeth. *Book Clubs: Women and the Uses of Reading in Everyday Life.* The University of Chicago Press, 2003.

Lynes, Russell. "Highbrow, Lowbrow, Middlebrow." 1949. *The Wilson Quarterly*, vol. 1, no. 1, 1976, pp. 146–58.

Macdonald, Dwight. "Masscult and Midcult." 1960. *Against the American Grain.* Da Capo Press, 1983, pp. 3–75.

Macdonald, Kate, editor. *The Masculine Middlebrow, 1880–1950: What Mr Miniver Read.* Palgrave Macmillan, 2011.

Macdonald, Kate and Christoph Singer, editors. *Transitions in Middlebrow Writing, 1880–1930.* Palgrave Macmillan, 2015.

Mackey, Allison. "Troubling Humanitarian Consumption: Reframing Relationality in African Child Soldier Narratives." *Research in African Literatures*, vol. 44, no. 4, 2013, pp. 99–122.

Mafe, Diana A. "Ghostly Girls in the 'Eerie Bush': Helen Oyeyemi's *The Icarus Girl* as Postcolonial Female Gothic Fiction." *Research in African Literatures*, vol. 43, no. 3, 2012, pp. 21–35.

Mandel, Ernest. *Late Capitalism*. Translated by Joris De Bres, Verso, 1975.

Mankekar, Purnima. *Screening Culture, Viewing Politics: An Ethnography of Television, Womanhood, and Nation in Postcolonial India*. Duke University Press, 1999.

Marcus, James. *Amazonia: Five Years at the Epicenter of the Dot.Com Juggernaut*. The New Press, 2005.

Marx, Karl. *Capital*. Vol. 3. 1894. Translated by David Fernbach. Pelican Books, 1981.

McGurl, Mark. *The Program Era: Postwar Fiction and the Rise of Creative Writing*. Harvard University Press, 2009.

—. "Everything and Less: Fiction in the Age of Amazon." *Modern Language Quarterly*, vol. 77, no. 3, 2016, pp. 447–71.

—. *Everything and Less: The Novel in the Age of Amazon*. Verso, 2021.

McLeod, John. "Extra Dimensions, New Routines: Contemporary Black Writing of Britain." *Wasafiri*, vol. 25, no. 4, 2010, pp. 45–52.

Michaels, Walter Benn. *The Trouble with Diversity: How We Learned to Love Identity and Ignore Inequality*. Metropolitan Books, 2006.

Monk, Claire. "Heritage Film Audiences 2.0: Period Film Audiences and Online Fan Cultures." *Participations: Journal of Audience & Reception Studies*, vol. 8, no. 2, 2011, pp. 431–77.

Moretti, Franco. *The Way of the World: The Bildungsroman in European Culture*. Verso, 1987.

—. "Conjectures on World Literature." *New Left Review*, vol. 1, 2000, pp. 54–68.

—. *Graphs, Maps, Trees: Abstract Models for Literary History*. Verso, 2005.

—. *The Bourgeois: Between History and Literature*. Verso, 2013a.

—. *Distant Reading*. Verso, 2013b.

Moruzi, Kristine, Michelle J. Smith and Elizabeth Bullen, editors. *Affect, Emotion, and Children's Literature: Representation and Socialisation in Texts for Children and Young Adults*. Routledge, 2018.

Mullaney, Julie. *Postcolonial Literatures in Context*. Continuum, 2010.

Murray, Simone. *The Digital Literary Sphere: Reading, Writing, and Selling Books in the Internet Era*. Johns Hopkins University Press, 2018.

Nadiminti, Kalyan. "The Global Program Era: Contemporary International Fiction in the American Creative Economy." *NOVEL: A Forum on Fiction*, vol. 51, no. 3, 2018, pp. 375–98.

Nakamura, Lisa. "'Words with Friends': Socially Networked Reading on *Goodreads*." *PMLA*, vol. 128, no. 1, 2013, pp. 238–43.

Newell, Stephanie. *Ghanaian Popular Fiction: 'Thrilling Discoveries in Conjugal Life' and Other Tales*. James Currey, 2000.

—. *West African Literatures: Ways of Reading*. Oxford University Press, 2006.

Noble, Safiya Umoja. *Algorithms of Oppression: How Search Engines Reinforce Racism*. New York University Press, 2018.

Norridge, Zoe. "Sex as Synecdoche: Intimate Languages of Violence in Chimamanda Ngozi Adichie's *Half of a Yellow Sun* and Aminatta Forna's *The Memory of Love*." *Research in African Literatures*, vol. 43, no. 2, 2012, pp. 18–39.

Nöth, Winfried. "Symmetries and Asymmetries between Positive and Negative Emotion Words." *Anglistentag 1991 Düsseldorf: Proceedings*, edited by Wilhelm G. Busse, Max Niemeyer Verlag, 1992, pp. 72–88.

Novak, Amy. "Who Speaks? Who Listens? The Problem of Address in Two Nigerian Trauma Novels." *Studies in the Novel*, vol. 40, no. 1/2, 2008, pp. 31–51.

Ogunyemi, Chikwenye O. *Africa Wo/man Palava: The Nigerian Novel by Women*. The University of Chicago Press, 1996.

Ommundsen, Wenche. "Literary Festivals and Cultural Consumption." *Australian Literary Studies*, vol. 24, no. 1, 2009, pp. 19–34.

Ortony, Andrew, Gerald L. Clore and Mark A. Foss. "The Referential Structure of the Affective Lexicon." *Cognitive Science*, vol. 11, no. 3, 1987, pp. 341–64.

Oruene, Taiwo. "Magical Powers of Twins in the Socio-Religious Beliefs of the Yoruba." *Folklore*, vol. 96, no. 2, 1985, pp. 208–16.

Ouma, Christoper. "Reading the Diasporic *Abiku* in Helen Oyeyemi's *The Icarus Girl*." *Research in African Literatures*, vol. 45, no. 3, 2014, pp. 188–205.

Owens, Trevor. *Designing Online Communities: How Designers, Developers, Community Managers, and Software Structure Discourse and Knowledge Production on the Web*. Peter Lang, 2015.

Pahl, Miriam. "Afropolitanism as Critical Consciousness: Chimamanda Ngozi Adichie's and Teju Cole's Internet Presence." *Journal of African Cultural Studies*, vol. 28, no. 1, 2016, pp. 73–87.

Pardey, Hannah. "Middlebrow 2.0: The Digital Affect and the New Nigerian Novel." *Imperial Middlebrow*, edited by Christoph Ehland and Jana Gohrisch, Brill, 2020, pp. 218–39.

—. "Middlebrow Postcolonialisms: Studying Readers in the Digital Age." *Postcolonial Cultural Studies*, special issue of *Anglistik: International Journal of English Studies*, vol. 31, no. 3, 2020, pp. 67–88.

Parry, Benita. *Postcolonial Studies: A Materialist Critique*. Routledge, 2004.

Partington, Alan and Anna Marchi. "Using Corpora in Discourse Analysis." *The Cambridge Handbook of English Corpus Linguistics*, edited by Douglas Biber and Randi Reppen, Cambridge University Press, 2015, pp. 216–34.

Pearce, Michael. "Investigating the Collocational Behaviour of MAN and WOMAN in the BNC Using Sketch Engine." *Corpora*, vol. 3, no. 1, 2008, pp. 1–29.

Pérez-Fernández, Irene. "Embodying 'Twoness in Oneness' in Diana Evans's *26a*." *Journal of Postcolonial Writing*, vol. 49, no. 3, 2013, pp. 291–302.

Ponzanesi, Sandra. *The Postcolonial Cultural Industry: Icons, Markets, Mythologies*. Palgrave Macmillan, 2014.

Pritzker, Sonya E., Janina Fenigsen and James M. Wilce, editors. *The Routledge Handbook of Language and Emotion*. Routledge, 2020.

Procter, James and Bethan Benwell. *Reading Across Worlds: Transnational Book Groups and the Reception of Difference*. Palgrave Macmillan, 2015.

Pucherova, Dobrota. "What Is African Woman? Transgressive Sexuality in 21st-Century African Anglophone Lesbian Fiction as a Redefinition of African Feminism." *Research in African Literatures*, vol. 50, no. 2, 2019, pp. 105–22.

Quayson, Ato. "Magical Realism and the African Novel." *The Cambridge Companion to the African Novel*, edited by F. Abiola Irele, Cambridge University Press, 2009, pp. 159–76.

—. "Africa and its Diasporas." *The Oxford Handbook of Postcolonial Studies*, edited by Graham Huggan, Oxford University Press, 2013, pp. 628–47.

Radway, Janice A. *A Feeling for Books: The Book-of-the-Month Club, Literary Taste, and Middle-Class Desire*. The University of North Carolina Press, 1997.

Ramone, Jenni. *Postcolonial Literatures in the Local Literary Marketplace: Located Reading*. Palgrave Macmillan, 2020.

Ramone, Jenni and Helen Cousins, editors. *The Richard & Judy Book Club Reader: Popular Texts and the Practices of Reading*. Ashgate, 2011.

Rauscher, Janneke. "Reading Readers of Crime Fiction? Potentialities and Limits of the Analysis of Online Reviews as Resource for Literary Studies." *Crime Fiction: A Critical Casebook*, edited by Stephen Butler and Agnieszka Sienkiewicz-Charlish, Peter Lang, 2018, pp. 307–24.

Rehberg Sedo, DeNel. "Richard & Judy's Book Club and *Canada Reads*: Readers, Books and Cultural Programming in a Digital Era." *Information, Communication & Society*, vol. 11, no. 2, 2008, pp. 188–206.

Renne, Elisha P. "Twinship in an Ekiti Yoruba Town." *Ethnology*, vol. 40, no. 1, 2001, pp. 63–78.

Rooney, Kathleen. *Reading with Oprah: The Book Club That Changed America*. The University of Arkansas Press, 2005.

Roy, Anindyo. "Auto/Biographer, Historian, *Griot*: Measures of Realism and the Writing of History in Helon Habila's *Measuring Time*." *ARIEL: A Review of International English Literature*, vol. 41, no. 1, 2011, pp. 5–26.

Rubin, Joan Shelley. *The Making of Middlebrow Culture*. The University of North Carolina Press, 1992.

Saha, Anamik. *Race and the Cultural Industries*. Polity Press, 2018.

Schmid, Hans-Jörg. "Shell Nouns in English: A Personal Roundup." *Caplletra*, vol. 64, 2018, pp. 109–28.

Schulze-Engler, Frank. "Fragile Modernities – History and Historiography in Contemporary African Fiction." *Postcolonial Studies across the Disciplines* [ASNEL Papers, 18], edited by Jana Gohrisch and Ellen Grünkemeier, Rodopi, 2013, pp. 263–82.

Scott, John P. "The Function of Emotions in Behavioral Systems: A Systems Theory Analysis." *Emotion: Theory, Research, and Experience*, edited by Robert Plutchik and Henry Kellerman, Academic, 1980, pp. 35–56.

Scott, Mike. "PC Analysis of Key Words – and Key Key Words." *System*, vol. 25, no. 2, 1997, pp. 233–45.

Scott, Mike and Christopher Tribble. *Textual Patterns: Key Words and Corpus Analysis in Language Education*. John Benjamins, 2006.

Seaver, Nick. "Knowing Algorithms." *Media in Transition*, vol. 8, 2013, pp. 1–12.

Shringarpure, Bhakti. "Digital Forms, Migrant Forms: Yaa Gyasi's *Homegoing* and Chimamanda Ngozi Adichie's *Americanah*." *Postcolonial Text*, vol. 15, no. 3/4, 2020, pp. 1–22.

Squires, Claire. *Marketing Literature: The Making of Contemporary Writing in Britain*. Palgrave Macmillan, 2007.

Staab, Philipp. *Digitaler Kapitalismus: Markt und Herrschaft in der Ökonomie der Unknappheit*. Suhrkamp, 2019.

Staab, Philipp and Oliver Nachtwey. "Market and Labour Control in Digital Capitalism." *tripleC*, vol. 14, no. 2, 2016, pp. 457–74.

Stedman, Gesa. *Stemming the Torrent: Expression and Control in the Victorian Discourses on Emotions, 1830–1872*. Ashgate, 2002.

—. "Sidelining Racism and Discrimination – Recent British Black and Asian Fiction." *Imperial Middlebrow*, edited by Christoph Ehland and Jana Gohrisch, Brill, 2020, pp. 206–17.

Stein, Lorin. "Preface." *The Unprofessionals: New American Writing from* The Paris Review, edited by Lorin Stein, Penguin, 2015, pp. ix–xi.

Steinbach, Susie. *Understanding the Victorians: Politics, Culture and Society in Nineteenth-Century Britain*. Second edition, Routledge, 2017.

Steiner, Ann. "World Literature and the Book Market." *The Routledge Companion to World Literature*, edited by Theo D'haen, David Damrosch and Djelal Kadir, Routledge, 2011, pp. 316–24.

Stone, Brad. *The Everything Store: Jeff Bezos and the Age of Amazon*. Little, Brown and Company, 2013.

Storm, Christine and Tom. "A Taxonomic Study of the Vocabulary of Emotions." *Journal of Personality and Social Psychology*, vol. 53, no. 4, 1987, pp. 805–16.

Stouck, Jordan. "Abjecting Hybridity in Helen Oyeyemi's *The Icarus Girl*." *ARIEL: A Review of International English Literature*, vol. 41, no. 2, 2011, pp. 89–112.

Strehle, Susan. "Producing Exile: Diasporic Vision in Adichie's *Half of a Yellow Sun*." *Modern Fiction Studies*, vol. 57, no. 4, 2011, pp. 650–72.

Striphas, Ted. *The Late Age of Print: Everyday Book Culture from Consumerism to Control*. Columbia University Press, 2011.

—. "Algorithmic Culture." *European Journal of Cultural Studies*, vol. 18, no. 4/5, 2015, pp. 395–412.

Stubbs, Michael. *Text and Corpus Analysis: Computer-Assisted Studies of Language and Culture*. Blackwell Publishers, 1996.

Sullivan, Melissa. "The Middlebrows of the Hogarth Press: Rose Macaulay, E.M. Delafield and Cultural Hierarchies in Interwar Britain." *Leonard and Virginia Woolf, the Hogarth Press and the Networks of Modernism*, edited by Helen Southworth, Edinburgh University Press, 2010, pp. 52–73.

Sullivan, Melissa and Sophie Blanch. "Introduction: The Middlebrow – Within or Without Modernism." *Modernist Cultures*, vol. 6, no. 1, 2011, pp. 1–17.

Suter, Christian, S. Madheswaran and B.P. Vani, editors. *The Middle Class in World Society: Negotiations, Diversities and Lived Experiences*. Routledge, 2020.

Taylor, Charlotte. "Searching for Similarity Using Corpus-Assisted Discourse Studies." *Corpora*, vol. 8, no. 1, 2013, pp. 81–113.

Taylor, Jack. "Language, Race, and Identity in Adichie's *Americanah* and Bulowayo's *We Need New Names*." *Research in African Literatures*, vol. 50, no. 2, 2019, pp. 68–85.

Toivanen, Anna-Leena. "Emailing/Skyping Africa: New Technologies and Communication Gaps in Contemporary African Women's Fiction." *ARIEL: A Review of International English Literature*, vol. 47, no. 4, 2016, pp. 135–61.

Tunca, Daria. *Stylistic Approaches to Nigerian Fiction*. Palgrave Macmillan, 2014.

Tunca, Daria and Bénédicte Ledent. "The Power of a Singular Story: Narrating Africa and Its Diasporas." *Research in African Literatures*, vol. 46, no. 4, 2015, pp. 1–9.

Turner, Jonathan H. *On the Origins of Human Emotions: A Sociological Inquiry into the Evolution of Human Affect*. Stanford University Press, 2000.

Turner, Jonathan H. and Jan E. Stets. *The Sociology of Emotions*. Cambridge University Press, 2005.

Ucham, Emelda and Jairos Kangira. "African Hybrids: Exploring Afropolitan Identity Formation in Taiye Selasi's *Ghana Must Go* and Chimamanda Adichie's *Americanah*." *Journal for Studies in Humanities and Social Sciences*, vol. 4, no. 1/2, 2015, pp. 42–50.

Wawrzinek, Jennifer and J.K.S. Makokha, editors. *Negotiating Afropolitanism: Essays on Borders and Spaces in Contemporary African Literature and Folklore*. Rodopi, 2011.

Weber, Max. *The Protestant Ethic and the Spirit of Capitalism*. 1904/05. Edited, translated and with an introduction by Peter Baehr and Gordon C. Wells, Penguin Classics, 2002.

Wierzbicka, Anna. *Emotions across Languages and Cultures: Diversity and Universals.* Cambridge University Press, 1999.
Williams, Abigail. *The Social Life of Books: Reading Together in the Eighteenth-Century Home.* Yale University Press, 2017.
Williams, Raymond. *Marxism and Literature.* Oxford University Press, 1977.
—. *Keywords: A Vocabulary of Culture and Society.* 1976. Revised and expanded edition, Oxford University Press, 1985.
Woolf, Janice M. "Reading Oprah: Gender and Literacy in Book Club Culture." *WILLA,* vol. 12, 2003, pp. 27–37.
Woolf, Virginia. "Middlebrow." *The Death of the Moth and Other Essays.* The Hogarth Press, 1942, pp. 113–19.
WReC (Warwick Research Collective). *Combined and Uneven Development: Towards a New Theory of World-Literature* [Postcolonialism across the Disciplines, 17]. Liverpool University Press, 2015.
Zabus, Chantal. "Introduction: The Future of Postcolonial Studies." *The Future of Postcolonial Studies,* edited by Chantal Zabus, Routledge, 2015, pp. 1–16.
Zuboff, Shoshana. *The Age of Surveillance Capitalism: The Fight for a Human Future at the New Frontier of Power.* Profile, 2019.

Index

Abani, Chris 15n19, 69, 133–36, 138–40, 145, 166, 192
  Song for Night ix, 52n35, 95, 117n11, 123–24, 127, 129, 131–32, 134–36, 138–40, 148–49, 160, 165
Achebe, Chinua xiv, 12, 28n11, 44, 46, 49
  Things Fall Apart 35, 41n28, 54
Adebayo, Ayobami 13, 133–36, 138–40, 145, 166
  Stay With Me ix, 33, 35, 46, 54, 84, 89–92, 94, 100–05, 114–15, 118–20, 122–23, 125–28, 131–40, 148–49, 160, 165
Adenekan, Shola 9n10, 14–15, 31, 60n6
Adichie, Chimamanda N. 13–14, 15n19, 23–26, 29, 31–32, 47–49, 102, 106n27, 110, 121, 123, 133–36, 138–40, 145–46, 166, 192
  Americanah ix, xv, 8n7, 22–26, 32–33, 43, 65, 69, 71n17, 72, 80n7, 82, 84, 87, 91n15, 92–96, 98, 102, 104, 105n26, 110, 114, 118, 120–26, 128–29, 131–32, 134–40, 148–49, 160, 165
  Half of a Yellow Sun ix, xiv, 24, 32, 35, 48–54, 65, 72n20, 92–93, 95–96, 102, 105n26, 114, 119, 121, 123, 125–29, 148–49, 160
  Purple Hibiscus ix, 8n7, 32–33, 35, 45–47, 50, 65, 71–72, 80n7, 87, 90, 92–93, 105, 110, 114, 118-19, 122–29, 148–49, 161

"The Danger of a Single Story" 31
"To Instruct and Delight" 24
"We Should All Be Feminists" 31, 96n20
affect *see* emotion
affect patterns 18, 110, 123–29, 137–40
affect style 120, 123, 137, 140
affective norms *see* feeling rules
affective online communities *see* online reading communities
affiliate links 1, 62n9, 104, 106
Afropolitanism 13, 14n17, 45n31
  see also hybridity
  see also Selasi, Taiye
algorithms xvii, 1, 17, 19, 25n5, 57, 59–60, 62–63, 65–66, 68–69, 73, 77, 81n8, 89–90, 92, 112, 135–36, 142–44
  see also ecosystems
Amazon ix–xi, 1–2, 10, 17–18, 25n5, 26, 29n12, 32–33, 55, 57–58, 61–71, 73, 77–79, 80n7, 81–82, 87–90, 91n15, 95, 97–98, 103–06, 111–13, 121, 123, 130, 136–37, 143
  badges 78, 105
  Kindle ix, 26n8, 62, 67, 78, 82n10, 97, 131
  middlebrow practices 64–66
  as publisher 61, 67
  relation to publishers 66–67
  reviewer interaction, investment and impact 78–79, 149
  Vine Voices 78, 82n10, 105–06

209

Anderson, Benedict 57, 88n14
AntConc xvii, 17–18, 74–75, 109–11, 117, 143
   see also CADS
   see also keyword analysis
Atta, Sefi 146, 192
   Everything Good Will Come ix, 35, 45–48, 80, 123, 148–49, 161
Aubry, Timothy 8n6, 9, 34n23, 36, 42, 59–60, 69, 73, 77, 83, 86–88, 96–98, 100, 102, 107, 114, 120
   see also book clubs
   see also literary festivals
   see also Protestant work ethic
   see also therapeutic paradigm
authenticity 7, 31–32, 66, 77n1, 124
authors 2, 12–19, 22, 26, 29–36, 43, 48, 50, 55, 69, 79, 89, 95, 106n27, 109–10, 113–14, 116, 123, 125–27, 129, 131, 133–38, 143–44
   creative writing 2–3, 14n17, 15, 17, 22, 26, 29, 31, 52, 55, 136n31, 139, 141, 143, 145–47
   emotion terms 135–36, 166–67
   online performances 24, 30–33, 143
   videos on YouTube x, 109, 133–36, 138–40, 183–92
   see also new Nigerian novel
autobiography 24, 31n15, 32, 36, 43n30, 54, 130, 131n23, 132, 139

Barker-Benfield, G.J. 58, 88n14
battle of the brows xvi, 5–6, 83n12
Bednarek Monika 74n25, 75, 110, 115, 117n11, 118, 120n14, 123n17, 124, 129, 130n22
Berlant, Lauren 58, 88n14, 119n13
Bezos, Jeff 63–66, 81
Biafran War see new Nigerian novel
Boehmer, Elleke xv, 4–5, 13, 46
Bongie, Chris xiv, 3, 7, 21, 60
book clubs xv, 7–8, 30, 80–81, 84, 94, 105n26, 117
   see also middlebrow
book haul 72, 91–92, 152
Book-of-the-Month Club xiii, 7
book trailer 134
Bookstagram see Instagram
BookTube see YouTube

Bourdieu, Pierre xvi, 59–61
   forms of capital 60–61
   habitus 60
   literary field 9–10, 30
Braithwaite, Oyinkan 13, 146
   My Sister, the Serial Killer ix, 22n2, 46n33, 69, 94, 123–24, 126, 128, 148–49, 161
   The Baby Is Mine 69
Brouillette, Sarah 3–4, 22n2, 24, 27, 32, 60, 131n23
Bucher, Taina 10, 61–63, 65, 68, 78, 107
buddy read 80n7, 92

CADS xv, xvii, 17–18, 31n15, 33n19, 59, 68–70, 71n18, 72–75, 109, 113, 115, 116n7, 117, 131, 133, 136, 142
   see also AntConc
   see also keyword analysis
capitalism 10–11, 12n16, 15, 17, 19, 21, 34, 57–59, 61, 66–69, 72n19, 75, 88, 95, 106–07, 109
   see also labour
   see also middle class
care 1, 18, 64, 78, 86, 103–07
Chibber, Vivek 12–13
class see middle class
Cole, Teju 13–14, 28n11, 31, 146
   Every Day Is for the Thief ix, 43n29, 92, 115, 120, 123–25, 127, 148–49, 161
   Open City ix, 43n29, 90, 115, 121, 123, 129, 131, 148–49, 162
Community Guidelines 32, 65–66, 70, 105
corpus linguistics see CADS
Cousins, Helen xiv, 7, 8n6, 15, 52
creative writing see writing workshops
cultural studies 2, 4, 6, 9, 14n17, 63, 75, 116, 144

Debray, Régis xvi, 2, 10, 21, 22n1
digital affect 2, 4, 17, 19, 59, 67, 141–44
digital companies see Internet corporations
digital humanities 2, 9n11, 22n1, 72–73, 116
digital literary economy xv, 2, 11–12, 14, 16–19, 22n1, 55, 57–67, 75, 78, 90, 93, 103, 105, 109, 114, 130n19, 131, 135, 141–44

digital literary sphere 2, 9–10, 14–17, 21, 26, 31, 39, 50, 59–60, 62n9, 63, 71, 72n20, 81–82, 89, 92, 94–95, 97–98, 100, 102, 104–05, 107, 109, 114–15, 129–31, 142–43
digital literary studies 73, 117
digital milieu of literary transmission 1–3, 14–15, 142
digital programme era 23–34, 28, 33
    see also creative writing
digital reading diaries 87–88, 90, 93
    see also middlebrow work ethic
digital review corpora 17, 67, 148
    corpus construction ix–xi, 2, 67–72
distant reading x, 12n16, 71, 73, 85, 98, 117
Driscoll, Beth xiii–vi, 8–10, 18, 30–32, 52n35, 57, 59–60, 63–64, 69–71, 73–74, 78–81, 83, 85–86, 92, 94–96, 98, 102, 113–14, 116n6, 119n13, 123, 134, 137

e-books ix, 19, 26, 81, 89, 104, 116, 130
ecosystems 17, 19, 59, 62–63, 68, 75, 77, 141
Emecheta, Buchi 12, 44
    Destination Biafra 48
    The Joys of Motherhood xv
Emezi, Akwaeke 13–14, 29n13, 31n15, 32n18, 125, 129, 133, 146, 193
    Freshwater ix, 31, 33, 35–36, 43–45, 69, 71n17, 72, 84, 87, 90–94, 96, 104, 105n26, 118–21, 123, 125, 127–28, 148–49, 162
    The Death of Vivek Oji 69
emotion
    definition 10, 74, 77
    history 2, 10, 17–18, 74, 116–23, 142
    hotspots 18, 109, 113
    ideologies 11, 18, 24, 30, 50–51, 58, 63, 74n25, 75, 77, 109–10, 115–23, 125, 129–30, 135, 140–41, 143
    research 10, 17–19, 60, 73–75, 95, 106, 115–18, 130, 142
    structure 2, 10, 17, 67, 129, 141
    talk 74, 77, 115, 119, 120n14, 126
    terms 18, 75, 113–17, 119–23, 131–37, 139, 156–67

work *see* labour
    see also affect patterns
    see also feeling rules
    see also middle class
Evans, Diana 28n11, 43n29, 136n31, 146, 193
    26a ix, 35–47, 119, 122–23, 127, 148–49, 162

Facebook 22n2, 33, 61–62, 68, 79, 80n6, 82, 133
Farafina Trust Creative Writing Workshop 29, 146
    see also Purple Hibiscus Trust Creative Writing Workshop
    see also writing workshops
feeling rules 9, 11, 58, 66, 69, 72, 74–75, 95, 97, 104, 109, 115–17, 124, 129–32, 135, 137–40, 142–43
Feldner, Maximilian 12–14, 16, 22n2, 34n22, 36, 39, 42, 45n31, 48, 50–51, 53

gender *see* middlebrow
global book market 12n16, 14, 59, 88
    see also digital literary economy
    see also digital literary sphere
Gohrisch, Jana xvi, 2, 3n1, 5, 7, 11, 14, 33n20, 58, 60, 116, 118, 130, 139–40
Goodreads ix–xi, 1–2, 9, 17–18, 32–33, 55, 57–58, 61, 62n9, 63–64, 66, 68–71, 73, 77, 79–82, 87, 90, 95, 97–101, 105–06, 111–15, 116n6, 121–23, 130, 136–37, 153
    NetGalley 82n11, 105–06
    page design 79–80
    reviewer interaction, investment and impact 79–81, 149
grammar of affect *see* affect patterns
group workshop *see* writing workshops

Habermas, Jürgen 57, 88n14
Habila, Helon 13, 69, 136n31, 137n34, 139, 146, 193
    Measuring Time ix, xiv, 35, 47–50, 54, 123, 148–49, 162
Hochschild, Arlie Russell 10–11, 58, 72n20, 77–78, 106, 117

Huck, Christian xvi, 11–12, 16n21, 25n5, 61, 63, 65, 67
Huggan, Graham 3, 7, 16, 18, 28, 34, 59, 97–98, 101, 114
Humble, Nicola xiv, 5–6, 23–24, 33
hybridity xvii, 13–14, 22n2, 35–36, 47, 98, 100

Illouz, Eva 10, 27n9, 29n12, 36, 42–43, 60, 62–63, 87, 107, 117
Instagram 1, 22n2, 32n18, 33, 68, 79, 82
Internet corporations x, xvi, 1, 3, 10n12, 11, 16–19, 25n5, 58–59, 61–62, 65–66, 68, 70, 73–75, 77, 83, 94, 103, 105–07, 135, 143
intimacy 18, 31, 80, 111n2, 123–29
  see also affect patterns
Iowa Writers' Workshop 16n20, 29–30, 147
  see also writing workshops
Iweala, Uzodinma 13, 146, 193
  Beasts of No Nation ix, 26n8, 32, 39, 52n35, 71, 82, 87, 90, 95, 98, 123, 125, 127–28, 148–49, 163

Jameson, Fredric 29, 46, 58n4, 120

keyword analysis xvii, 10n13, 18–19, 71n18, 72–75, 101, 109–14, 116n7, 117n10, 130, 154
  see also AntConc
  see also CADS
Kindle see Amazon

labour 18, 59, 69, 75, 77, 85, 94, 103–07, 141, 143
Leavis, Q.D. xvi, 5, 30
literary festivals 9, 102, 116n6, 133
  Melbourne Writers Festival 9n11, 74, 98, 102
  see also middlebrow
literary prizes 92, 94, 111
  BookTube Prize 107n28
  Man Booker Prize 1, 8n8, 30, 35, 94, 104
  Women's Prize 1, 94, 134
  see also middlebrow
literary public sphere 57–58, 88n14
literary studies 11, 16–17, 21, 131

literary world-system see digital literary economy
Long, Elizabeth 8, 71, 86

Marcus, James 65, 136
mass reading events 8
McGurl, Mark 17, 23, 26–31, 42, 64–67
media studies 9, 25n5, 89
mediology 2
middle class
  globalisation 1, 18, 29, 31, 36, 43, 85, 93, 100, 107, 124
  self-fashioning 2, 5, 97–103, 106
  see also emotion
middlebrow
  2.0 8–10, 83, 95
  amateur 18, 24, 36, 77–85, 87, 90, 103–07, 136n1, 137–38, 143, 151
  and class see middle class
  consumption contexts xiv, 1, 72, 77, 85–98, 101, 111–12
  and gender 6, 18, 78, 80n7, 96n20, 97–99, 103–07, 131–32, 141, 143, 153
  historical xvi, 5–6, 10, 23, 30, 33, 83, 142, 144
  and race 1, 18–19, 23, 25, 36, 50, 63, 93–95, 97–98, 100–02, 153
  reader xiv–xv, 8, 10, 22, 24, 33, 42, 44, 52, 54, 68, 81–82, 86, 89–90, 94
  reading practices xv, 1, 8n6, 11, 16–18, 22, 57, 59, 72, 77–97, 112
  work ethic 85–98, 106, 112
Moretti, Franco 12, 33, 73, 116n6, 117–19, 141
Murray, Simone 8–10, 18, 32–33, 59–60, 62n9, 63, 65–67, 73, 78, 80n6, 81, 105, 107, 133n26, 134n28, 135

Nadiminti, Kalyan 15, 27–29
Nakamura, Lisa 66, 68, 70, 74, 81
Ndibe, Okey 15n19, 193
neoliberal university 2–3, 15, 26, 28–29, 143
  see also writing workshops
Netflix 52n35, 63
NetGalley see Goodreads
netiquette see Community Guidelines
new African diaspora 12, 34

new economy 29, 64
 see also Internet corporations
new Nigerian novel ix, xiv–vi, 1–2, 4n3, 8, 12–19, 21–55, 58, 63, 65, 67, 69, 72, 73n21, 74, 77, 80–83, 85–87, 90, 94–97, 100–01, 104–05, 109–10, 113–14, 118, 119n13, 120–21, 125, 130, 133n26, 134n28, 135, 136n32, 137, 140–43
 allegorical realism 46, 49–50
 Biafran War 47–55
 bourgeois realism 34, 36, 42, 142
 emotion terms 133, 135–36, 165–67
 generic identity 23, 33
 magical realism 35–36, 38–39, 42, 44
 twin trope 35–47
 see also Afropolitanism
 see also hybridity
 see also new African diaspora
 see also therapeutic paradigm
new Nigerian novelists see authors
newspaper blurbs x–xi, 19, 71, 109, 130, 136–39, 143
Nwaubani, Adaobi T. 146, 193
 I Do Not Come to You by Chance ix, 22n2, 32, 123, 127, 148–49, 163

Obioma, Chigozie 15n19, 28n11, 133–36, 138–40, 146, 166
 An Orchestra of Minorities ix, 69, 87, 91, 104, 123–24, 129, 148–49, 163
 The Fishermen x, 33, 46, 48n34, 80, 87, 92, 94, 104–05, 115, 119, 121–23, 125–26, 129, 131–32, 134–40, 148–49, 163, 165
Okigbo, Christopher 49
Okparanta, Chinelo 13, 49, 133–36, 138–40, 147, 166
 Under the Udala Trees x, 31n15, 48–50, 53–55, 80, 84, 89, 91n15, 92, 95–96, 99, 101, 104, 114, 118–20, 122–28, 131–32, 134–36, 138–40, 148–49, 164–65
Okri, Ben 12, 39
 The Famished Road 35, 42
One City One Book 8n7
 see also mass reading events
online literary communities see online reading communities

online reading communities x, 1, 8, 10–12, 16–18, 22, 26, 31, 34, 36, 47, 53–55, 57–59, 61, 63, 71n17, 74–75, 87, 88n14, 96, 102, 106, 110, 113, 119, 129, 142–43
online reviews see reviews
Onuzo, Chibundu 13, 133, 147, 193
 Sankofa 69
 The Spider King's Daughter x, 46n33, 82, 123, 126, 128n18, 148–49, 164
Oprah Winfrey Show 43, 83
Oprah's Book Club 8n6, 8n8, 30, 81, 117
Oyeyemi, Helen 13, 43n29, 147, 193
 Peaces 69
 The Icarus Girl x, 35–47, 98, 104, 123, 125, 128, 148–49, 164

Parry, Benita 3n2, 13
postcolonial
 exotic 3, 7, 18, 34, 97–98, 101–02, 114
 middlebrow xiv, xvi, 6–7
 reader 3–5, 8, 142
Protestant work ethic 18, 77, 85, 143
publisher blurbs x–xi, 19, 71, 109, 130, 136–38, 143
Purple Hibiscus Trust Creative Writing Workshop 29n13, 146
 see also Farafina Trust Creative Writing Workshop
 see also writing workshops

Radway, Janice A. xiii–xv, 7–8, 10, 46n32
readathon 1, 92–93, 95, 111–12
readers see reviewers
Rehberg Sedo, DeNel 8–10, 59, 63, 69–70, 73, 79, 81, 113–14, 116n6, 123
reviewers
 demographic data 34, 71n17, 75, 77, 97–103, 153
 interaction 79, 149
 see also middle class
 see also middlebrow
reviews
 emotion terms 121–23, 156–60
 keywords 112, 154–55
Richard & Judy Book Club xiv, 7, 8n6, 81, 92

Saro-Wiwa, Ken 52n35
Selasi, Taiye 13–14, 147
  Ghana Must Go x, xv, 35, 44–45, 87, 90, 94, 96, 102, 114, 123, 125, 127–29, 132, 148–49, 164
  see also Afropolitanism
sentiment analysis *see* SentiStrength
SentiStrength 9, 73–74, 116n6
service economy *see* new economy
Smith, Zadie xvi, 4, 34
social media 1–2, 9n10, 10–11, 14–15, 18, 22n2, 31, 32n18, 33, 54, 58–59, 65, 68n15, 69, 73, 80n7, 83n12, 96n19, 112, 133, 137, 142–43
  see also media studies
sociology of literature 5, 7, 26, 60
Soyinka, Wole 35, 41n28, 49
Staab, Philipp 10–11, 17, 61–62, 65–66, 78, 106
Stedman, Gesa xvi, 11, 34, 58, 60, 115–20, 130
Striphas, Ted 17, 63, 78

tag 1, 80n7, 92–93, 95, 111–12
TBR 72, 81n9, 91–92, 94, 111–12, 152
theory of combined and uneven development *see* world-systems theory
therapeutic paradigm 27n9, 31, 34n23, 36, 39, 41–42, 43n29, 43n30, 44–45, 47, 60n6, 72, 87–88, 91n15, 92, 94–98, 107, 120–21, 132, 134, 137, 139, 143
third-generation Nigerian writing *see* new Nigerian novel
Twitter 1, 32n18, 33, 68, 74, 79, 80n6, 82, 133

Vine Voices *see* Amazon
vlogs 1, 90–91, 104, 112, 152

Web 2.0 *see* middlebrow 2.0
Web 2.0 businesses *see* Internet corporations

Weber, Max 88, 91
Williams, Raymond 3, 5n4, 19, 116
Winfrey, Oprah 8n6, 8n8, 30, 32n16, 43, 81, 83, 117, 137
  see also Oprah Winfrey Show
  see also Oprah's Book Club
Woolf, Virginia xvi, 5–6
world-systems theory 3, 11–13, 16, 25–26, 67, 106n27, 141, 144
wrap-ups 72, 91–92, 94, 111–12, 152
WReC (Warwick Research Collective) 3, 12, 144
writing workshops 2–3, 14n17, 15, 17, 22, 23n3, 26–27, 29–31, 42, 55, 64, 102, 134, 136n31, 139, 141, 143, 145–47
  author function 17, 143
  imperatives 27, 32
  relation to middlebrow 30–33
  see also middle class
  see also neoliberal university
  see also therapeutic paradigm

YouTube xi, 1–2, 10, 17–19, 31–32, 33n19, 55, 57–59, 61, 62n9, 63, 66, 68–72, 77, 79, 80n7, 81–87, 89–106, 107n28, 109, 111–13, 121–23, 130, 132–33, 134n28, 143, 150–51, 153, 169–92
  amateur channels 83–84, 151
  collaboration with publishers, retailers and literary prize organisers 94, 103–07
  lifestyle channels 72, 86
  professional channels 83–84, 150
  reviewer interaction, investment and impact 79, 81–82
  types of video 90–94, 111–12, 152

Zuboff, Shoshana 10, 61, 66

www.ingramcontent.com/pod-product-compliance
Lightning Source LLC
Chambersburg PA
CBHW071408300426
44114CB00016B/2228